GOD'S

HEALTH CARE PLAN

Biblically Balanced & Absolutely Affordable

By father Boyd

fB Publishing, LLC

God's Health Care Plan, Biblically Balanced & Absolutely Affordable
Copyright © 2012 by Boyd Berends, (father Boyd)

Most books offered by fB Publishing are available at special quantity discounts for bulk purchase by religious organizations. For details contact fB Publishing via the contact page listed on the Website.

fB Publishing, LLC
10519 Summer Grove Ct, Zeeland, Michigan 49464
Website: www.fatherboydsbooks.com / Email address: fatherBoyd@fatherboydsbooks.com

Library of Congress Control #2012948971
ISBN: 978-1-4675-4615-7

Unless otherwise indicated, Scriptures are taken from the New Kings James Version.
Copyright © by Thomas Nelson Inc. Publishers.

First Printing, October 2012
Printed in USA, by Color House Graphics

12 13 14 15 16 / 15 14 13 12 11 10 9 8 7 6 5 4 3 2 1

Acknowledgements

It is most fitting that the Father, Son, and Holy Ghost receive the first and highest acknowledgement for the writing of this book. Over three score years ago Father God began what has turned into a life long exposure and experience in His healing ministry.

Some years later the Son made it a personal relationship with the Father through His death on the cross for me. It was at that time the Holy Spirit also moved into my life in a significant way.

How does one acknowledge the person who was directly responsible for the direction and contents of this book, 'God's Health Care Plan'? The Holy Spirit provided the inspiration, the words, the memories, the arrangement, and the corrections. I can only apologize for the inexperience that He had to work with.

I would like to acknowledge my uncle Mink. It was he who directed me to the Saint Mary's Prayer community meetings when I wanted more of Jesus Christ. It was also my uncle and aunt who had thousands of teaching tapes available in their basement and a duplicating machine to make copies. It was these teaching tapes on faith, healing and a whole lot more which shaped my religious understanding.

I have a special word of thanks to my wife Linda who has put up with me for over fifty-five years. Linda walked with me through all the years with the trials and health problems leading up to this book. For the past two or three years Linda has tolerated this husband with the insane notion that he could write a book. Thank you so much Linda.

I would also like to acknowledge three pastors that have had significant input in the content of this book: Pastor Dave Guerrin of Manna Fellowship, Pastor Fred Gulker of Faith Christian Center, and Pastor Brian Aulick of Engedi Fellowship. Thank you each so very much.

Along the way there have been so many other people who have had a significant impact in my spiritual life. Some of these were aware of that impact, but many were not even aware of their influence in my religious understanding.

I am sorry that I can not identify each of you by name, but I would not know where to stop. So please accept my appreciation.

In Him,
Boyd Berends (father Boyd)

Contents

Introduction

This book, **God's Health Care Plan**, is being written primarily to Christian brothers and sisters in Christ Jesus. **However, God's healing power is available to all, not just to Christians.**

Much has been written over the years about 'faith'healing, but very little has been written about what the 'entire' Bible teaches about healing.

Biblical healing needs to be a 'balanced' approach, using 'balanced' God-given practices, and with 'balanced' opportunities that allow God to heal in any of the ways that He created.

In my life there have been numerous times where I have been miraculously healed. There have been times where I have been used in the miraculous healing of others. There have been times when healing occurred in ways that I never expected.

And I have also prayed for healings, believed for healings, and expected healings that did not happen. **This simple fact is not only true in my life, but I am sure for countless others as well.**

I would also venture a guess that when healing has not occurred as believed for and as expected, this has often turned people, especially Christians, away from asking for, and/or expecting healing.

The fact that everyone is not healed every time they pray or are prayed for, has also kept many (clergy & laymen) from the Biblical directive of believing for their healing and for the healing of others.

This fact has also resulted in keeping many preachers, pastors, and teachers from preaching and teaching on the subject of Biblical healing. And because of what we have, or have not, been taught, our expectations have been lowered, or even locked-down when it comes to our God-given healing and the gifts of healing that should be flowing from all Christians.

Over the past sixty plus years I have had the experience of attending denominational churches where the Biblical subject of miracle healings is ignored. I have also spent many years in charismatic fellowships and prayer groups, Protestant, Catholic and Charismatic, where miracle-healing was expected and Biblical healing passages were taught.

I have listened to numerous sermons, tapes, and teachings where it was stated that 'all' sicknesses and diseases are from the devil. The devil has been defeated, and all one has to do is claim healing in the name of Jesus, or plead the blood of Jesus.

I have attended numerous healing services that were emotional in nature. Some people at these 'healing-style-meetings' have indeed been healed. But what about all the others who came to these meetings and seemingly were not healed?

That same question can be asked of Jesus when He walked this earth. The Scriptures are often quoted saying He (Jesus) healed them all. But did Jesus really heal ALL? Does the Father through Jesus really heal everyone today?

Notice that I did not ask if Jesus can heal everyone today. Of course He can, but does He?

As we walk through the Word of God, the answer to these questions seems to be, **NO**, Jesus did not heal everyone then, nor does He heal everyone now.

At least not in the physical sense or in the time frame we expected Jesus to do it when we prayed.

I have often asked myself this question when I have prayed for personal healings, or when I have prayed and believed for healing of others, and no miraculous healing followed.

I would venture a guess that you have asked these or similar questions. In the course of this book we will work to get answers for the question of' **why not**' from the Bible, itself.

The lack of answers directed me to ask Father God what I was missing, or what I did not understand. Why had not all of the personal healings I had asked for, and then claimed in the Name of Jesus been received?

Why haven't all the people I have prayed for and believed with over the years been healed? Why haven't all the sick and diseased people who attended healing services led by note-worthy people such as Katherine Kuhlman, Bennie Hinn, Rod Parsley, Oral Roberts, Hobart Freeman, and others not been healed, **only some.**

Why did these same Jesus' Anointed individuals so often have health and sickness issues within their own lives, or in the lives of their family members?

Personally I do not think it was due to a lack of faith on their part.

How can the Bible state so boldly that Jesus paid the price for healing, and then Christians remain sick? How is it that healings have actually taken place, continue to take place in Jesus' name, and yet in every believing community one finds so much sickness, disease, mental problems, addictions and failed relationships?

There are many Christians who believe and teach that healing is part of the Biblical atonement, and that healing should automatically follow because of Grace and Mercy. Yet in daily observation of Christian communities the opposite appears to be the case.

Why have I personally received so many healings, in so many different ways; and yet in many instances where I thought I was praying and believing in the same way, I was not miraculously healed? By faith have I been healed, but have not yet experienced the healings that I have prayed and believed for? That of course is one possibility, but is it the only one?

When I asked Father God these questions, He directed me into His Word and said through the Holy Spirit, He would direct my search.

For the last several years I have gone through the entire Word of God.

Starting in Genesis, I began combing through the Bible, verse by verse, chapter by chapter and book by book.

Everything I read related in any way to healing, I made a note of. Every sermon or teaching I heard, when I was quickened by the Spirit, I made a note of what was said.

Finally after reading the entire Bible through twice and then rereading certain books and/or chapters through numerous times, the Holy Spirit said, "Now is the time to start writing."

I discovered miraculous healing is contained not just within the New Testament, but found through out the entire Bible. Even before Jesus came to earth and paid the price for our healing, there were many miracle healings recorded in the Old Testament.

With healing, as with so many other subjects, I learned what has often been said. ***"The NEW is in the OLD concealed; the OLD is in the NEW revealed"***.

As we delve into the topic of healing, I urge every reader to keep in mind the words of Proverbs 16:25. A belief or teaching may seem right to us, but maybe the belief or teaching is incorrect in God's sight.

There is a way that seems right to a man, but its end is the way of death.

As we journey together through God's Word, there may be times when a concept or idea will be new to you. Your thinking could very well be challenged. But we must always look to God's Word for our answers.

Relying on our own ideas may seem right at the time, but in the end, our own ideas could lead to death, both physically and spiritually.

One needs to be keep in mind when dealing with a Biblical subject such as healing, the Bible not only provides the promises of God; **the Bible also contains the conditions of Father God.**

God is the God of Love and Mercy, but God also has many more attributes. All the attributes of God must be included or one does not have a balanced understanding of who God is, what God does, what God will do, or what God wants to do.

We must also understand that there may be conditions or expectations that He imposes on each promise, **and we may not like these conditions or God given expectations.**

Another key principal to keep in mind is that every Biblical passage has one primary meaning, but may have two or more applications. We must first seek to understand what the Biblical author meant for that time or age. Then look at how that meaning is to be applied today for you and for me.

Another thing to keep in mind when studying Scripture is the issue of 'context.' Dr. Ben Witherington III, a leading author and professor said in a recent seminar that **"a text without context; is a pretext for the text to be whatever you want it to be."**

If the text used is then used in a larger subject application, the context then needs to include more than just the passage wherein it is contained. At that point we need to keep the entirety of the Scriptures in mind as we try to honor the need to keep a text and passage in context.

David Turner of the Grand Rapids Theological Seminary when teaching a session entitled, 'Bible 101' said, "a given Bible translation should not be considered an end in itself; we should study other versions as well."

Certain versions such as the KJV, NASB and the ESV, are closer to the original in their translation. The NLT is a reworking of the Living Bible, while the NIV is still a fairly faithful rendering of the original. The Living Bible and the Message are paraphrases of the big idea.

As we study the subject of Biblical healing, I would encourage the reader to consult different translations for a broader understanding of a given passage.

The Holy Spirit has made it very clear to me that all my personal experiences involving healings have been for a purpose, and that these experiences needed to be written down, along with those things He still is teaching me.

Quite a few years ago our youngest daughter took a phone call from an evangelist friend of mine who inquired if brother Boyd was at home. Quick as a whip she replied that brother Boyd was not at home, but father Boyd was. From that humorous response by my daughter a moniker was coined, and one which has stuck through time, and one that I have chosen for the author of this book.

However this is not a book about father Boyd, but a book about how father Boyd was used and taught by God in the healing ministry. These experiences through the guidance and direction of the Holy Spirit have been used to pen this book.

Several years ago I was on a 'working' mission trip to Honduras. We were building a church and as we were raising the fourth roof truss, the truss split, and as the entire, 45-foot long, extremely heavy truss, began to fall. I yelled for everyone to run.

One of the pastors on this work trip was directly beneath the falling truss. He heard me yell to run, but he also heard Father God tell him to "stay put". He obeyed what he heard from God and bent over while he waited to be crushed by this heavy wooden truss. Instead the truss fell completely around him and then broke in pieces without hitting or crushing him.

What did we learn from that misfortune? Two things: One, when God speaks, **listen**, and second, don't attempt God's work without inviting Him to oversee, direct and watch over those doing the work. After that, we started every work day with specific prayer and asking Him to direct the work.

As I began to pen this book on God's Health Care Plan I remembered the lesson learned a number of years ago in Honduras. I never start a writing session or an editing session without asking the Holy Spirit's input.

Many are the mornings when I awake early for one reason or another. If I can not quickly go back to sleep, I ask Father God what He wants. In these very precious times when He and I are talking, He will give me an insight, a scripture, recall an incident, etc. I have learned that if I do not get up and immediately write down what I have been given, later I will not be able to recall what I was given.

We will touch on the supporting scriptures all through this book, but the Bible is very clear that God is a Spirit, and we can not contact

God except through our own spirit. As God's spirit talks with our spirit, a wonderful 'conversation' develops.

I can talk with Father God and Father God talks to me through His Spirit. **This is not a special privilege reserved for only a few. We all have this rare privilege, to talk with Him and we should know that He desires to talk with us as well.**

I do not claim to have the final word on healing. What follows in this book should be considered an introduction. I urge every reader to take what you are reading, study the Word for yourself, and then trust God's Spirit to lead you into all truth. Acts 17:11b says of those in Thessalonica that:

They received the word with all readiness, but they searched the Scriptures daily to find out whether these things were so.

Dr. Witherington said, "Our culture today, especially our Christian culture, is Biblically ignorant." I would add that far too many Christians are perfectly content to believe whatever they read or hear if they feel the author, pastor, or teacher is in their eyes, 'credible'.

Acts 17:11 makes it very clear that we are not to take what we hear at face value. **What we hear must coincide with what the Bible says, and it is our duty to check out what we hear with what is written.**

Part of the inspiration for writing this book came from Psalm 71:17,18 *O God, You have taught me From my youth and I (will) declare Your wondrous works. Now that I am old and gray-headed, O God, do not forsake me; until I have declared Your strength (to this generation) and Your power to everyone who is to come.*

God did not stop with the inspiration directing me to write down all the things that I had experienced and/or learned. He also directed me to the passage in Jeremiah 1:6b & 7b where I read the following:

Behold I cannot speak - but the Lord said to me: "You shall go to all whom I send you. And whatever I command you, you shall speak.

In my case that also included the word 'write'. As you will see in the pages that follow, God (even before I came to personally know Him) has been teaching me about healing from my youth.

Over the years I have had the privilege of experiencing and declaring His wondrous works involving healing. And now that I am old, God has promised not to forsake me, **or take me in death,** until I have told what

I have experienced, and what I have learned, to this generation and to the next.

In the first chapter of Acts, the first and second verse we read,

"The former account I made, O Theophilus of all that Jesus began both to do and to teach, until the day in which He (Jesus) was taken up, after (which) He through the Holy Spirit had given commandments to the apostles whom He had chosen.

In order to be an apostle one had to have seen Jesus. The apostles were to continue the work of Jesus which He both taught and practiced while here on earth with them. The book of Acts reveals the transfer of Christ's authority and mission to His disciples. The original apostles and disciples have passed on from this life.

However as a follower of Jesus Christ you and I are considered to be disciples. According to the commandment of Jesus Christ found in the gospel of Mark; as disciples we are supposed to be doing what Christ did on this earth, and teaching others to do the same.

As followers of Jesus Christ, the responsibility to both **'teach and to do'** the things that Christ Himself taught and did has been placed upon each of us.

"The Spirit of the Lord is upon Me. Because (the Holy Spirit of God) has anointed Me to preach the gospel to the poor; He (the Holy Spirit) has sent Me to heal the brokenhearted, to proclaim liberty to the captives, and the recovery of sight to the blind. To set at liberty those who are oppressed; to proclaim the acceptable year of the Lord. **Luke 4:18 & 19**

These words were written by the prophet Isaiah in the sixty-first chapter and were read in the Synagogue by Jesus Himself. Isaiah prophesied one of the purposes Christ Jesus would have in coming to this earth was to heal the body, the soul, and the mind.

Jesus promised to transfer this same power, **administered by His Holy Spirit to His children,** so that they could continue His work. Every aspect of healing was included during the time of Christ Jesus while He was on this earth. And Jesus expected His disciples to continue to do the same things that He did.

We will deal with these aspects of healing in greater depth as we proceed, but it is clear that Jesus came to heal, as well as to teach. In fact, Jesus often considered healing to be a form of teaching. Often times Jesus taught and then He healed, and later we will explore why teaching is so very important to a person that is healed.

Again, the Bible makes it abundantly clear that as disciples of Jesus, we are expected to do as Jesus did.

Let's look at just a few of the Bible passages outlining how Jesus preached the kingdom of heaven.

And Jesus went about all Galilee, teaching and preaching the gospel of the kingdom, and healing all kinds of sickness and all kinds of disease among the people. Matthew 4:23

Matthew 10:7,8 – And as you go, preach, saying, The kingdom of heaven is at hand. Heal the sick, cleanse the lepers, raise the dead, cast out demons.

Luke 9:2 -He sent them to preach the kingdom of God and to heal the sick.

These are just a few of the many verses and passages where Jesus equates the preaching of the 'good-news' to more than just words. Jesus adds credibility to His teaching and preaching by healing and casting out demons.

There are numerous scriptures where Christians are considered disciples and as Christians we are told in Matthew 28:19,20 –

Go and make disciples of all the nations, baptizing them in the name of the Father and of the Son and of the Holy Spirit, teaching them to observe all things that I have commanded you;

John Bevere in his book the 'Bait of Satan' wrote, 'Jesus did not compromise truth in order to keep people from being offended'. If in reading this book you encounter a teaching, or explanation that offends you or that you find hard to accept, study the passages yourself and determine if what you are reading is truth according to God's written word?

In second Timothy the third chapter we read:

All Scripture is inspired by God and profitable for teaching, for reproof, for corrections, and for training in righteousness.

Acts 17:1b says it even better:

--and they searched the Scriptures daily to find out whether these things were so.

In the book of Isaiah the 55th chapter, we learn that God has not promised to bless oratory or clever preaching, or even staged healing events.

Instead, God has promised to bless His Word, and He has said that His Word will not return to Him 'empty' (or void). It is precisely the Word of God that the Holy Spirit uses to accomplish healing.

Herb Stewart in his book The Mighty Hand of God put it this way, "A God-ordained author or teacher does not rely on self-satisfying displays of extravagant theological jargon or endless definitions of the Greek and Hebrew root meanings."

When Jesus taught, He used the simple things of life to illustrate deep truths. **And isn't that how one should write as well?**

In summary, this is a book about Biblical healing, written mainly to brothers and sisters in Christ Jesus. It is written because Father God through the Holy Spirit has told me to do so.

When the Holy Spirit points out something to you in a special way as you read this book, then listen and obey, as these could be words or an action that Father God is directing to you.

Just as I am learning to trust when Father God says in effect, 'Jump', so you must be willing to trust what Father God tells you to do, and then to 'Jump' when it comes to your healing.

In the gospel of John, Jesus is referred to as "the Word" and Jesus is available for all people. When reading the Word there is no distinction between Christians and non-Christians in what God promises. The same **"WORD" or Jesus** also applies to your healing.

When faced with the need for a healing, always remember that with God, ALL things are possible. There is nothing that God cannot do. Jeremiah 23:3 says it much better than I ever could:

I am the Lord of all flesh. Is there anything too hard for me?

As I mentioned earlier, this book is directed more towards brothers and sisters in Christ Jesus than those that do not personally know Him. **But that does not exclude anyone from God's grace and mercy.**

Despite the focus of the book directed towards the children of God, I would like to take this opportunity to share with you a bit of my own personal journey to find God, and then to follow up with a question.

I was born and raised in what would be regarded as a Christian home. In addition, I attended parochial, or what is known as a Christian school all the way from the 1st grade though high school. Then I continued my education at church related colleges for several years.

My wife Linda and I married at an early age and we formally joined the church. Over the next few years we had five children. The church denomination we were members of at that time practiced infant baptism by sprinkling. Linda and I had received infant baptism and we had our children baptized as infants.

In trying to do all the correct things, I taught Sunday school, served on the church board, etc. **But from the time I was eighteen years of age, I knew that if I were to die, I would be spending eternity in hell.**

All of that changed for me when I committed my life to Christ as my Lord and Savior. I will share more of my spiritual change in greater detail later on.

My larger concern is where you are in your relationship with Jesus the Christ right now, today. Do you know where you will spend eternity if you should leave this earth today, tomorrow, or even next year?

If you can not answer that question with a resounding YES, please keep reading for the answer to how you can change your maybe, I don't know, or I am not sure, to **YES I am sure.**

My uncle who went to be with Jesus a few years ago had an insert added to the order-of-service for his funeral entitled, "THE FORK IN THE ROAD." If you are not a follower of Jesus Christ, then as you read this, you too are at a fork in the road.

Maybe this is not the first time you have been asked the question of your future destination, but each time you were asked, or even thought about the question, you were at a fork-in-the-road in your life. God is full of grace and mercy, but He has also said that He will not strive forever.

"As you travel this journey of life – you soon realize that your journey must come to an end. And somewhere along the way you will come to a 'fork-in-the-road'. At that point in time we must each make a decision. (a non-decision for Jesus Christ is a negative decision) The "fork" you chose to take will determine your **'ETERNAL DESTINY'.**"

This can be very simply shown by the following diagram:

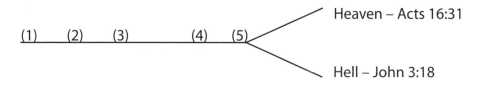

Heaven – Acts 16:31

(1)   (2)   (3)   (4)   (5)

Hell – John 3:18

1. Life begins and the Bible states that all have been born with a sin nature. Psalm 51:5
2. At best we will live for a 'few-years'. Here today and gone tomorrow. James 4:14
3. There is no question, we will ALL die; Hebrews 9:27
4. Then what? Heaven or Hell for all eternity.   Acts 16:31 and John 3:18
5. Finally, there will be a judgment... Hebrews 9:27

Where you will spend ETERNITY depends on which fork in the road you choose to take. One leads to HEAVEN and the other leads to HELL!

The Choice is Yours!! Joshua 24:15

If you have never made the choice for Heaven, and you are reading this, you are at your 'FORK-IN-THE-ROAD'.

You can take the fork leading to heaven, or you can simply go on as you are.

If you want to take the road towards heaven you can do so by simply saying to Father God that you realize that you are a sinner and that you want to accept His Son, Jesus Christ as your Lord and Savior. Thank the Father for sending His Son Jesus into this world for the express purpose of dying for your sins. Your sins will then be removed as far as the East is from the West. Ask Jesus to take control of your life from here on until you die and go to be with Him. Then thank Jesus for what He has done for you.

You are now on the road with so many others that will lead you into heaven for all eternity. Find a Bible believing community, church or fellowship to fellowship with and start reading the Bible.

For those of you who believe that just because God is Love, full of Grace and Mercy and we all are going to Heaven; I would submit that you HAVE NOT CONSIDERED everything THAT THE Bible says about God. John 3:16 says it so clearly:

For God so loved the world that He gave His only Son that whosoever believes on Him shall live and shall not die.

God's love is so great for you and I that He was willing for His Son to die in order to cover the sins you and I commit. But the choice of believing that He loved us that much, as well as the choice to believe that Jesus Christ is the one and only way to be made right with God, is yours to believe or to not believe.

You can believe that because God is Love, He could not possibly reject you, or that He would never send anyone to Hell. But your belief does not change what God has clearly said.

By referencing only parts of the written Word, one can make anything sound right, or as stated earlier, "A text without context is just a pretext for the text to be whatever you want it to be." **The truth is that God is both loving and just.**

Suppose you told your son or daughter, or for that matter a stranger, that you had deposited a hundred thousand dollars in the local bank in their name. All they had to do was go to the bank and fill out a withdrawal slip and the money was theirs. However, before they go to the bank they would have to make a few decisions:

- First, do they believe you have the funds to make a deposit of this much money,
- Second, would the bank really give them the money,
- And finally, do they really want what has been offered enough to go to the bank and get it?

That is basically what Father God is saying.
- I have what you need,
- I am offering what I have to you;
- Now do you want it enough to do what is needed to claim it for yourself?
- Your call!

Having reviewed this most important question of all, it is now time to dive into God's Word. I encourage you to FORGET what you think you know, or any preconceived notions you might have about healing. The only thing that counts is what Father God has told us in His word.

Please, do not think this book on healing is complete in all that God can do, has done, or what He will do, because there is not one of us that can know or understand -----

HOW GREAT IS OUR GOD!!!

ONE

Before we can begin any study of God's word, we need to understand who God is. You would think as a Christian that would be an easy thing to understand and agree to, but I have found the answer to this question can be as varied as the people who try to answer that question.

The same holds true within the various religious groups, churches, denominations or other affiliations. There are times within the same religious groups when there will be significant differences as to who God is, or in how that relates to us as individuals.

This book entitled, 'God's Health Care Plan' is based on a balanced Biblical approach and taken from the Word of God. One must first agree on two basic understandings of the Bible starting with who God is, and why the Bible should be used as the basis for our study of God's healing desires for the people He created.

Through this entire book we will provide greater detail who our God is, but first the question, "Is the Bible, really God's word to His people? Is this Book really written by men, and written as God told them or inspired them to write?

Or is it just a book like any other book, and we can read and believe what suits our fancy.

I recently read a very popular book written on God's love where the author used a number of texts without considering the context. The texts used were reference texts only and the author used the texts in a manner which sounded very religious, and even quite pious. But I could not find where the author ever said he believed the entire Bible was the Word of God.

Christians should have a problem with an author, pastor or teacher using texts out of the Bible to explain their way of thinking; without out making it clear that the entire Bible is the Word of God. It appears

that this author did not use his chosen texts within the context of the passage.

And with a subject as large as 'God's Love'; not taking the passage in the context of the entire Bible is a **biased** approach, not a **Biblical** approach.

In addition to the 'context' issue is the fact that the God sometimes puts expectations and conditions on His promises? **Christians often want the promises, but choose to ignore the conditions.**

As we try to answer the question, "is the Bible really the authoritative Word of God," we need to keep in mind that the Bible is composed of many kinds of literature: narrative history, epistles, poetry, prophecy, etc. In the case of history, most of that can be verified. The people and places named in the Bible can be checked against the historical record. There has been a large number of documents found in the past one-hundred years that lend great support for the reliability of the Biblical writings.

But the larger question is, "Is the Bible authoritative, and is it really the "Word of God?"

Engaged in a speaking seminar at a large university during the 'question-and-answer' session, Rev. Jason and Dr. Ron Carison were asked a question by one of the students. Rev. Jason Carison took over as President of Christian Ministries International with the death of his father, but prior to Dr. Ron Carison's passing they presided jointly at various seminars.

The student asked a question that I have also asked. "Why do you believe that the Bible is the inspired word of God? What is so special or so unique about the Bible that Christians believe it is literally the inspired word of God?"

In answering the student's question, Carison said that he encouraged the student to consider the following facts about the Bible:

First, The Bible is not just one single book. This is a more common misconception than many people realize, especially with people who do not come from a Judeo-Christian background. Rather than being a single book, the Bible is actually a collection of 66 books, which is called the 'canon-of-scriptures.' These 66 books contain a variety of things: history, poetry, prophecy, wisdom, literature, letters, and apocalyptic.

Second, these 66 books were written by 40 different authors. These authors came from a variety of backgrounds: shepherds, fishermen, doctors, kings, prophets, and others. And most of these authors never knew or collaborated with one another in writing these books.

Third, these 66 books were written over a period of 1500 years. Yet again, this is another reminder that many of these authors never knew or collaborated with one another in writing these books.

Fourth, the 66 books of the Bible were written in 3 different languages. In the Bible we have books that were written in the ancient languages of Hebrew, Greek and Aramaic; and include a reflection of the historical and cultural circumstances of God's people.

Finally, these 66 books were written on 3 different continents; Africa, Asia, and Europe. Once again, this is a testament to the varied historical and cultural circumstances of God's people.

To summarize, 66 books, written by 40 different authors, over 1500 years, in 3 different languages, on 3 different continents. What's more, this collection of books share a common storyline – the creation, the fall, and the redemption of God's people; a common theme – God's universal love for all of humanity; and a common message – salvation though the Son of God that is available to all who repent of their sins and commit to following God with all their heart, soul, mind and strength. In addition to sharing these commonalities, these 66 books contain no historical errors or contradictions. God's word is truly an amazing collection of writings!

After Carison had shared the above facts with this student, he offered him the following challenge: Carison said to him, "If you do not believe that the Bible is the inspired word of God, and if you do not believe that the Bible is of a supernatural origin, then I challenge you to a test." "I challenge you to go to any library in the world; you can choose any library you like, and find 66 books, which match the characteristics of the 66 books in the Bible. You must choose 66 books, written by 40 different authors, over 1500 years, in 3 different languages, written on 3 different continents. In addition, they must also share a common story-line, a common theme, and a common message, with no historical errors or contradictions." Carison went on to say, "If you can produce such a collection of books, I will admit that the Bible is not the inspired word of God."

The university student's reply was almost instantaneous as he emphatically stated, **"But that is impossible!"**

And yes, it truly is impossible, for any collection of human writings. However, the Bible passes this test. The Bible does indeed contain 66 different books complied under one cover. The Bible was indeed written by 40 different authors, written over 1500 years, written in 3 different languages, on 3 different continents, with no historical errors or contradictions. The entire Bible, from the first book of Genesis to the last book of Revelation, does indeed bear the mark of Divine inspiration.

Now I will issue you the same challenge as the challenge given to that university student, **and if you cannot find anything to challenge the Divine inspiration, then accept by faith that this Book,** the Bible that I am using as the basis for this book on healing is the authoritative and inspired Word of God.

This same book says that **God does not lie**, and if that is so, then we can take what we learn, and use the same faith to both believe it, and to apply it to our lives.

If you cannot accept that the Bible is the word of God and accept what is written within the pages of the Bible is from Him, then you might as well close the cover of this book and forget about your healing outside of what the medical profession can do for you. For the purposes of this book on healing, one must accept that God's Word has been provided for us in what we know as the Bible.

Sometimes various translations of the Book may say the same things using different words, but in fact, there is remarkable agreement. Unless otherwise noted, the Scriptures quoted will be from the New King James Version, as that is the study Bible that I have become the most familiar with. If you, as you read this book prefer to compare what is written with your version, I would encourage you to do so, keeping in mind not just the individual comparative passages, but more importantly the overall subject comparisons.

Our quest for a Biblical understanding of healing begins where God's Word begins, in the book of Genesis. Before we begin our study we need to interject a few things the Bible notes about God Himself. In Isaiah 44:6 and Isaiah 45:5,6 we read the following:

I am the First and I am the Last; Besides me there is no God.—(vs.8b)
Is there a God besides Me? Indeed there is no other Rock.

And in Isaiah 45:5,6 we read:

I am the Lord, and there is no other. There is no God besides me. - That they may know from the rising of the sun to its setting that there is none besides Me. I am the Lord, and there is no other.

God is the I AM and not the I Was. The book of Genesis 1:1 begins as follows:

In the beginning God created the heavens and the earth.

The basic assumption, the assumption upon which every other teaching is based, is that God created everything. It doesn't matter if you can explain God or not. It doesn't matter if one believes that this happened instantaneously, or over a period of time. The bottom line is that it all started with God creating what we know as the heavens and the earth.

Then God created the different things related to heaven and earth, and said that what He had done was 'good'. The crowning achievement of God's creative efforts is found in Genesis, the first chapter the 27th verse:

So God 'created man in His own image; in the image of God He created him; male and female He created them. Then God blessed them.'

In the future when we refer to "man" we will always be referring to both man and woman, not just the male gender.

The New Testament also supports this idea of God creating all things. Paul writes in Acts the 17th chapter and 24th verse, the following:

God made the world and everything in it.

Paul sums it up very nicely and in a very few words. Throughout the entirety of the Scriptures there is the assumption that God is responsible for creating the world and everything in it. One cannot help but notice that God's creative energies were expressed differently when it came to the creation of man. That part of creation was not only 'good' but in addition He **'blessed'** this work of His creation and declared it was "very good."

It is interesting that Father God blessed the only part of what He had created that involves you and I. The rest of the creation He only declared as good.

I wondered about the word bless, or blessed, so I got out my big Webster's dictionary and looked up the word. According to Webster the word 'bless' means to invoke divine care on something, to confer happiness upon, to protect or to preserve, and finally to endow with favor.

It should be fair to assume that if everything that was created was "good" and humans were "very good", then there was no sickness involved.

If blessed according to Webster can be defined as covered with divine care, given happiness, being able to protect and to preserve, and to finally endow with favor, then sickness, disease and anything relating to less than perfect health, or wholeness, was not part of creation.

Upon reflection you could say, 'these negative things did not enter the world until sin became a part of the world', and of course you would be correct.

Moving on a bit to the book of John, in the first chapter we read the following:

In the beginning was the Word, and the Word was with God, and the Word was God. He was in the beginning with God. All things were made through Him, and without Him nothing was made that was made. (John 1:1-3)

Biblical scholars tell us that the 'Word' refers to Jesus Christ. Jesus Himself made man as part of the creation. Although I have never created something out of nothing, I have often built or constructed things. If it broke, I could probably fix it as well. Keep this principal in mind as we spend time in this book on healing.

Recently I received an email that I had never given any thought to. Jesus, according to the Bible literally came to this earth over 2000 years ago. He died and physically left this earth. Yet NO Christian has ever referred to Him as the <u>late</u> Jesus. Even those who do not personally believe in Jesus do not refer to Him in the past tense! **<u>Jesus is the Living Jesus!</u>**

In the beginning of God's Word we read that at least two principal parties were involved with Creation. Now it seems that there is one more entity involved. In the second verse of Genesis the first chapter we read:

And the Spirit of God was hovering over the face of the waters.

Now we have the third person of the God Head involved. First God the Father spoke the words of creation. Then we have the Son taking that 'Spoken Word', and making the actual creation. Now the action arm of the God Head, the Holy Spirit is carrying out the nuts and bolts of creation.

Although the doctrine of the Trinity is impossible to completely comprehend, let me share my definition or understanding with you.

- God the Father is the top four star general if you will. In essence all four star generals (except for seniority) are equal. However, no one would question the statement that some are more equal than others. Father God basically calls the shots.
- Jesus is another four star general, but He is also the Son of the Father. Jesus carried out the directive of the Father by coming to earth to suffer death as the Father's penalty for our sins.
- The Holy Spirit is another four star general who delivers the messages, enlightens and empowers the troops, as well as providing the faith (the guns and ammunition if you will) to fight the battles.

Before we move on, let's do a brief recap. First, one must believe that there is a God. Second one has to accept the fact that this God made the heavens, the earth and everything in them. Third, we have acknowledged that our Bible is the inspired and authoritative Word of God. If there is a God, and if that God made the heavens and the earth, and if that God also made man, then it seems likely that the record of what follows was also written under His control and direction.

We are going to move forward with the assumption that the Book we are going to be using really can be considered the 'inspired word of God'.

As I look back I found it interesting that in all of my health related situations, even the ones that were 'life-threatening', I only once thought I was going to die. The time I suffered a stroke, I really expected to suffer a second stroke and that I would die. Although the second stroke never occurred, I started to question what I believed. Was the God I professed to know, really who He said He was? Were other religions just as good? What made me think that what I believed was the only correct belief? The questions continued -- but where would I find the answers?

I decided I would need to start by examining other religions. Fortunately in this day and age with computers and internet search engines to do this, it is much easier to find information than it was just a few years ago.

So I started my research with the major religions. Whenever I could, I read their equivalent of the Bible. I looked at the leaders of each religion and how they practiced their religion. I looked at what they taught regarding their beliefs. Then I took a look at the long-term results, or effects, that those beliefs offered the world. It was an interesting study and if you are convinced that Christianity is not the answer, then I would suggest that you do what I did and see for yourself.

To start with I could not find another religion where God is called a person's father. Other religions call their god great, or give him other attributes, but to call their god their father?

I could not find any other religion where its leader is credited with giving something to His followers. In the Christian religion, Father God gave His Son to those who would be willing to follow Him. If you or I were to give our life for one of our children, would you do so for any reason other than 'love'?

God gave His greatest gift not to His sons and daughters, but He gave His greatest gift to those who only later by adoption would become sons and daughters. That same great love is the basis for all the teachings of Jesus Christ. I can not find one other religion where love is not only the foundation, but plays a significant role in that religion.

Of the major religions I could not find any that claim to have a leader who died and then came back to life. Not only does the Christian religion claim a leader that died and then came back to life, *but it is a religion* that also claims the religion's leader plans to come back again to the place where his followers are.

In the introduction I mentioned an email that I had recently received, and I think it bears repeating. Jesus died over 2000 years ago yet no one ever refers to Jesus as the 'late' Jesus. **Jesus is the Living God!**

Let's return briefly to the statement that the God of this Christian religion is called 'Father'. Again I hauled out my big ole Webster's to find the definition of 'father'. Webster defines father as, (1)a man who has begotten a child, (2)the first person of the Trinity, (3) one related to another in a way suggesting that of a father to a child, and finally (4) the word father is used as a respectful form of address.

Well, dah, of course a child has a father, and a father can be either biological or a father through adoption. And most everyone knows that the word 'father' can be used as a respectful form of address, especially when used in the religious aspect.

So what does the term father mean for a Christian? Obviously if a Christian uses and applies that term personally, it can not be considered in the biological sense, so it must mean the adopted form of fatherhood. In all the other religions that I studied, I never found one where the follower called the God of that religion his or her father.

But the religion that has Christ as its leader not only call God, Father, but His followers may talk directly with Him, and even more importantly, a follower may call God 'Father' in those communications.

In no other religion could I find where their god or leader communicates <u>directly</u> with his followers.

I could find no other religion where music is an essential part of its religion. The Christian can not only praise God in words, but also in and through songs. And in the process of examination, I came across a song that I have sung so many times in my Christian walk, and a song that sums it all up so well. The song is entitled, **"Bring <u>everything</u> to God in prayer. "**

We mentioned earlier that in the Christian religion, we can speak directly to God ourselves. In this song, we are told that we can bring everything to God in prayer, and that includes sickness and disease.

Why bring something to God in prayer if you don't think He can, or will, do anything about it? When you go to a doctor do you do so with the expectation of his/her being able to help you? It should be no different when you bring something to Father God.

Christianity is also the only religion where its leader claims to be the Son of God. All religions claim that there is a God and the leaders of the various religions claim to be special in the eyes of God. Most of the religious leaders claim to have a special revelation from God. <u>BUT NO OTHER RELIGIOUS LEADER CLAIMS TO BE THE 'SON' OF GOD.</u>

I could not find any other religious leader that ever offered his life for his followers. Only Jesus Christ did that, and not for just His followers, but for the entire world. No other leader preached, as well as commanded that we must have love for one another.

Jesus then went even further and made love an integral part of what He expected from His followers. No other religion teaches women being equal with men. In no other religion did I find where the husband is commanded to love his wife.

And the list can go on and on, but the bottom line for me was, **NO OTHER RELIGION OFFERS WHAT CHRISTIANTY OFFERS.** In every other religion, one has to personally earn the right to heaven, or paradise. In the Christian religion that is offered to an individual as a free gift. Only after a person accepts the free gift, is he or she then out of gratitude expected to live in a manner described in the Bible.

And even then, when a person messes up and falls short of Father God's expectations, Father God will forgive him or her.

Although at the time I was not looking for this, I could not find any reference to miracle healings in the religions that I researched. However, in my Biblical study of healing I found that the free gift of salvation is available to everyone, regardless of race, color or ethnicity.

This is also true for the gifts of healing which are also free and available to everyone.

An honest, even cursory study of science and the world around us should quickly make a person realize that this world and all that is in it really could not have originated by itself.

Because the limited and finite mind of mankind cannot understand God as the Creator, mankind needs to find a beginning for the world that he can grasp, or get a handle on. Most often the solution that one comes up with takes more faith to believe than the faith it takes to believe there is a God who put all of this together.

Keep in mind, when a person is looking for an alternative to creation, he or she has all the resources of Satan to help them believe in an alternative. And Satan will use all kinds of deceptions and pressure, whereas the Holy Spirit is a gentleman and allows a person to make his or her own decision without any deception or pressure.

When a person's natural mind can not 'compute' or understand the God of creation, he then tries to bring God down to a level that he can understand.

I have noticed this same process happens even among Christians. If there is something that a person can not his or her mind around, then just rearrange that particular thing to where you can get your mind around it. **It will not take much faith to believe, if we can understand the problem or question.**

I concluded from my research of other religions that NO other religion measured up. To summarize, here are ten things I have found that sets Christianity apart from all other religions:

1. It is the only religion where God is called Father and is a personal God we can converse with; a God who will also communicate with us.
2. It is a religion that unequivocally states that the founder created the world and everything in it.
3. It is the only religion whose leader is credited with giving something to His followers, namely His son Jesus Christ.
4. It is the only religion founded and perpetuated both in and with 'love'.
5. It is the only religion where the founder, Jesus, is love personified, or has come in human form.
6. It is the only religion where man does not have to do something in order to obtain eternity with God the founder.
7. It is one of the few religions where women are held in high esteem, and where the husband is commanded to 'love' his wife.
8. It is the only religion that uses singing as a way of praising the founder. (singing as compared to chanting, etc.)
9. It is the only religion where the founder dies and then comes back to life.
10. It is the only religion where the founder, Jesus Christ, is going to return to this earth.

I challenge you to take the time to investigate other faiths, beliefs, or religions as I did. See for yourself how different they really are.

TWO

I n the previous chapter we studied some basic foundational facts about God, Creation and the Bible. If you are still with me, then you are either in agreement or else you have some questions and you wonder if this crazy author has any answers.

I will make no apologies for telling you that I will only provide answers that can be found in the Word. I will share with you what I have found and then it will be up to you to decide what to do with the answers that are found there.

In the introduction I wrote that this book is being written especially for my brothers and sisters in Jesus Christ. With this in mind, and before we can talk about having faith in Father God through His Son Jesus about matters such as healing, we probably should check on who we really are, in or through Jesus Christ.

And the only way that I know of to check this out is by going to the Holy Word, or as we know it, The Bible.

It is here that we can, and hopefully we will, see ourselves as Father God sees us.

One of the things that I have learned in my walk with the Lord is if I wanted to understand the Word I needed to ask the Holy Sprit to open my eyes, open my understanding, as well as to open my heart.

When I read my Bible, I have found if I wanted to understand what I was reading, I needed to begin my reading by asking the Holy Spirit to open my eyes to see what I was reading, and to open my heart to understand the words that I would be reading.

I have found that if I do not do this, I usually end up just reading words; words that most often had little or no meaning. Unless I ask the Holy Spirit to help me, I found my mind wandering to other things as I read the Word.

I am sure you can guess who has access to my mind and interjects other things for me to think about. And the list of things that can take my mind off what I am reading is endless.

So, before we go any further in this book, I want to take just a minute to pray. I invite you to join in, either as I have written it, or in your own words.

Father, what a privilege it is to be able to address you as Father, We know that You name each of us as Your child, and we ask that You would help us to see not only who You are, but whom we are in Your eyes.

Father through the simple words printed in this book on healing, and through the words printed in Your Holy Book, help us to both understand and to claim that what you say is ours. Both because You have said it and because of what Your Son, Jesus Christ has done for us.

And because Jesus said that He gave us His authority, we use this precious, powerful, and authoritative name of Jesus to come against anything that would hinder that which You would have us to know and understand.

Amen.

Billy Graham in his book The Journey said and I quote, 'Whenever Christians have lost sight of a teaching of Jesus; they have betrayed their Lord and brought dishonor to His name." Let's make sure that we have not lost sight of this basic teaching of who we really are in God's eyes.

In God's eyes as Christians do we qualify as a 'saints' instead of 'sinners'? Does it make any difference in God's willingness to heal us if we see ourselves as 'saints or sinners'?

Personally, I do not really think it makes much difference to God how we see ourselves as He can and will heal under any circumstance. However, just as with salvation, a person needs to accept what God has made possible in order to accept that which He is offering.

God has made healing available to you, but you have to accept it. **If the devil can keep convincing you that you are a sinner, that will make it harder for you to accept the healing that Father God is offering to you.**

To find out how God sees us, one needs to start way back at the beginning of mankind. In Genesis, the very first book of the Bible is recorded an account of what God did in creating the heavens and the earth.

When God finished creating the heaven and the earth, He went on to create everything else in the earth, ending the creation story with the creating, or bringing into existence man and woman.

Somewhere back in the beginning God planted a really nice garden, great to look at, and filled with good things to eat. The Bible doesn't tell us who gave it the name, but this garden was located Eastward in what God called Eden, so the name 'Garden of Eden' stuck.

Then we read that God Himself took the man and the woman He had created and placed them in the garden to look after it and to enjoy it.

There was only one restriction that God gave to Adam and Eve. Father God said to eat all they wanted, enjoy all that they saw, with one exception. God placed a 'no-no' sign on the fruit of one tree and said that one was off-limits.

Now the story gets really weird, and we are only getting started in this book called the Bible. It seems that God the Creator has some competition. I don't know exactly where this being came from, but we do know this entity was not part of the creation of heaven and earth as we know it. According to what we read, this entity preceded the creation. Elsewhere in the Bible this entity was given the name of Satan so we will call him that.

How Satan got into the garden, we are never told. How Satan took on the form of a serpent, we are never told. But we are told he was a sneaky one and slicker than the worse lawyer to ever practice.

This sneaky creature twisted the truth to the point where he sounded rather convincing. And you know the story. Eve ate of the fruit and so did Adam. Sin at that point entered into the perfect creation of Father God.

The Bible never says how much time passed before sin entered into the perfect creation, but until that point it is safe to assume that Adam and Eve would have qualified as saints as they had not sinned.

When they disobeyed, sin entered into the perfect creation, and at that point mankind became sinful in both his character and in his actions.

That mankind was separated from God at this time is a subject we are not going to discuss. There are people called theologians far more knowledgeable than I on this subject. This subject has been studied and written about for many years. But it is safe to assume that along with the entrance of sin into the creation of God, sickness, disease, sorrow and pain became part of the separation from God that was caused by this first sin.

A lot of history and information can be found in the pages of the Bible. The history starts with the creation of the heavens and earth and everything in them. History continues on with sin entering into the world, and continues with the One who brought the world into existence coming into this same world to provide a way out for this now 'sinful' mankind.

And it doesn't stop there as the Bible continues on with the promise that the One who came to provide a way out of this sinful mess, will be coming back to this earth. At which time this earth will again be as it was originally created.

At the beginning of this chapter we asked the questions who are we; 'Sinners or Saints'? There are many different answers to that question, depending on who is making the judgment call. What do I mean by that?

Early on in the Bible, after the incident with the fruit, man is often referred to as a sinner. Today either from secular reading, such as the newspapers, watching the TV, or any other presentation of things mankind does, or in how mankind behaves, it would be very difficult to say that mankind is not a sinner.

Over the years there have been those who have stated man is evolving into a better creature. However, given the passage of time, it would seem that man has not changed his nature or his actions; man is just as sinful and bad as he has ever been.

Satan knows that all of mankind are sinners and he does everything in his power to make sure we continue to sin. If a person is a Christian, Satan will work even harder to make sure that person continues to sin. And if he can lead a Christian even deeper into sin he will do so.

If we were to look closely at our lives and then ask the question of who we are; if we are honest we will have to conclude that we are sinners. Oh maybe not as bad as some, but we are sinners.

All mankind has one thing in common, all have sinned, continue to sin, and will continue to sin until we die. The only thing different is the degree to which we sin.

But the degree of the sin does not matter in God's eyes, sin is sin and that condemns each of us and with no exception.

So the real question is how Father God sees us, and that is the question we are going to answer from the Bible. **According to the Word, God sees His kids as 'saints'?**

Really, how can this be, I know what I am, and I am sure you know what you are. And I know that I should not be seen as a saint, and I suspect you should not be either.

Satan would have all Christians believe they are sinners, and of course he is correct. Satan will also do everything he can to convince each of us we are such a bad sinner that Father God wants nothing to do with us. Surely God cannot forgive whatever sin it is that you or I see as our worse sin.

So who should qualify as a 'saint?' I checked this word out in my Webster's dictionary and Webster defines a saint as a 'holy person'. I do not see myself qualifying as a holy person, so according to Webster; I am out of the running.

Of course it isn't Webster's definition we should be concerned about. I understand the Bible to indicate a saint according to Father God is someone He has called. So let's see who in the New Testament is called a saint.

In Acts 9:11 we read, *'To you saints in Jerusalem'* – in the context of this greeting Paul seems to be greeting the regular Christians. And then in Acts 9:32 we read:

As Peter went through all parts of the country, that he also came down to the saints who dwelt in Lydia.

The context here is that the saints are just plain everyday working people. In Romans 1:7 we read:

To all who are in Rome, beloved of God, called to be saints.

Would you agree that it seems anyone who is loved by God, He considers a saint? The list goes on in Romans 12 and 15 where the church was to distribute or minister to the needs of the saints.

These were needs of just everyday Christians, but those Christians had needs that needed to be taken care of by others.

In first Corinthians the 1st chapter we are called to be saints. And in Second Corinthians the 1st chapter Paul is addressing the church and refers to the church members as 'all the saints'.

In Ephesians 1, the Christians are referred to as saints that enjoy the riches of glory of the inheritance along with Christ Jesus.

In Ephesians 4, Paul refers to the 'equipping of the saints for work of the ministry', and he indicates that he is referring not just to bishops and deacons.

Whoops, if Paul is correct, then you and I, not just the pastors, teachers, elders, etc. are to do the work of the ministry. As saints we will be equipped by the Holy Spirit to serve in ministry. And as we will see, the work of the ministry was defined by what Jesus said and did, and then commanded his followers to do also.

And finally in Ephesians 3 verse 8 we read,

"—to me, the least of all saints".

If Paul considered himself the least of all saints, given who Paul was, what he did, and the books he wrote, it makes it very hard for me to consider myself a saint. Yet the Word says that is exactly what you and I are through Jesus Christ.

We are considered to be saints in the eyes of Father God, but what makes this the case? Again I checked this out in the Bible and here is what I found in Romans 5:1:

I have been justified and completely forgiven and made righteous.

Webster' says that to be justified someone must put up the bail or surety. Jesus Christ did that for us, and because the surety was satisfied, we have been forgiven, and because we have been forgiven, in the eyes of Father God we are now considered by Him to be righteous. If we are considered to be righteous, then it would seem we also could be considered **'saints' as** Romans 8:1 reads:

I am free forever from (any) condemnation.

There are two things I see here, the first being that I am in this state-of-forgiveness or forgiven, and second that this state-of-forgiveness will last forever. If this state of being free from sin lasts forever, that means it starts here in this world and then follows me as I move to the heavenly world.

Please note this does not mean that I will not sin again as long as I live. It just means the **'keep-out-of-jail'** card is <u>not</u> a one time deal. This is a done deal and that is it, period.

Bottom line is if we are called by Father God, then as far as He is concerned, you are a saint because of Christ Jesus; we, <u>you and I</u>, are not considered to be sinners.

But all these benefits from Father God come with a price tag. The gifts are free to us, but they were not free for God. Father God sent His Son to cover the price tag, but if we accept the gift, then Paul tells us in I Corinthians 2:

'I have been bought with a price; (but) I am no longer my own; I (now) belong to God'.

If you have become a child of God, then you and I are saints, not sinners. And as saints, you and I now belong to God. The reverse would then also be true. If you are not a saint belonging to God, then you must be a sinner, and if a person does not belong to God, he or she must then belong to the enemy which we have identified as Satan.

I was just looking at a number of verses I compiled some time ago, and I am going to summarize the essence of these verses that are scattered throughout the New Testament.

I am the salt of the earth and the light of the world. I am a child of God as well as a friend of Jesus. I have been chosen by Father God who made me and I am a new creation, an heir of God. As His child, I am both righteous and holy in Christ. I have been chosen by God and I am loved by God. I am a son of light and not of darkness. I am an enemy of the devil and while I am not the great, "I AM", by the grace of God I am what I am.

Because we are in Christ, every one of these characteristics is completely true of you, and of me. It is my choice to make these traits more meaningful and productive in my life by simply choosing to believe what Father God has said is true of me. And by believing what Father God has said in His Word, you can make these same characteristics true for you as well.

Summary:
If you have accepted what Jesus Christ has done for you and asked Him to forgive your sins, <u>then you are a saint.</u>

THREE

What is Health & Sickness?

In the first chapter we learned some basic Biblical foundations, and then we took a side trip to determine if we are sinners or saints.

The answer to the question of whether we are sinners or saints seems to be that we are both. That would seem to be a strange paradox, or to put it differently, how can a person be both. The answer to how a person can be both a sinner and a saint depends on who is making the call.

With one exception, all of mankind everyone from the first Adam to every person living today or that will ever live in the future, we have said are sinners. Of course to make such a statement there needs to be an established base line. The baseline we used was the Bible and without exception, we all qualify as sinners. And that includes the leader of any religion, with one exception, and that is Christ Jesus.

There are people who live more 'saintly' than others; but **only one religious leader has ever claimed to be the Son of God and without sin.**

Okay, what if this present life is all there is; we live and then we die. If that is the case then a person has two options. A person should do the best he or she can do, be the best he or she can be, and then depart this earth and be done with it.

The reverse is also true. Why live as best we can if it doesn't matter anyway. Let's live for today regardless of who we hurt or what we do.

Most of mankind believes that life does not end when we stop breathing this polluted air that surrounds us. Much of mankind believes a much different life is waiting for everyone.

For many the coming existence is divided into two basic parts. One is known as heaven and the other is commonly referred to as hell.

Books have been written, preachers have preached, evangelists have extended the invitations, and people have shared the way to the heavenly life, but that is not the basic purpose of this book.

This book, 'God's Health Care Plan', is being written about just one aspect of how a loving God has put things in motion regarding health for people while they are living here on this earth.

There is no health care plan in heaven as there will be no need for one.

Even here on this earth God has only one health care plan; **He wants you well!**

Unfortunately the understanding of God's Health Care Plan for His kids here on this earth seems to be another 'Hole-in-the-Gospel' given the fact that so many Christians are sick physically and mentally, instead of being whole and healthy. So let's get directly to the subject at hand starting with:

What is Health?

I have said we would use the Bible as the base line, but there is an organization which has stated the definition of health so well, and because the World Health Organization's definition lines up so perfectly with the Word of God we are going to use their definition.:

Health is a state of complete physical, mental and social well-being and not merely the absence of disease or infirmity.

I do not know who came up with this definition, but it sure seems to cover all the bases of the human body health wise.

When it comes to healing, Christians especially seem to be fragmented on their approach to the subject. Christian understanding can range from the far left that believes all sickness is the work of the devil, Jesus defeated the devil and faith now conquers all sickness.

The opposite extreme is found on the far right that teaches healing occurs when we die and go to heaven. **And of course there is everything in between.**

The Bible states that God is not the author of confusion, so somewhere there had to be a balanced answer. Where better to find this answer than within the Word of God.

Confusion often arises when Bible texts are taken out of context and taken to extremes in either direction.

God is a God of balance and one must look for this balance throughout the entire Bible.

For example, prophecy is often taught as that which is yet-to-come. In truth the same prophecy more often refers to an event that happened in a shorter time frame of when the prophecy was originally written.

Daniel for one wrote of many prophetic things to come. Most if not all of Daniel's prophecies have already come to pass. It is also possible in another sense these same prophecies will again occur in a different setting.

The churches that John wrote to in Revelation had the problems at that time, but what John wrote also applies to both individuals and churches that were yet to come.

God is a God of grace and mercy, but God is also a God of justice. His grace and mercy have conditions that must be considered and the prophecy of His judgment can happen more than once. In every Biblical teaching one needs to find God's balance.

Not only does the Biblical teaching and understanding of healing need to be balanced, but we also should allow Father God the opportunity to heal in any of the numerous ways He set up from the time of creation.

There is a basic Biblical principal that does not change or waver; **all healing originates from Father God.** But as pointed out, God is always a God of balance, and that also includes health and wellness.

As we study more from God's perspective, we will find God is interested in the physical body ailments such as sickness and diseases, the mental aspects such as depression, addictions, sadness, etc. and finally in our interpersonal relationships, including loneliness.

The Bible also includes discussions regarding the absence of disease or infirmity.

In the book of Exodus the 15th chapter we read:
If you diligently heed the voice of the Lord your God and do what is right in His sight, obey God's commandments and keep His laws, (then) I (God) will put none of the diseases on you which I have brought on the Egyptians. For I am the Lord WHO HEALS YOU.

God can not only heal, but God also promises that if His conditions are met, then He will keep sickness and diseases from His kids. We will address this aspect of God's healing later on in the book.

Far too often healing is only thought of from a physical view point. Charismatic healing ministries pray for miraculous physical healings; probably because this is what can be seen with the naked eye. The healing of the mind and the healing of relationships cannot be easily or quickly seen.

Our youngest son, probably due to drugs and satanic involvement, was estranged from us for many years. Many years of prayers were involved before changes took place and healing began.

With our daughter a situation occurred that resulted in a very cool relationship for seven years and only recently is a loving relationship is starting to bloom.

Often the healing of the mind and/or relationships will occur over a longer period of time so these sicknesses most often are not addressed in 'healing' crusades.

But know that Father God is just as interested in the healing of mind and relationships as He is in the healing of the body.

We have referred to Billy Graham's quote in his book, 'The Journey' where he says, **"Whenever Christians have lost sight of a teaching of Jesus, they have betrayed their Lord, and brought dishonor to His Name"**, and with the subject of healing this quote is worth repeating.

With some limited exceptions it would seem, both as a church, and as a people called by His Name, by and large we have lost sight of the healing teaching of Jesus Christ. However, when one reads the Gospels it is clear that Jesus came to bring Good News, and the Good News that Jesus preached, taught, and did, **included a full range of healings.**

As I reflected on this statement by Billy Graham, I realized that when it involves healing, his statement is literally quite true. I asked myself why the body of Christ seems to dance around the subject of healing. I came up with would appear to be a simple explanation.

When a Christian, be it a pastor or a lay person, using the Name of Jesus or pleading the blood of Jesus, prays for someone to be healed and the person is not healed, then the blame must fall somewhere, because God's word clearly seems to teach that a person will be healed if there is faith.

The same should be true when you pray for healing for yourself or your family. If the miracle does not occur it must be because you did not have enough faith.

So if a person I pray for does not get healed, it is either lack of faith on my part, or lack of faith on their part. Either way, the person who did the praying loses.

The easy way out is to just not to get involved, and I personally think that with some variations, this is what has happened in the Christian community. **Don't teach it, don't preach it and don't practice it** and you won't have to answer the question of what went wrong.

I would suggest there is considerably more involved than just a lack of faith. Please do not get me wrong, **faith for healing is very important,** and God's will is for all to be healed. In addition Jesus Christ paid the price for all sicknesses and diseases. He then gave to all His disciples the power and authority to heal using His Name.

But my study of Biblical sickness and disease goes way beyond just faith to be healed. Why sickness, why this sickness, why now, who caused the sickness, is faith the only way to get healed, what is faith, and so forth. The subject of healing turned out to be much more involved and complicated than I had first thought.

Dr. James D'Adamo in the introduction to his book the D'Adamo Diet prefaced the introduction by saying that many people when they get sick ask the question; **'Why is this happening to me?'**

Dr. D'Adamo went on the say that most of us consider ourselves to be healthy. We are busy and active, and we contribute to life. We are absorbed in our work, our play and our relationships.

When we are healthy we often take health for granted, and we are excited about being alive.

Then one day we have an ache, perhaps in our back or elsewhere. Or we have a stroke or heart attack and this comes as a shock as we have seemingly been healthy. Often we ask, **"Why is this happening to me?"**

We don't feel so good; we are depressed; the back hurts, and so on. What happens next is that we schedule an appointment with the doctor, or if we cannot wait; we head for the hospital emergency room. After some poking, prodding, and a bunch of tests, we are told that we really do have a problem, a BIG problem.

A completely different life style begins at that point, our life can change, our thoughts can change, our attitude can change, and the list goes on.

Dr. D'Adamo went on to say that we need to honestly examine our attitude towards illness. A person is likely to say something like: "Poor me! Or isn't it terrible? Just when everything was going so great, look at what has happened?"

Dr. D'Adamo went on to say that some people enjoy their illnesses. They do not really want to give them up. It is easier to say, "I am sorry, I just can't do that today or I am not feeling well, perhaps you can do this for me."

This 'poor me' attitude towards a sickness usually occurs over time. Some people use their sickness to gain attention. Look as what I have now.

Some people use their sickness as a source of spiritual pride. Look at what the Lord is putting me through now. And the list can continue.

Some people Dr. D'Ademo also said use illness to control those people closest to them. Being sick becomes a way of solving problems for them. For example if a person is sick, it is easy to say 'I can't deal with this right now, or I am too sick to make a decision like that right now, etc.'

In a recent article written by Kris Frieswick in a business magazine that I read, she made a comment that I thought was most appropriate for this article. Kris related the Bible passage where Jesus went up to a blind man and asked the question, "Do you want to be healed?" To Kris this seemed like an idiotic question to asked, as of course you should want to be healed.

But in reality the truth may be quite different. The blind man was being taken care of somehow, but if you were no longer a blind man or a leper you would then have to provide for yourself. If you were a blind, crippled or a leperous person that was healed, you would now be expected to care for yourself.

That same consideration has to be taken into account by any person that has been sick, had a disease, had back trouble, trouble with walking, been in a wheel chair, or other physical or mental problem.

Do you really want to be healed, or do you like being cared for, the center of attention, or not having to provide and do things that a healthy person has to do?

When someone has an attitude towards sickness like this, they really, consciously, or subconsciously, do not want to be healed. It should be obvious that these persons, Christians or non-Christians, will never have faith for God to heal them, **as long as that attitude persists.**

They may say they wish to be healed, and they may even ask people to pray for their healing, but in fact they really do not wish to be healed.

Assuming this is true, no matter how much faith the person praying for them has, healing will probably not occur as long as that attitude continues, **unless God has something else in mind.**

Even if that person comes to a healing service or meeting and asks for prayer to be healed, no amount of faith by others can overcome the iron curtain that has been raised.

So when physical or mental sickness attaches itself to you, or if sickness has been your companion for a long time, it would be a good idea if you were to take a step back and asked yourself the hard question, **do I really want to be healed?**

Oh I know, if your sickness is one that could lead to death in the short term, the answer may be entirely different than if your sickness, disease, or whatever is not a terminal illness.

Then there are those who have resigned themselves to having arthritis, heart trouble, cancer, or something else, simply because your mother, your grandmother, an aunt, or some other relative have all had this problem before you.

Neal Anderson in his books would call this a generational sin that has been passed on. The Bible describes this as 'visiting the sins of the father unto the 3rd and 4th generation.

Both Dr. D'Adamo and Neal Anderson have indicated that some forms of sickness or disease need to be indentified as these may need to be addressed in different ways.

Just eating differently, praying the prayer of faith, taking authority over the devil, or to believe that Jesus Christ will just heal the person, may not be the way in which the problem needs to be addressed.

<u>Please do not get me wrong, Jesus Christ can and will deal with your sickness or disease, and you should pray.</u> But your prayer of faith may have to approach the problem from a different direction. Your answer could be answered in a different way than you might have expected.

Many times we need to know what the sickness or disease is, in order to pray properly. Just asking Jesus to heal us quite often will not do the job. If the sickness or disease is generational in nature, that generational sin may have to be broken before healing can take place.

I would like to return to what Dr. D'Ademo mentioned in his book. Often people when they are told they have a life-threatening problem ask; **'why is this happening to me?'**

Dr. Ed Dobsen the former senior pastor at Calvary Undenominational church in a series of sermons he preached added to the question of 'why is this happening to me?' He said that when he was diagnosed with ALS he identified two additional questions we often ask. In addition to Why Me, he added **Why this, and Why now.**

Dr. Dobsen went on to say that when a person is faced with a life-threatening disease such as cancer, ALS, stroke, heart problem, etc., there are really two big questions that always seem to come up.

The first big question contains the three 'Whys'. The second big question for a Christian is, **"Where is God in all of this"?**

I am a Christian and Christ paid the penalty not only for my sins, but also for my sicknesses and diseases, **so where is God?**

Dr. D'Adamo is a physician and his approach to the question 'why me' is from the human viewpoint. Dr. Dobsen on the other hand is a pastor and he approached the three 'why' questions from a Biblical viewpoint.

Later when I share my personal experience with multiple occurrences of prostate cancer, I will have more to say about Dr. D'Adamo, but for now I would like to address the two questions that Dr. Ed Dobsen asked when he was diagnosed with ALS.

Dr. Dobsen addressed these questions from the Biblical viewpoint and I would like to share his understanding on these. The first contains three parts, the first being; <u>**Why Me?**</u>

In Ecclesiastes the third chapter we read:

To everything there is a season, a time for every purpose under heaven: a time to be born and a time to die; a time to plant, and a time to harvest; <u>a time to kill (or to be sick) and a time to heal</u>; a time to weep and a time to laugh; a time to mourn and a time to dance. A time to keep silence and a time to speak, a time to love and a time to hate, a time of war and a time of peace, etc."

What the prophet is saying in Ecclesiastes is that there is a normal 'Cycle-of-Life'. There is a time for everything including sickness. You and I do not control the time we are born, nor do we control the time we will die. Dr. Dobson went on to say that we do not control very much in between either.

Oh we like to think we are in control, or that we make decisions as if we can control the outcome. But when you think about it, is there any time in which you have thought you were in control that a small thing you had not even considered, messed up what you thought you had control over?

Getting back to the passage in Ecclesiastes, there are many books that have been written that will tell you that it is never the will of God for a person to be sick, and that would be correct in the world that existed before sin entered the world.

According to this Biblical passage that is just not true; sickness is a part of the normal life cycle for each of us.

But you say, 'that passage is in the Old Testament and we now live under grace so that does not apply anymore.'

So please show me where God has negated what He has said in the Old Testament and I will then agree with you.

God is a God of balance and that means God is also a God of justice, even as He is a God of Mercy and Grace. Just because Jesus Christ paid the atonement for our sicknesses and diseases does not change the fact that God is also a God of justice.

Nor does the appearance of Jesus Christ negate a principal of God. This passage in Ecclesiastes is a **principal** that God established after He created the world and sin entered in.

No, the words in Ecclesiastes remain. The difference for us today is that Christ has suffered and paid a price for our sicknesses and diseases. For us Christ has provided additional ways and means in which we can be healed.

Along with this **'right-to-be-healed'** there now comes additional responsibility. Along with the 'cycle-of-life' things listed in Ecclesiastes we also read that in every season there is a purpose. It could be God has a purpose for the sickness and disease in your life.

Where I can easily see it, I have a note that reads, 'God has a plan and a purpose for our lives, **BUT He usually gives it to us on His installment plan, ONE installment at a time.'**

Please do no misunderstand me, God is a loving God and God's will is to heal; and He is entirely able to heal in every situation. But when sickness happens, it might be a good idea if you were to ask the question of WHY me?

Is God trying to tell you something, to teach you something, or to use the situation for some other reason? Or is it just the normal cycle-of-life that happens to each of us all through our lives and is the result of the fall of man?

So go ahead, when sickness enters into your cycle-of-life, ask God WHY? Only remember to listen for the answer, as it may come from where you might not expect the answer to come from. **And it just might not be the answer that you expected either.**

I am going to share a story with you that you may have heard before, but it illustrates my point that when you ask God for His help He expects you to be aware of His answer to your cry for help.

This guy gets caught up in a raging flood and is being swept down the river calling out to God to rescue him. A tree comes floating up along side of him and he just ignores it, and keeps crying out to God to rescue him.

About that time a small boat floats along side of him and he ignores that also. A few minutes later a helicopter flies overhead and a rope ladder is dropped down. The guy in the helicopter hollers for him to grab hold and they will pull him up.

The floating guy, crying out to God to rescue him, looks up and hollers back, "No that's okay; I am waiting for God to rescue me.

Just about then, he hears a loud booming voice from heaven, **"I sent a tree, a boat and a helicopter. What more do you want?"**

The moral is, when God sends you an answer to your prayer; don't miss it because that was not the rescue you had in mind.

Why This?

In James 1:5 we read that

if any man lacks wisdom, he should ask and the Father will answer.

Recently I was suffering with a very painful shoulder. I prayed for healing, I prayed for the pain to go away and when neither of those prayers resulted in the pain leaving, I figured that the devil was involved, so I took authority over him in the Name of Jesus. That did not work either.

So when the normal Biblical healing methods did not work, I figured I needed some wisdom, and where better to find wisdom than from the Boss man. Here is where you have to listen because the answer can come from a least expected source.

In this case it came from my wife. She said my shoulder pain sounded exactly like what she had experienced some years ago; a rotator cuff problem. I had no idea what a rotor cuff problem even was. I went on the internet and checked it out and sure enough the symptoms bore out the fact I could have a rotor cuff problem.

If I had not been listening for an answer I would have missed it. An MRI confirmed I did indeed have a rotor-cuff-tare and the exercises that I had been doing to overcome the problem were in fact making the situation worse.

I thanked God for His answer, stopped the exercise, and within days the pain was gone. In the process, I learned there is one rotator cuff tare that will never heal, and the normal use of the arm will not aggravate it. I didn't know that, but from now on I will not exercise in the manner I did.

There is another lesson to be learned from this. When the normal Biblical ways which God often uses to heal do not work, try going directly to Him and ask Him what the problem is.

This question, 'why this', is a bit more difficult as it may be caused by our actions, our habits, our heritage, and so on.

I remind you again of the scripture in the first chapter of James where we are told to ask God for wisdom. When the normal ways or methods of God's healing are not working, then I would suggest spending some time in prayer and ask God for His answer to the question of why this.

Please keep in mind that God will always answer our prayers, but not always when we expect them to be answered, or even in the way we want them to be answered.

There have been a number of times when my prayers were answered long after I prayed, but I always knew that I would receive an answer.

If you are doing well, then you should praise God, as it just may get worse. If you are hurting, praise God as it will most likely get better.

In addition to the 'cycle-of-life' aspect is the Biblical fact that Jesus has suffered and paid the price for sickness and disease. And He can certainly shorten the length of this part of the cycle-of-life for us, **but sickness is result of the fall of mankind.**

We should also keep in mind that Father God can, and often does, use sickness, disease, mental health and relationships to increase our faith, test our faith, or to point out a particular sin.

Some years ago I was diagnosed with prostate cancer. I will discuss this more later on, but for me God killed the prostate cancer tumor the first time. Then when the cancer again resurfaced, He killed it the second time, and He did it again the third time.

I was getting spiritually a bit proud that I had such great faith that three times God had killed the cancerous tumor, and in between the bouts with cancer, God took care of a bad heart problem, a stroke and numerous less life-threatening problems.

Then this little health problem came along. Somehow I developed a cold with a very sore throat problem, and a cough that just racked my whole body. The coughing was deep and racked my body worse than what I experienced following the by-pass heart surgery.

I prayed, I cursed the devil, everything I knew to do, I did; but nothing changed. Again, back to the Boss and asked Him what was going on. Oh boy, I was sorry I asked as He let me know that I had a pride problem.

What God had been doing in my body in answer to my prayers, had evolved to the point where subconsciously I was feeling pretty proud spiritually.

Nobody knew it because I was always careful to give God the credit, **but it was how I was giving God the credit.** What I said and how I was saying it was putting as much glory on me because of what I wanted others to think, than the glory that was being given to God.

I had to do some serious repenting, and that pride had to go. There is no question in my mind that Satan was behind this example of 'religious pride'.

In John 11 we are told the story of Lazarus. You will remember in the story Jesus was told his friend Lazarus was sick. Keep in mind that this was the same Jesus who had been going around healing all manner of sickness, and all kinds of diseases.

You would think the fact that Lazarus being a personal friend of Jesus that He would rush right over and heal Lazarus. But no, Jesus did not hurry and Lazarus died. Do you remember what Jesus said when He heard Lazarus had died? He said this was a sickness that was not unto death, but this death was going to be for the glory of God.

I will throw this in for you to think about. When you are healed, no matter how God heals you, God should be getting the glory. When someone prays for you to get healed and God heals you, both parties should be giving God the glory.

Remember, **it isn't about you; it is about Father God getting the glory.**

And God was glorified when Christ brought Lazarus back to life. But the fact remained; for Lazarus this healing was only temporary. The same is true for you and for me.

God will heal us of our sicknesses, but any healing is only **temporary.** Sickness, suffering, pain, and death, is eventually going to get us all. We are all going to die, no one is exempt; **Death will get us all.**

The answer to the question of 'why me' and 'why this' is simply, **WHY NOT?** God can and will do what He wants, when He wants, and to whom He wants.

Not out of viciousness, but out of love. He wants what is best for us **eternally**, even if we think it is not fair now.

The question of 'why me' and 'why this', is more than just 'why not.' Do you think you are any better than anyone else? Do you think you are living the perfect Christian life? If Jesus Christ suffered, are you or I any better than He is?

<u>**Why Now?**</u>

You know God; it is just not convenient for me to have to go through this right now. If your diagnosis is terminal it is natural to think of all the things you still have to do, or want to be involved in.

Just let me raise my children, I really want to see my grandchildren, I have a business to run, and so forth. What it comes down to, there really is no good time to be sick, or to die; <u>not at least according to our timetable.</u>

In the cycle-of-life there may be sickness, but God has provided a way for your healing. Believe the words of promise written in the Bible, and ask Father God for the faith to believe that He will heal you.

Then accept that the 'why now' of your sickness has been allowed or sent for a purpose. Allow God to show you His purpose for the 'Why Now'.

Father God wants to heal you and He will give you the answer as to why you are sick. He will also provide you with the faith you need to be healed.

There is one other thing you should keep in mind. In the fourth chapter of James, we are told that we have not because we do not ask. **So do not be afraid to ask to be healed,** as this is also part of Biblical healing.

The second question of where is God in the midst of my sickness or disease? **He is right there with you.**

Have you ever read the story of the 'foot prints in the sand?' When the person was walking with God there were two sets of footprints in the sand, those of the person walking and those of God's as He was walking beside the person. When the person got into a bad situation and he looked behind in the sand, there was only one set of footprints. The question he asked of God, 'where did you go' as I only see one set of footprints. Jesus replied, "That is because I was carrying you."

Psalm 3 verse four reads:

I cried to the Lord with my voice and He heard me from His holy hill.

I love this passage from Psalm 18:1-6 because of the way it finishes.
I will love You, O Lord, my strength, my rock and my deliverer. My God is my strength, in whom I will trust, -- I will call upon the Lord, who is worthy to be praised. - In my distress I called upon the Lord and cried out to my God; and He heard me - <u>and the earth shook.</u>

In Psalm 34:6-15 we see again where God is in the midst of our troubles; sickness, disease, relationships, marriages, and mental health problems, all which surely qualify for troubles.

This poor man cried out, and the Lord heard him, and saved him out of all his troubles. The angel of the Lord encamps around all those who fear, or reverence Him, and delivers him. - Oh fear the Lord, you His saints! There is no want to those who reverence Him; -- they shall not lack any good thing. - The eyes of the Lord are on the righteous, and His ears are open to their cry.

In Psalm 147:3-5 we read that it is God who heals and binds up, simply because He is Lord and He can.

He heals the broken hearted and binds up their wounds, -- Great is our Lord and mighty in power; and His understanding is infinite.

In Hebrews 13 the fifth verse Father God has the greatest words of hope any Christian will ever hear:

"I will never leave you nor forsake you."

No maybes in there that I can find; God said it and that settles it as far as the Christian is concerned.

And finally in Romans 15:13 Paul tells us how to have joy, peace and hope:

Now may the God of hope fill you with all joy and peace in believing that you may abound in hope by the power of the Holy Spirit.

Trust the power of the Holy Spirit in your life that you may be filled with joy, and peace, as well as hope, in what ever situation you find yourself in.

Where is God?
Right in the Middle of it All!

Four

We now transition from the foundation setting of first three chapters into the real issues of this book, namely; Biblical Health Care and Biblical Healing. The first chapter of this transition addresses the first of the three basic questions that have been asked by numerous Christians and non-Christians ever since Jesus Christ walked the surface of this earth.

The first question being, 'Can God heal?' The second being, 'Does God heal today?' And finally the one that affects both you and I, **'Will God Heal Me?'**

On the surface, this question of whether God can heal would seem to be a 'no-brainer'. Of course God can heal because most everyone will agree that God can do anything. We even read this in the Book,

"With God all things are possible?"
Matthew 19:26

In my numerous years of being exposed to creative people, it has always been my experience that if a person designed or made something, and if the thing ever malfunctioned, quite working or broke, they could either figure out what was wrong, or they themselves were able to fix it.

So let's return to the discussion we had earlier in this book. Who made this world we live in? Who created or made everything in this world? And who created or made mankind, which is also saying **'who made you'?** In Genesis 1:26 we read where God said:

Let us make man in Our image, according to Our likeness –

Now if God created man in His image, do you think there was any sickness or disease found in him? Most likely you would quickly say, 'of course not.' So then by inference, man was made without any sickness or disease in his body.

It would also not be far-fetched to say that somewhere after creation the body of man became broken? That should also be a 'no-brainer' question.

Then going back to my earlier analogy, the person who created the 'thing' would also be the person who could fix the broken thing.

So if God created or made it, then He surely ought to be able to fix it. Early on we said the Bible would be the basis for our study so let's see what we can find to support this supposition, or claim that God can fix what He created.

In the 16ᵗʰ chapter of Genesis we read that Abram's wife had no children. According to Sarah it was because the Lord had restrained her from having children. When God promised Abraham and Sarah they would have children, both of them were very old, way too old to have children and they both thought this was not only unbelievable, but for Sarah it was also a laughing matter.

What Abraham and Sarah thought did not matter to God. He had made them both. According to Sarah, God had shut her womb, but when God wants to fix something He doesn't seem to have any problem in doing so, and Abraham and Sarah had a son and named him Isaac.

In the 20ᵗʰ chapter of Genesis we read of another account where God had closed up the wombs of Abimelech's entire household. In this case Abraham was instructed to pray and when he did, God reversed Himself and opened up the wombs so that once again the ladies could bear children. **God again fixed that which was broken.**

In Numbers the 12ᵗʰ chapter, Aaron and Miriam spoke against Moses, and we read the anger of the Lord was aroused against them. Just that quick Miriam became leprous and after a prayer offered by her brother Moses; God healed her.

But God only healed after seven days giving Miriam and Aaron time to think about it. Once again, the body was broken and God fixed it.

In the 13ᵗʰ chapter of I Kings is a story that really gets to me. Jeroboam was the king of Judah and he was going to offer a sacrifice on the alter of God. Even though he was the king, he was not supposed to do this, only the priests could offer sacrifices on God's alter.

God sent a man of God to tell Jeroboam he should not do this. The king got a tad bit angry, to the point where he pointed a finger at the man of God and told his people to arrest him. God caused the king's hand to wither up so badly the king could not even pull his arm back. **Care to make a guess who was the King in charge here?**

It did not take king Jeroboam long to figure things out and he begged the man-of-God to entreat, or pray, to the Lord God for restoration.

God who had created Jeroboam in the first place and had now caused the withered arm, could of course fix the problem.

A brief rabbit trail here but as I read this, God Himself caused the withered arm. Remember this incident for a later discussion in the book.

I will close the list of examples but not because there aren't additional stories; with the story found in the 5th chapter of second Kings.

In this Biblical story we have an important man in the army of Syria. Syria was not considered part of God's chosen people. In other words, using today's understanding, Naaman was a man who would be considered a Gentile or an outsider. He was considered a mighty warrior, but somewhere along the line he had contracted leprosy.

Naaman had a young female Jewish slave who knew the power of God. She suggested that if Naaman were to go to Israel and find the prophet in Samaria, the prophet would heal Naaman of his leprosy. The young female Jewish slave girl may have had her theology incorrect as to who would do the healing, but she knew that somehow Yahweh was involved, and what He could do.

Naaman may have thought this was a bit ridiculous, but he also probably thought, 'what have I got to lose?' So he asked for a letter of reference from the king of Syria and traveled to Samaria where he found the prophet.

Now you have to give Naaman credit as he was not looking for something-for-nothing. He was perfectly willing to pay for what he desired.

An interesting side note here, when you come to Jesus for healing are you willing to pay for what you desire or are you looking for a freebee? Do you come promising Jesus that if He will heal you, you will do this or that for Him? If you did, and Jesus healed you, did you keep to your promise to Him?

Let's return to the story of Naaman. God has a sense of humor and the story is really quite funny as it progresses.

Our story started when the Syrian army took a young Israelite girl captive. One of the important Syrian army generals has her as a slave. This young girl tells Naaman about this man in Israel that she says is a Man-of-God who could heal him of leprosy. Naaman gets a recommendation letter from the King of Syria and heads to Samaria to see this

Man-of-God. Naaman probably expected this holy man to come out, sprinkle a little holy water around, dance a few jigs, mumble hocus-pocus, kowtow to Naaman, and he would be healed. Naaman had big expectations because of his exalted position in the Syrian army.

When Naaman finally arrives, Elisha the Man-of-God would not even come out to meet with him. He just sent a messenger out to him with a message. And what a message it was. Elisha simply told Naaman if he wished to be healed, then go and wash in the river Jordan.

That wasn't what Naaman wanted to have happen. Naaman was an important person and he wanted to be treated in a manner that showed he was important. Besides the river Jordan was considered a dirty river. In short, Naaman was a bit put out, but finally one of his servants convinced him that he had nothing to lose, so he went.

And once again, God proved who was top dog and Naaman was healed. Once again God showed that if He made it and it broke, He was able to fix it.

In this biblical story Naaman was upset with the way in which God wanted to heal him.

If you find yourself in a situation where you would like God to heal you, **let Him heal you in whatever way He wants to do it, not the way you think it should be done.**

These few incidents taken from the Old Testament showed that even before the coming of Christ Jesus, God was involved in the healing ministry.

Now let's travel to the early New Testament time and see if Father God, through His Son was still in the healing business.

We begin our travel by taking a look at what Matthew wrote in the 17th verse of the 5th chapter. There we read words directly from Jesus Himself:

Do not think that I came to destroy the Law or the Prophets; I did not come to destroy but to fulfill.

In a sense the coming of Jesus was to bring to completion the partial revelation written in the Old Testament, and to give true interpretation of the Old Testament writings.

The healings recorded in the Old Testament were now being included in the healing aspect of Jesus' ministry, and in fact they became a major part of the 'Good News'.

Jesus is considered part of the God Head, or the Trinity. Healing now continues directly through God the Son, and is a fulfillment of the Old Testament promises.

God, through Jesus proved that He is not only able to heal; He continues healing and calls it part of His preaching the kingdom of God.

Shortly after Jesus announces that the kingdom of heaven has arrived, we read in the 4th chapter of Matthew the following:

And Jesus went about all Galilee, teaching in their synagogues (or churches), preaching the gospel of the kingdom, and healing all kinds of sickness and all kinds of disease among the people. Then His fame went throughout all Syria; and they brought to Him all sick people who were afflicted with various diseases and torments, and those who were demon-possessed, epileptics, and paralytics; and Jesus healed them.

Wait a minute Syria was not in the land of Israel nor was Syria part of God's chosen people. Jesus has hardly started bringing the message of the Kingdom of God to the Jews and he is **where?** Buried in the passage above is the reason why Jesus went about all of Galilee healing people. We read:

then His fame went throughout all Syria—

This is the first recorded healing in Matthew and what was the result? Jesus not only got their attention by healing sick people but the people apparently spread the word.

Read the context in which a miracle occurs and you will almost always find the reason for a given miracle. In this recorded healing the miracle healing fame of Jesus went through out all of Syria.

In every recorded incident in the Bible where God is involved in a healing miracle, there is always a reason why God did the miracle. This principal of God's healing has not changed today; there is always a reason for the healing that occurs.

Wow, here we are in the early part of the recorded account by Matthew where Jesus not only heals, but He is healing Gentiles, or more emphatically He is healing those who today would be considered as non-Christians. One of the reasons for healing is obviously to **focus peoples' attention on Jesus.**

The question for this chapter is whether God can heal. As we move on from the Old Testament we see the healing power of God has now moved into the next age; the age of the New Testament. It certainly would appear He is still in the business of healing thorough His Son Jesus.

God through His Son is now more than ever involved in the healing ministry. In fact He has made it a <u>preaching</u> part of His kingdom coming to earth. We will continue to see this healing trend of miracles continue as we recount several stories of healing during the time of Christ. Remember, we are still answering the first of the three questions, **can God heal?**

The pastor at a church Linda and I attended in the past often said that one must interpret, or understand the Bible by using the Bible. In other words, to interpret the Word one must use the Word.

To better understand a verse, one must read it in context, and then also to understand what the Bible has to say in related texts or passages elsewhere throughout the Bible.

I quoted Dr. Ben Wirthington earlier and I am going to repeat what he said as it has such a direct bearing on how a person reads and understands the Bible. Dr. Wirthington said, **'A text without context is a pretext for whatever you want it to be'.**

I will add that while there is the immediate context, there is also the understanding of the passage as it relates to the entire context of the Bible, and that also needs to be kept in mind.

If we were to read Luke 4:18 putting the text within the passage and then expand this meaning within the larger Biblical context we would have to include the following:

The Spirit of the Lord is upon Me. Because He has anointed Me to preach the gospel to the poor; He has sent Me to heal the brokenhearted, to proclaim liberty to the captives and recovery of sight to the blind, to set at liberty those who are oppressed: to proclaim the acceptable year of the Lord.

For those of you who recognize this passage, you know that it is taken from the Old Testament book of Isaiah the 61st chapter. Originally Isaiah's prophecy in this passage referred to the deliverance of Israel from Babylon.

However, all through the Old and New Testament, God is in the business of healing. Jesus makes it clear that there is a secondary application by saying in verse 21:

Today this Scripture is fulfilled in your hearing.

So Jesus has come to preach the kingdom, to the poor, to the brokenhearted, and to the oppressed. This description of **whom** Jesus came to preach-the-kingdom too seems to cover everyone except those who think they just might be something special or somebody important.

The first four books of the New Testament tell us how Jesus went about preaching the Good News that the Kingdom had arrived. Let's review a few of the many times Jesus included healing in His preaching about the arrival of the Kingdom.

We have just shown from one Biblical passage an example of now as we move into the kingdom age, God not only can but that He continues to heal.

Let's take a look at a passage in the 8th chapter of Matthew where God not only demonstrated He can heal, but where He makes it clear He also wants to heal. In the 2nd verse of the 8th chapter we read:

And behold a leper came and worshiped Him, saying, "Lord, if You are willing, You can make me clean." Then Jesus put out His hand and touched him, saying, "I am willing; be cleansed." And immediately his leprosy was cleansed.

The Greek word used for 'willing' is translated: to wish, to desire, to will, to take delight in. The word also carries the idea of being ready to do so. **What is God's will for healing? Seems simple to me, <u>He is willing.</u>**

When someone offers a prayer for healing by saying, "God if it is Your will, please heal so-and-so", then I say shame on them for not knowing what the Word says.

If you are praying to God to heal you and you pray, God, if it is Your will, please heal me. Then shame on you as the Word makes it very clear that it is God's will to heal.

The Bible is very clear that it is God's will to not only heal, **but to heal <u>you</u>**. Jesus Christ in all of His recorded healings never once turned anyone away that came for healing,

And for that matter no one who has ever come to Jesus for salvation has ever been denied either.

In this transition from the Old Testament period to the New Testament time, we have learned that God not only can, but that He continues to heal.

From the verse it is clear that it is also the will of Jesus to heal. Let's examine some more healings that took place during the ministry of Jesus. Please give me a break as there is no way in which we have the time or space to touch on all the recorded healings of Jesus. You can read the first four books of the New Testament and review these for your own foundation of knowledge and understanding. You will also find a list of the healings found in the Bible in the Appendix.

I love this healing recorded in Matthew 8: 6-13:

A centurion came to Jesus, pleading with Him, saying, "Lord, my servant is lying at home paralyzed, dreadfully tormented." And Jesus said to him, "I will come and heal him." The centurion answered and said, "Lord I am not worthy that You should come under my roof. But only speak a word and my servant will be healed."

The story gets better as Jesus marveled that even among the chosen people, He could not find anyone who had the same measure of faith that this Gentile showed.

Inverse 13 Jesus said to the centurion:

Go your way; as you have believed, so let it be done for you." And his servant was healed that same hour.

There are a number of things that jumped out from this passage. First is the reaffirmation that healing is for more than just the Jews. Second, here faith for healing was not the faith of the sick person. And finally, it was not even necessary for Jesus to do as He said He would do and go to the centurion's home to heal the sick servant. The centurion was the head of his house and the servant was his responsibility. **The centurion believed and it was a done deal.**

Again in the 8th chapter of Matthew we read of Jesus going to Peter's house. It is obvious that Peter was married as Jesus was made aware of Peter's mother-in-law lying down, sick with a fever.

So He touched her hand, and the fever left her. And she arose and served them.

I found this story interesting because she did not ask Jesus to heal her. Jesus saw a need and responded. Then Jesus just touched her hand, and the fever left her. Jesus just touched her hand, she was healed, and she then gets up from whatever she was lying on.

She then used the same hand that Jesus had touched to serve them. In this case Peter's mother-in-law was healed to serve, and I would suggest that **one of the reasons for healing is for the healed person to serve.**

Oh boy, we can't even get out of the chapter when we read of another interesting incident starting with the 16th verse where we read:

When evening had come, they brought to Jesus many who were demon-possessed. And He cast out the spirits with a word, and healed all who were sick, that it might be fulfilled which was spoken by Isaiah the prophet saying: "He Himself took our infirmities and bore our sicknesses."

The first thing that comes to my attention with this passage is the words, many who were demon-possessed. To my understanding there is a difference between what is understood as demon-possessed and demon-oppressed.

I am going to take a side trip here because within the church there is often an argument regarding demon possession and demonic oppression. I suggest that one more designation needs to be added and that is use of, or possession without ownership. Let me explain.

When a person invites Jesus Christ into their life, at that point in time the Holy Spirit becomes the title holder, or if you prefer, the Holy Spirit is the owner in terms of the deed but the Christian allocates the usage of the rooms. Kind of like a Bed & Breakfast, you can let out the use of the rooms as you see fit.

As long as the Holy Spirit holds the deed, Satan and his demonic cohorts do not have ownership, only usage.

My brother was in a situation that may explain how this works in a practical way.

In trying to help a person recently released from jail, he thought if he could set this person up in the lawn care business that would be a good thing. My brother purchased a used van and mowing machine for this person to use. Things went sour between them and an altercation ensued and my brother thought he was going to be killed in the process.

Now this other person has the van and the mower and uses them, but he does not have the title. In reality my brother holds the title and the ownership, but the other person has the access and usage. Allow me to put this all into an analogy for better understanding.

My brother is the holder of the title of the property, so let's cast him as the Holy Spirit.

The ex-con has the property and is using it, so let's place him in the position of the devil.

My brother and his family would like the property returned but for one reason or another are hesitant to go get it.

However, there is the authority that operates in situations like this known as the police. They have the authority and the power to go get the property so let's cast the police force as Jesus Christ.

My brother and his family have the right to use this power to take back what is theirs. But if they are not willing to press the charges against the ex-con who has in effect stolen the property, the police are hand-cuffed and cannot take action.

Do you think the ex-con who has use of the property cares who holds the title? Having the use of the property is all he cars about. And he has the use without ever having to pay to purchase the property.

Earlier I used the term 'Bed & Breakfast'. The situation I just related had Satan taking physical possession without the title holder's permission and in effect is using the property that he stole by acquisition.

With a Bed & Breakfast the property holder invites people to come and use rooms within the house. The property holder can invite good people or bad people, and can even have both in attendance at the same time.

For sake of clarity let's cast the bad people that you allowed into your home as part of the demonic kingdom. In effect you gave them access into your home.

Satan will work to gain access either by subtle means like promising you good feelings, fame, an ego trip, or what ever, but he gains entry into parts of your home because you invited him in. The demon once he gains access will invite his friends in as well.

Satan does not care if he has to steal the property or if you are willing to just allow him the use of rooms. He has the use of the property that he stole or he has the use of the rooms you let him use, but he has no intention of giving back the stolen property or of moving out of the rooms you are providing.

The problem for the Christian is how do you get back what you own? How do you get the bad parties out?

<u>Do you even want them out</u>? Are you willing to use the police force to do what you can not do on your own? These are interesting questions or problems and we will discuss this in further detail later in the book.

The term mental illness and all the words associated with mental illness had not yet been coined when the Bible was written. When the Bible refers to the demonic or demon-oppressed it usually references mental illness.

At the time of Christ, the Holy Spirit had not yet been given. And if the demonic was involved it was considered demon-possession.

After Jesus ascended into heaven and when a person became a Christian, the Holy Spirit entered that person's life.

However, Christians can still be demon-oppressed. The demonic forces can still occupy a room or use the property.

But I do not know if I could support a Christian being demon-possessed because that refers to ownership.

I do think that a Christian can take back the title from the Holy Spirit and freely give it to the devil. In that case, the person would no longer be considered a Christian and would most likely be considered demon possessed.

In reading the tenth chapter of Hebrews Paul seems to be addressing the situation I just mentioned, and Paul concludes the chapter in the 38th verse by saying:

Now the just shall live by faith; but if anyone draws back, My soul has no pleasure in him.

God is making it very clear that the Christian can withdraw from all that God has offered, but if he or she does, the favor of God will be withdrawn.

In my opinion, based on the Word and many personal experiences, demons did not just disappear when Christ was crucified and Satan was defeated. The demonic kingdom of Satan is still active and the Christian must learn to deal with that kingdom when operating in the arena of healing.

What really got my attention in this story was who was in charge even of the demons. **Jesus is here, and Satan is going down.** Jesus never pulled any punches when He dealt with the Devil or the demonic beings.

Just an aside here; Jesus never laid hands on the person to get rid of the demon, or demons. Jesus seems to think they are beneath His even touching the person that had the demon problem,

Jesus has enough power and enough authority to kick the demons out just by using His mouth. **Get out, and out they went.**

We continue to examine the question of can God heal by looking at additional times when God through Jesus Christ did indeed heal.

What should get your attention is the passage in Isaiah 53:5 where Isaiah said:

He Himself took our infirmities and bore our sicknesses.

Matthew makes it very clear that Jesus Christ took on all our sicknesses and diseases, and that also included mental sickness and strained relationships.

The provision of divine healing must rest on clear Biblical grounds and we understand from this passage in Isaiah, **divine healing is for us.**

Divine healing was prophesied long before Christ the Healer came. As we see in Isaiah, the Servant of Yahweh would bear sickness in the same way in which He (Jesus) would bear our sins, and to use a big word, 'vicariously'.

The word 'our' in the prophecy means all of mankind and just as the well known verse found in John 3:16 says:

"For God so loved the world that He gave His only begotten Son, that whoever believes in Him should not perish but have everlasting life".

This passage is very clear that a person who believes in God's Son will be saved and has everlasting life. This same loving God who sent His only Son Jesus to bear the sins of mankind, is the same loving God who allowed Jesus to be whipped.

And with the stripes Jesus would bear on His back at Calvary, Jesus would also pay the price to cover all of the sickness and disease that had entered this world through the sin of Adam.

By faith anyone who is willing to believe that Jesus died for their sins is promised everlasting life. By faith anyone who is willing to trust that this same Jesus suffered for their sickness and disease **will be healed.**

The death of Jesus Christ on the cross was more than enough to provide for the salvation of everyone who lived, is living or is yet to come. **And the stripes that Jesus bore at Calvary were also sufficient**

to cover every sickness or disease for everyone who lived, is living, or is yet to come.

But let me ask you a question. Is everyone saved, and will everyone go to heaven? If not, then why not?

Regardless of what some people think of the controversial book 'Love Wins', not everyone is going to end up in heaven.

Yes God is love, and Father God may have more than one way to get you to put your faith and trust in Him through Jesus Christ. But His great love for mankind, while it provided the opportunity, also left it up to each of us to decide if we wanted to be a part of that great love.

Read verse 16 again:

whoever believes in Him should not perish but have everlasting life.

It is clear that the death of Christ was sufficient for everyone, but it also clear that there is a condition. Yes God loves everyone, but He still attached a condition in order for a person to obtain everlasting life.

God is love, but God is also just. **He provided the way** to eternal life, **but leaves the choice up to us.**

Isaiah prophesied that the death of Christ for sins covered everyone. The suffering and humiliation of Jesus was also sufficient for the healing of everyone. But as we will see there are conditions. Not everyone will be saved because not everyone will believe.

While the suffering of Jesus was sufficient for everyone to be healed, **not everyone will be healed.**

We are still on the second of the three questions and we will continue to look at various healings that took place while Jesus walked this earth.

In Matthew the ninth chapter we will touch on four healing incidents. The first was the paralytic man whose friends broke a hole in the roof of the house where Jesus was and then let him down inside. Here Jesus did two things, Jesus told the man that his sins were forgiven him and now that his sins were forgiven, he was told to pick up the bed he was laying on and go home.

Was this man sick because of his sins? The answer is not given in the text; just that his sins were forgiven and he was healed. Isn't it interesting that the paralytic man's faith in Jesus for healing also seems to be the catalyst which earned him the forgiveness of his sins and life eternal?

The next healing incident involved a woman who had a blood issue for 18 years and was so humiliated that all she could bring herself to do was to get near enough to touch the clothes of Jesus.

She did not have much faith, but it was enough. Her little faith was enough and when she touched the robe of Jesus, He healed her. (later I will share the story of how a lady in India with a similar issue was also healed)

Then we read the story where a ruler came and worshipped Him saying:

"My daughter has just died, but come and lay Your hand on her and she will live (again).

Jesus went to the home of the ruler and did indeed lay His hand on her, and life came back into the ruler's daughter. The story ends with the words that this report went out to all the land. Again it would appear that one reason for this miracle was so the entire land would hear what Jesus had done.

But stop and think about it, the report of the miracles of Jesus did not stop there. They are still being told today to everyone who reads the Bible.

A couple of things I noted from the passage. The girl was dead and not just sleeping as some would like to say. Second, it was the father, the head of the house, who had the faith that was sufficient for Jesus to return his daughter to life.

Obviously it could not have been the faith of the daughter as she was dead. Faith residing in the head of the house moves Jesus to action. **Father's faith, daughter lives again**.

Matthew 9:27-31 tells the story of two blind men who were following Jesus begging Him to have mercy on them. These two men were really persistent; they even followed Jesus into a house where I am sure they had no business entering.

Jesus finally acknowledged the two men and asked them if they believed He was able to heal their blindness. They replied that yes they believed that Jesus was able to heal them.

So Jesus put what they had said to the test. Jesus said,

"According to your faith let it be to you."

I would surmise that they had enough faith because just like that they could see.

When I read this passage, being the skeptical person that I am, I asked myself what would have happened if their faith to believe was not there. After all Jesus asked them if they believed He was able to open their eyes and they said that yes they believed that He was able.

What if the words of their reply had just been empty words, would they have been healed?

These men did not give up asking, even though it appears that Jesus was ignoring them. And second, I don't know how much faith they had, and Jesus did not ask them that question. Jesus only asked if they believed He was able to open their eyes, and when they said He was able, they were healed.

Was it their faith that was responsible for their eyes being opened, or was it the fact they believed Jesus was able to open their eyes the reason for the miracle? **Or doesn't it make any difference?**

The final thing that I found interesting in this passage is that Jesus told them to be quiet about what He had done but they could not keep quiet and told the entire country. When you are healed by Jesus, give God the glory and spread the news wherever you go.

I am going to include the next miracle because it seems the devil was often the cause of sickness Jesus had to deal with. This story is also found in Matthew, and involves only two verses.

Matthew 8:32 & 33 reads:

As they went out, behold they brought to Jesus a man, mute and demon-possessed. And when the demon was cast out, the (tongue-tied) mute opened his mouth and spoke.

Again we are not going to deal with whether the man was possessed or oppressed. It is enough that the demon seems to be the entity that was behind the man not being able to speak. What is interesting is that Jesus had the power to tell the demon to get lost and it did.

It is also interesting that the Pharisees saw this and attributed Jesus' power to Satan, the ruler of demons. At least the Pharisees knew where demons came from, even if they did not know, or would not admit to, the power Jesus exhibited over Satan and the demonic.

The heading for this chapter is; Can God Heal and we are answering the question with the record of Jesus actively involved in the healing ministry.

Up to this time we have only read where Jesus was doing the miracles. The ministry of bringing the Good News now seems to be expanding.

In the tenth chapter of Matthew we read where Jesus empowers and sends out the twelve. I am not going to write the entire passage, but pick out what I think is important.

> And when Jesus had called His twelve disciples to Him, He gave them power over unclean spirits, to cast them out, and to heal all kinds of sickness, and all kinds of disease. – These twelve Jesus sent out and commanded them, saying, "Do not go into the way of the Gentiles, and do not enter a city of the Samaritans. But go rather to the lost sheep of the house of Israel. And as you go, preach, saying, the kingdom of heaven is at hand. Heal the sick, cleanse the lepers, raise the dead, and cast out demons."

Jesus is moving out beyond Himself. He gave the disciples the power, which is to say **He passed on to them the anointing of the Holy Spirit.** Then He sends them out to preach, and notice what the preaching included.

I am going to insert something here that I will touch on again later in the book. A disciple is a learner and one who follows both the teaching, and the teacher. **Jesus taught and Jesus healed**. He now tells the disciples to go out and say what He has been saying and do what He has been doing.

The word disciple is first used for the twelve and later of Christians generally.

Interestingly Jesus did not send them out to preach primarily with words. They were to preach the kingdom of God, but they were to do so with more than words. Jesus said, "The kingdom of heaven is at hand, heal the sick, cleanse the lepers, raise the dead, and cast out demons."

The Bible states that God is the same today as He was yesterday, and that He will be the same forever. If this is so, then could it be that Jesus expects the preaching of His kingdom to be conducted in the same manner today?

In the book of Luke we read that Jesus sent out seventy with the same instructions. I don't know if the twelve were sent out at the same time or if this was a different time, but the instructions given in Luke are the same as those given to the twelve in Matthew.

What I like about the sending out of the seventy is their response when they get back to home base. These disciples came back bubbling over with joy at what had taken place. Everything that Jesus had sent them out to do, preach, heal the sick, etc., happened. But what really astounded these seventy disciples has been recorded in Luke 10:17-19.

Lord, even the demons are subject to us in Your name. And Jesus said to them, "I saw Satan fall like lightning from heaven. Behold, I give you the authority to trample on serpents and scorpions, and over all the power of the enemy, and nothing shall by any means hurt you."

Jesus went on the say that this power over the camp of the enemy is nice to have and experience, but listen to what Jesus said is really important.

nevertheless do not rejoice in this, that the spirits are subject to you, but rather rejoice because your names are written in heaven. vs. 20

In this book we are going to be talking about your healing, your healing of others, and your power over all the camp of the enemy.

But all of the power that resides in the Name of Jesus pales to insignificance when compared to having your name in the book of life.

Healing the sick and the casting out of demons, as exhilarating as they are, are not top priority and you need to keep your priorities in the proper order.

Eternal life for yourself, or others, is more important and you should have that as the top priority in your life.

In the book of John in the first part of the 5th chapter is recorded a healing by Jesus that needs to examined. On the porches that surrounded the temple one could find a 'great multitude' of sick people, blind, lame, and paralyzed, all waiting for the moving of the waters. When the waters moved, if you were fortunate enough to get into the waters while they were moving, you were healed.

In these five porches lay a great multitude of sick people, blind, lame, paralyzed, waiting for the moving of the water. Now a certain man was there who had an infirmity for thirty-eight years. Jesus said to him. "Do you want to get well?"

Jesus zeroed in on one man, a lame person unable to walk for the past thirty-eight years and lying amongst the great number of sick people that were also waiting to be healed. Jesus looked at him and asked him a simple question. Do you want to be made well, or as we would say, healed?

Obviously the man must have thought this was a very stupid question because he never did answer the question asked by Jesus. He just gave Jesus the reason he thought he had not been healed. Jesus ignored the excuse and simply told the man to pick up his bed and start walking.

When you read the rest of the story, it becomes evident why Jesus healed this man. There was no faith for healing on the part of the lame man, nor did he ask to be healed. **Jesus just did it**. The reason Jesus healed this lame man comes later as this healing was done on a Sunday, and it really ignited a fire storm with the Jewish religious leaders.

What I want to bring out of this story is the following. There are Christian people who say that Jesus always healed everyone. Not according to this recorded incident. The lame man was only one person in the middle of a large number of sick, blind, lame, and paralyzed, waiting for the waters to move so that they might have an opportunity to be healed.

If Jesus healed everyone every time, why was only one person selected to be healed?

And if Jesus wanted to really make a statement about healing on the Sabbath, wouldn't the healing of all those who were waiting for the water to move have caused a stir? But Jesus only chose one person to heal at this time. There are many more examples of Jesus healing when He was here on earth that I could include, but as John said,

'If all the things that Jesus did were to be written one-by-one, even the world itself could not contain the books that would be written.

In summary of the question, **Can God Heal,** the only conclusion that one can arrive at, is <u>**YES HE CAN and yes, Jesus did.**</u>

God healed in the Old Testament and Jesus healed in the New Testament. Now let's turn our attention to the second question and that is the question: **Does God Heal Today?**

Five

The second question is one that I have labeled the 'Bigger Question' is the question of whether God heals today.

By today I mean the time starting when Jesus left the earth and includes up to the present time.

There has long been a group of Christians that are convinced when Jesus returned to heaven, the healing ministry left with Him. We are told we now have the Bible and should no longer need the miraculous. In theory this sounds very spiritual, and maybe even a bit pious.

But if the suffering of Jesus covered all sickness and disease, then, at least for Christians, shouldn't the problems of sickness and disease have also disappeared when Christ went to heaven?

Let's take a journey back in time to see what the preaching of the kingdom of heaven looked like after Jesus physically left this earth. We have already observed that Jesus sent out His disciples, not only the twelve, but at least seventy more disciples as well.

One would think these disciples would now have direct experience in preaching the Kingdom of God in the same manner that Jesus had been preaching it.

Assuming this to be the case, Jesus now had a core of trained and experienced disciples sufficient to continue the healings of Jesus.

I would like to start the journey into the question of does God heal today by going to the words that were given to the disciples of Jesus when He went to take His seat at the right hand of God the Father.

In the last few verses found in Matthew we read the instructions that Jesus left with His disciples:

And Jesus came and spoke to them, saying, "All authority has been given to Me in heaven and on earth. (You) Go therefore and make disciples of all nations, baptizing them in the name of the Father and of the Son and of the Holy Spirit, teaching them <u>to observe</u> all *things that I have commanded you; and lo, I am with you always, even to the end of the age.*

Those that heard the instructions of Jesus were told to Go and Make disciples. According to Ray VanderLaan an expert and teacher on the Jewish Talmud, Jewish beliefs, and the rabbi called Jesus, a disciple is called a Talmidim, and a Talmidim is a follower of the Rabbi.

Jesus was definitely a Rabbi and by definition that makes the Christian both a follower and a disciple. Ray VanderLaan went on to say that a Talmidim not only listened and learned what the Rabbi said, but also learned to do what the Rabbi did.

Assuming this is the case, and assuming we Christians are also disciples, then it is not enough that we only teach and preach the words of Christ, **we also need to emulate the works of Christ.**

The final instructions given to the apostles and disciples in Mark the 16th chapter expand on the commission that is written in Matthew.

And He, Jesus, said to them, "Go into all the world and preach the gospel to every creature. He who believes will be saved, but he who does not believe will be condemned. And these signs shall follow those who believe; In My name they will cast out demons; they will speak with new tongues; they will take up serpents; and if they drink anything deadly, it will by no means hurt them; they will lay hands on the sick, and they will recover." After Jesus had spoken thus with them, He was received up into heaven; and they went out and preached everywhere, the Lord working with them and confirming the word through the accompanying signs.

There has long been a discussion whether the last part of the Great Commission in Mark was really included in the original manuscript.

I asked this question of a pastor who studied the original. His comment was, even if it were not in the original, is it consistent with the rest of what is printed in the Bible?

My reading of the Bible for this book on healing found the words to be consistent, even if they were not included in the original.

In both Mathew and Mark the disciples were told to go out and preach the good news. The good news included the fact Jesus came to earth and the disciples certainly preached the words leading to repentance.

But the disciples did not stop with just sharing the words which Jesus spoke. The disciples preached using the 'works' just as Jesus did which included doing all the miracles of Jesus that are recorded.

Certainly the Good News included the fact that Jesus Christ suffered, died, rose from the dead, and ascended into heaven. Those were powerful words, but the disciples were told to go out and preach the Good News **but not by only using words**. Jesus said He would confirm what they were preaching by doing miracles through them. A footnote in my study Bible has this to say about the word 'confirming'. The miracles that accompanied the disciples' preaching confirmed to the people that the messengers were telling the truth, that God was backing up their message with supernatural phenomena, and the age of grace had entered the world.

Jesus has now departed this earth so let's skip forward to the book of Acts and see what takes place now that the disciples are left without their physical Rabbi.

Keep in mind our question is, does Jesus heal today, two thousand years which have followed His sojourn on earth.

Acts records events following the ascension of Jesus and we will look at some of those things that took place, especially in the arena of healing. In reading through the book of Acts I made a note to myself that I would like to share with you.

The book of Acts is the story of the disciples receiving what Jesus received, in order to do what Jesus did; namely to preach the gospel and to demonstrate the kingdom power through the use of miracles.

Jesus received the Holy Spirit at His baptism and His ministry began. The disciples of Jesus received the Holy Spirit in the upper room and their ministry began.

The place to begin is with the Promise found in the first chapter of the book of Acts. In Acts 1:4 Jesus told his disciples to wait for the Promise of the Father. The 'Promise' Jesus gave the disciples was that they would receive the Holy Ghost, accompanied with all of the power which Jesus had displayed during His time on this earth. In verse 8 of the first chapter Jesus said,

"You shall receive power when the Holy Spirit has come upon you; and you shall be witnesses to Me in Jerusalem, and in all Judea and Samaria, and to the end of the earth."

I am going to inject something here that you may want to think and pray about. If a Christian is really a disciple, then this same Holy Spirit power is available to each and every Christian.

Assuming this is the case, a Christian has no excuse for not preaching the Word accompanied with 'signs and wonders'.

What does it mean to **'receive the power of the Holy Ghost?'** First it should be noted that the Holy Spirit just like Jesus is a person, the third person of the God head. The Holy Spirit provides the Power and ability (the guns and the ammunition so to speak) for serving God. The power of the Holy Spirit is also to be used in sharing the gift of God's kingdom with others. Scripture tells us that when a person receives Christ they also receive the Holy Spirit. This initial gift of the Holy Spirit is the actual person. When the Bible refers to subsequent gifts of the Holy Spirit given to the Christian, these gifts are the actual power gifts, or the guns and the ammunition if you prefer.

Sharing the Good News of the kingdom with others should include not only preaching and teaching with words, but also the use of the confirming power miracles just as Jesus did when He presented the good news.

It should be noted that Biblically the Holy Spirit's power must be **'received'** by the recipient; it is not an automatic experience. The gift of the Holy Spirit is received at the time a person accepts Jesus Christ as their Saviour, but there is a distinction between the gift of the Holy Spirit that is given at the time a person accepts Jesus Christ, and the gifts of the Holy Spirit found in I Corinthians 13 and in Romans 12.

These special gifts of the Spirit are separate from the initial gift received at the time of his or her accepting Jesus Christ as the giver of eternal life.

It is the initial gift of the Holy Spirit that later provides the faith for a person to receive the special enablement and power 'gifts-of-the-Holy Spirit'.

When a person reads about the gifts of the Spirit, it quickly becomes evident that not everyone, **and probably not anyone,** has been given ALL of the gifts.

Digging deeper, one will find that Christians may be given a particular gift, at a particular time, for a particular need.

When the need has been fulfilled, the special gift can be withdrawn until that gift, or another gift is needed to fill a particular need.

I say 'May-be-Given' because if the Holy Spirit wishes to give a particular gift to a Christian and the gift is rejected or not received, then the gift will not be forcibly shoved on the person. The Holy Spirit will never force a gift, **including the gift of salvation**, onto anyone.

This aspect of the Holy Spirit giving specific gifts as needed within the ministry and life of a disciple is far more prevalent than the bestowing of a specific gift to preach, teach, evangelize, or leadership, which can result in a full time ministry gift.

When the Holy Spirit fills a Christian with a special gift for a special purpose, **I guarantee you will know it.** Jesus said that He would send the Holy Spirit and **the power** that would accompany the gift. The disciples certainly found this to be the case.

Just as each person must believe and accept that Jesus Christ died for their sins, each Christian must accept the promise of the Holy Spirit that will be given for use within the kingdom. We must **'receive and then implement'** these special anointing gifts of the Holy Spirit just as Jesus commanded.

Sometimes the Holy Spirit will supply a needed power gift, but the Christian may be fearful and not accept the gift and/or the implementation of that special gift. We will discuss this in further detail in the chapter entitled, Faith, Doubt and Unbelief.

The initial gift of the Holy Spirit came as the apostles and a number of other believers were waiting and praying together. The story goes on to say that **as they were waiting** things began to happen which they realized was the coming of the Promised Gift, the Holy Spirit.

You can read this account in the second chapter of Acts, but this initial infilling of the Holy Spirit resulted in the ability to boldly proclaim the wonderful works of God. This bold preaching resulted in amazement and then conviction by those that heard the apostles speak with both words and with miracles.

In the 22nd verse of Acts 2 Peter sums up the ministry of Jesus while He walked around Israel. We read Peter's words,

"Men of Israel, hear these words; Jesus of Nazareth, a Man attested by God to you by miracles, wonders, and signs which God did through Him in your midst."

Peter made it very plain to those who were hearing him that Jesus' credibility was based on His miracle ministry.

Without exception, miracles, signs, and wonders accompanied the ministry and preaching of the early church leaders. We are examining the second question, 'Does God Heal Today' so let's take a deeper look at some of the things that took place after Jesus left His disciples to carry on the ministry of Jesus.

It doesn't take long to see what followed when the power of the Holy Spirit goes to work in a believer.

Acts 2:43 simply reads:

Then fear (awe) came upon every soul, and many wonders and signs were done through the apostles.

One of the things the apostles did while they remained in Jerusalem was to go to the temple daily to pray. The way into the temple used by the apostles was probably the same route that Jesus used when He went into the temple to pray. The gate through which they entered was called Beautiful. It seems to have been the place beggars used when asking for a gift from those going into the temple. The story reads:

And a certain man lame from his mother's womb was carried, whom they laid daily at the gate to ask alms.

This man had been lame and had been begging here for a long time. As Peter and John were going into the temple he asked them for a little money. The lame man did not get any money; what he got instead was the result of the gift of healing.

Peter, in the power of the Holy Spirit said that what he had he would give. In the name of Jesus Christ of Nazareth, get up and start walking. This time the 'gift' of healing that Peter exercised was the gift to heal a lame person.

In Isaiah 35, 5-6 we read:

God will come and save you. The eyes of the blind shall be opened, and the ears of the deaf shall be unstopped. The lame shall leap like a dear, and the tongue of the dumb will sing.

Peter and John, through the power of the Holy Spirit and the Name of Jesus, were doing what God in Isaiah had said Jesus would do. The Bible describes the healing gift as 'the gifts of healing'.

I believe the use of the plural 'gifts' is because when the Biblical healing goes out for others, or is given for a personal need, God usually provides it one individual gift at a time.

The plural gifts can also mean that there are many different healings that will be needed in the world. It will take a multiple number of disciples exercising one gift at a time to fill all the different needs of healing that people have.

Here is a question for you to think about. If this man had been placed here daily for a long time surely Jesus had to pass him by and probably more than once. Why didn't Jesus heal him when He entered the temple through this gate? After all we read that Jesus healed everyone, **but then again maybe Jesus did not heal everyone.**

This is the first recorded miracle preformed by the disciples after Jesus had left them. Here is the really interesting part. Peter takes him by the hand and lifts him up even as his bones were becoming stronger. The man completes his healing by walking into the temple with Peter and John. However, the no-longer lame man was not content to just walk. He walked, he leaped, and he jumped, all the while praising God.

And all the people saw him walking and praising God. Then they knew who he was and they were filled with wonder and amazement at what had happened to him.

When a person is healed, he or she should react by praising and giving God the glory. But the purpose of a miracle goes further as we see here. Miracles often happen so that others may be filled with wonder and amazement at what God can do.

As I was engaged in study and research for this book I asked myself the question, did Jesus heal everyone? I came to the conclusion that Jesus did not heal everyone. Could Jesus have healed everyone? **You better believe He could have.** Later we will take a deeper look as why everyone is not healed, every time.

I noted that Jesus did in fact heal everyone who came expecting; as well as all who asked.

Jesus healed in response to a person's faith, either for themselves or others. He also healed to demonstrate His power.

Other times He healed so that glory would be given to God.

• Sometimes Jesus healed to make a statement.

• Sometimes Jesus healed to start a confrontation.

• And finally, Jesus healed to establish His God given credibility.

Isn't it interesting that here Peter healed to demonstrate God's power? After the lame man was healed, the glory was given to God. This healing miracle surely established Peter's God-given-credibility through the use of Jesus' name. Five out of seven reasons for the lame man to be healed is not too bad.

The boldness and power that followed the influx or anointing of the Holy Spirit not only continued, but the Holy Spirit given power seems to increase as pressure is applied. In the fourth chapter the Jewish leaders are issuing threats to the apostles, but how do they react. Acts 4:29-33 reads:

> "Now, Lord, look on their threats, and grant to Your servants that with all <u>boldness they may speak Your word</u>, (how) by stretching out Your hand to heal, and that signs and wonders may be done through the name of Your holy Servant Jesus.

The passage goes on to say the place was shaken and they were all filled with the Holy Spirit, and they all spoke with boldness and great power.

It was interesting to read, "They were all filled with the Holy Spirit".

I thought that had already happened. Why did they again get a filling of the Holy Spirit?

It would appear we receive the Holy Spirit at the time of our conversion, but we need special fillings or anointing by the Holy Spirit for times of special needs.

To preach the word with boldness may also include speaking a strange language. And the preaching that is accompanied with signs and wonders seems to require that the disciples receive special fillings of the Holy Spirit given at the time of need.

The Greek word for boldness is 'parrhesia' which in this application denotes a divine enablement that comes to ordinary and non-professional people by exhibiting spiritual power and authority. Parrhesia is not a human quality but is the result of being filled with the Holy Spirit.

This special power or anointing is described again in Acts 5:15,16 where we read:

> --so they brought the sick out into the streets and laid them on beds and couches, that at least the shadow of Peter passing by might fall on some of them. Also a multitude gathered from the surrounding cities to Jerusalem, bringing sick people and those who were tormented by unclean spirits, and they were all healed.

The more we read, the more evident it becomes that God did not stop His healing ways just because Jesus left. Instead of Jesus alone doing the healings, the gifts of healing have now been greatly multiplied because there were now large numbers of disciples engaged in the ministry of preaching the Good News that included healing and casting out demons.

I am going to take a little rabbit trail here and insert the passage found in Acts 6:3.

"Therefore, brethren, seek out from among you men of good reputation, full of the Holy Spirit and wisdom, whom we may appoint over this business."

Pastoral leaders, Christian teachers, and even the elders, should not be expected to be all things to all people. Growth of the kingdom work, and that would include healing, probably should be appointed to others in whom the Holy Spirit has bestowed the anointing and the power to use in the gifts of healing.

An astute pastor would encourage and support specific ministries under his leadership and guidance. Most churches have elders, deacons, Sunday school superintends and so forth. Maybe there should be a faith healing church ministry as well.

Okay back to 'Does God heal today'. Take a look at the passage found in Acts 8:5-8. Philip was one of those appointed to do work that the apostles were not getting done. Philip has graduated and his ministry had moved from serving tables.

Then Philip went down to the city of Samaria and preached Christ to them. And the multitudes with one accord heeded the things spoken by Philip, hearing and seeing the miracles which he did. For unclean spirits, crying with a loud voice came out of many who were possessed; and many who were paralyzed and lame were healed.

Two things leap off the pages of Scripture. God had used Philip in the ministry of serving tables and then God moved Philip out. Philip learned more than just serving tables and God once again had a purpose in mind through the use of miracles.

In Acts 9:34,35 we read that a healing through Peter affected many:

"Aeneas, Jesus the Christ heals you. Arise and make your bed"
Then he arose immediately. So all who dwelt at Lydda and Sharon saw him and turned to the Lord.

One of the signs mentioned in the Great Commission found in Mark 15 that were to follow included the raising up from the dead. Here in the ninth chapter of Acts we read of this happening.

At Joppa there was a certain disciple named, Tabitha, which is trans-
lated Dorcas. This woman was full of good works and charitable
deeds which she did. – she became sick and died. – Then Peter arose
and went with them. – and knelt down and prayed. And turning to
the body he said, "Tabitha, arise." And she opened her eyes, and
when she saw Peter she sat up. --- And it became known throughout
all Joppa, and many believed on the Lord.

The list of healings that Jesus promised have now been completely placed into practice or carried out by the disciples.

As a disciple of Jesus Christ we first believe, then receive, then do that which Jesus did. Jesus said that what He did, **we would also do** and that is exactly what the early disciples were doing.

But I think it goes well beyond the 'can' do. Jesus said that greater works than He did **we will do.** Probably a better rendering of the text here would read, 'greater in number would be the works that the disciples would do.

From my reading of the Word, I don't think a Christian is truly a disciple if he or she ignores the healing ministry of Jesus Christ.

If I were to leave Acts without including the incident found in Acts 13:9-12 I would miss sharing a story that gets goose bumps running up and down my back.

Paul is sharing the good news with the head man, and the head man had a local sorcerer, a false prophet who was doing his best to block the good news that Paul was sharing with the head man. I love the next part:

Then Saul, who also is called Paul, filled with the Holy Spirit, looked
intently at Elymas and said, "O full of all deceit and all fraud, you
son of the devil you enemy of all righteousness, will you not cease
perverting the straight ways of the Lord? And now, the hand of the
Lord is upon you, and you shall be blind, not seeing the sun for a
time."

Elymas was the sorcerer and Paul told him he was full of the devil. Paul didn't bother casting the devil out of Elymas, he just said that Elymas was going to be blind for a while. Maybe he would get the message that way, but at the very least Elymas would be out of the way.

In the footnote of my Bible is a reference to this passage as found in the Old Testament book of Habakkuk the 1st chapter the fifteenth verse, where we read,

"Behold, you despisers, marvel and perish! For I work a work in your days, a work which you will by no means believe, though one were to declare it to you."

Could this New Testament story and the reference to the Old Testament passage have a meaning for us in this age? I think there are numerous disciples, teachers, pastors and other religious leaders that have set aside the work done in past days, and which they either ignore or ridicule.

If this is so, then what does it mean for these despisers? Will they also perish, or just never receive the power of the Holy Spirit as promised to 'all' believers?

Paul filled with a special filling of the Holy Spirit just said what he was directed to say, and the Lord carried out the sentence. Paul told Elymas exactly who he was, who he was representing, and oh-by-the-way, just so you know I am not making this accusation up, you are going to be blind for a while, **and so it was.**

The list of healings goes on through the rest of the New Testament. I think it is safe to say that as far as the time shortly after Jesus left, miracles and healings continued. In fact from everything I read miracles and healings were the norm, **and not the exception.**

Let's move into today and see if God is continuing to work miracles and healings.

I mentioned early on that I believe that God had a purpose for allowing all the health problems and the resulting healing experiences I have personally experienced in my life.

Having said that, I am going to share a number of miracles and healings that have taken place in my family, and other times in which God has used me in the gifts of healing.

I will not apologize for the numerous stories related to the things that have happened, either to me, or those with whom I have been involved. Earlier in the book I shared why I thought so many things revolving around healing had happened in my life. God was preparing me for this particular task of writing this book.

Moses led the Israelites in the wilderness for forty years while God prepared them for His purpose. God has also led me in the realm of healing for over forty years while He prepared me for this God-given task. Having said that, understand that much of what you read will be of personal incidents.

We are still on the bigger question of 'Does God Heal Today' and it is my intention to answer the question by sharing numerous times when God has used me in healing. I am still living as I write this and I have to assume you would agree with me, these things should be considered as happening today.

One of the earliest experiences where I was used by God in the area of healing involved our youngest son. Our son was and still is, great when it comes to working with his hands.

He was not yet a teenager when he was helping (or hindering) a friend of ours who was teaching him to weld. Our son thought he could get away without using a welder's mask by looking away from the welding flame.

As you have already guessed, this does not always work. That night our son awoke with a great pain in his eyes, and told us what he had done.

I called the doctor and told him what had happened. The doctor told me our son was probably going to have eye problems, and to bring him immediately to the local hospital.

My wife Linda took our son to the hospital while I stayed home with the other children. At this time in my life I had become what is sometimes referred to as a born-again-Christian. But as yet I had very little understanding of how God could, and would, work in the area of healing.

Sometimes even with limited understanding about a given subject, God will work anyway. I did know my Bible and understood that I was the head of my house. In other words I was the responsible one when it came to my family.

I started to pray for my son as soon as my wife and he had left for the hospital. When they arrived, the doctor examined our son's eyes, and then he examined them again.

Finally he said, "I do not understand this. I should be seeing something other that what I am seeing. I don't think any damage has been done, and he sent them home."

Can I say for sure that God answered my prayers with a miracle? No, I cannot, **but this I know**, when our son went to the hospital his eyes were really hurting, he could not see, plus his head was splitting.

These are all signs that usually follow when the eyes have been exposed to the effects of welding without using the welder's protective mask. When our son arrived at the hospital, all the symptoms had disappeared.

Okay, I know what I think, but it is your call as to what you think happened. But as head of the house it was my responsibility to serve as the cover for my family, and I did the only thing that I knew to do. **And as they say, the rest is history.**

I am going to share another story with you that also involved our youngest son which took place a few years later. This is a story that has a number of miracles, including physical healing. I trust you will see God's hand in the things that happened.

Over the years our youngest son has given Linda and I gray hair long before we were old. That statement is not true; it is just a figure of speech. Our hair did not really begin to gray until we were well up in years, but you get the idea.

One day our youngest son told us he had impregnated a young lady. When the young lady told her family, her father told her she was not welcome in his house. As we had a spare bedroom she came to live with us. The young lady had a number of health problems that had started when she was quite young. Among other things, she was a diabetic and often found herself being committed to the hospital because of it.

A few months into the pregnancy, she went in for a regular checkup. The doctor did his thing and before she left his office he told her that given her health circumstances, there was only a 50/50 chance of the child being born normal and healthy.

Later in the day when I returned home, I found her crying and asked her what was wrong? She shared with me what the doctor had said about the possibility of the baby not being born normal and healthy.

I asked her if it would be okay if I were to pray over the situation and for our unborn grandchild. She agreed, and I laid my hand on her stomach and prayed for this unborn child. Again I prayed with the knowledge and understanding I had at this time.

Did I feel any different for having prayed? No, but that was the only thing I knew to do in the situation. I had to pray and trust Father God to understand what was needed. This story then took some funny twists and turns before we ever learned the outcome of that afternoon time of prayer.

This was a time when the economy in Michigan was very uncertain. People were putting bumper stickers on their car that read, 'Will the last one to leave Michigan please turn out the lights.'

Our future daughter-in-law had a sister living in Texas. She told our son she could get him a job as a chef if he came to Texas. So the two of them left for Texas, but of course the move did not solve the health issues and Nancy spent a lot of time in Texas hospitals.

One evening Linda and I received a phone call from the hospital in Texas. It was Nancy and she told us that she and our son had been talking. They had decided when the baby was born they were going to place the child up for adoption.

Needless to say this hit us hard as this child was going to be our first grandchild. The Lord and I had a number of discussions regarding this situation. I must admit I was not happy with God and I did not use a lot of tack as I let the Lord know that I was not happy.

It finally dawned on me that I was not getting very far in these discussions with the Boss, so I grudgingly gave in. But I asked the Lord for just one thing; would He please see that the baby was adopted into a Christian home?

I may not have won any of the arguments, but I finally had a peace about the situation that had been evading me.

A short time after I had come to the point where I was willing to let God do His thing, we received another phone call from the hospital in Texas. We could hear tears in the voice on the other end of the line as our daughter-in-law tried to tell us what had just happened.

It was after visiting hours and our son had already left the hospital; when the door to her room opened and a man came in. He said, "You do not know me, and I do not know you. But I have been visiting my wife two floors up and as I left, God directed me to this floor and to this room. God told me that there was a young lady in here that was going to have a baby and she had decided to give her baby up for adoption. God told me to tell you **NOT** to do this."

Later we learned this unidentified man was a Jew who knew Yahweh personally. And he had also learned to listen to the Lord.

After all the time I had spent arguing with the Lord, He then made my arguments a moot point.

A few weeks later, our daughter-in-law gave birth to a good size, healthy, and normal boy, our first grandchild. Those prayers regarding the health of the baby prayed so long before had been answered. BUT that is not the end of the story. Remember the prayer I had asked of God regarding the Christian family for the baby's adoption?

Shortly after the birth of our grandson, our son and his family moved back to Michigan. We were blessed to be able to spend a lot of time with our first grandchild.

The marriage did not last, and our daughter-in-law and our grandson moved out. She had a hard time caring for her son, and on a 4th of July evening she showed up on our doorstep and asked us to take her son.

A number of things happened legally after that, but the bottom line was we ended up with our grandson on a permanent basis. Although we never legally adopted him we had the privilege of raising him for twenty years. In actuality he became more like one of our sons, than an adopted son.

The second big prayer was answered in a way that I would have never expected. I realize this rabbit trail has nothing to do with physical healing, but healing covers so much more than the physical. It has to do with the body, mind and soul, and it all started with a prayer for healing that took place many months before ever seeing God's answers to my prayers.

What am I trying to say with all of this?

NEVER UNDERESTIMATE GOD. If you are willing to trust Him, He will see you through. And when you look back on the experience, you too will say, "Thank You Lord for what I have experienced."

Remember the opposite is also true. If you rebel, fight, and rail against God because of your circumstance, you will end up bitter and disappointed.

I read somewhere that trial and tribulations are supposed to make you better, not bitter. It is only when you are willing to trust God, that you will find peace.

One of the experiences that I have been blessed with over the years was to be included on a number of mission trips. The church where Linda and I attended for many years had a ministry that was heavily involved in Honduras.

It was during these trips to Honduras where my faith and understanding grew in relation to healing. On numerous occasions I had the privilege of occupying the pulpit.

Honduras does not have much in the way of any health care plans, and the people are needy when it comes to sickness and disease. Along with sickness and disease we have to include the demonic oppression of the kingdom of darkness.

After every service, whether I led the service or someone else did, there was always a time when people came forward for prayer. The faith of these Christians often put mine to shame. Even so I had the privilege of seeing God answer numerous prayers for healing of all manner of sickness and disease.

It was here in Honduras that I often came face to face with brothers and sisters under the oppression of the devil. Sometimes it was fairly easy to use the Name and Power of Jesus to command the enemy to get out. Other times it was hard work, time consuming, and messy.

I say messy because sometimes when the demons finally came out, they came out through vomiting. Other times it was necessary to hold a person firmly to keep them from hurting themselves.

Why do I share these demonic experiences with you the reader? The demonic Kingdom, and that includes not just Satan himself, but also the lesser demons, has not gone away.

I have come to the conclusion that here in the Western world, Satan has for the most part gone underground and he has been quite successful in fooling Christians that demons no longer have to be a concern to Christians. That is simply not the case. There are any number of addictions that can not be overcome, sicknesses that resist the healing power of God, and diseases that run out of control, because the Church and the Christians within the church never come to grips with their real enemy, Satan.

We will deal with the demon problem in greater detail a bit further on, but for now we are still working through the question of 'Does God Heal Today'.

I am going to share some healing experiences I had a few years ago when I went to India with Herb Stewart the founder of New Harvest Ministries.

When Herb and I arrived in India, brother Herb informed me that I would begin every service. That meant I would have to teach or preach about 30 minutes before every meeting.

What a blessing that turned out to be for me. I enjoyed the opportunity to teach, but what was even more exciting was after every meeting the people would surge to the front to be prayed for. I did not speak any of the native language so it was often necessary to rely on the Holy Spirit to show me what was needed, and how I was to pray.

One evening after the service a young couple waited until I was finished praying for those who had come forward. They shyly came up to me and in very halting English they let me know that there were newly married.

Just that quick the Holy Spirit told me that they were expecting a baby, and they were worried because they had no money for a doctor. When I asked them those questions I was told that, yes that was their concern.

The word of knowledge from the Holy Spirit, and the confirmation by this couple, made it easy to know how to pray for them. They left the meeting completely at peace, knowing that God would not only take care of them, but their baby would be a fine healthy child. Some day I hope to find out just how well God answered the prayers of that night.

One Sunday morning we held a service at a village church. After the meeting the local pastor introduced me to a lady who a few years before had leprosy.

Pastor Herb had prayed with her and she was completely healed of leprosy. She wanted prayer and I sensed, again by the Holy Spirit, that she needed to feel the love of Jesus, and prayed accordingly.

The point I want you to see is that God physically heals today and the evidence of that was standing before me. My prayer was for this lady to feel the love and presence of God, and as I watched her face and demeanor change I knew God had again met her need.

Healing may not always be physical in nature, but the physical healing had taken place a few years earlier, now came a different kind of healing.

We were holding the final evening meeting at the ChittiGadda orphanage before we were to travel to Kanjrathukonam. It was 9:30 that night before everyone arrived and Pastor Herb began preaching on the availability of the Holy Spirit in their lives.

How this evangelist can take a message on the subject of the Holy Spirit and turn it into an alter call is beyond me, but he did. Over 200 first time responses for the gift of salvation followed the invitation. But it was after the preaching came to an end that the fun started.

You have read in the gospels where the people pressed in, and that is exactly what happens after meetings in India. Sometimes we would have to pray our way down the steps from the platform because the people were pressing in just wanting us to pray with them.

This night again was no exception. Except that on this night the crowd was much larger, and they seemed even more insistent when they pushed forward.

There was one man in the line before me patiently waiting to be prayed with. I did not understand the Indian language and there weren't any available interpreters, so I was just doing the best I could. When this man arrived at the front of the line, I laid my hands on his head and began to pray.

But he removed my hands from his head and placed them on his eyes. I am not very smart, but it did not require a rocket scientist to figure that he wanted me to pray for his eyes. **So I prayed and asked God to heal his eyes, not knowing what I was really asking God to do.**

After prayer the gentleman moved on. I went on praying with others, when suddenly I realized this man was again back at the front of the line. This time he took my hands and placed them on just one eye.

I remembered the story in the Bible where Jesus healed the blind man, but the first time the man only received a partial healing. Jesus then prayed again and the blind man was completely healed. So I prayed for that one eye, and then continued on, praying for others.

I don't know how long I had been praying for people, but I do know it was a long time before I finally got to the end of the line.

Finally I came to the end of the people wanting prayer. But when I looked up, the man whose eyes I had twice prayed for was back. This time he had four large Indian men with him. He was talking and gesturing up a storm and I thought surely I must be in trouble.

I had no idea what to do and I started to panic when I noticed old brother Matthew a few yards away. I motioned for him to come over. Matthew was Indian but he could speak both English and the local Indian dialect. I explained what had taken place and that I could not understand what was being said, but I thought I might be in trouble. Matthew said he would take care of it. He led the men over to the side of the meeting area. Later I asked Matthew what that was all about and this is what he told me.

It seems this man really was legally blind, and the first time I laid hands on his eyes and prayed, he began to see out of one eye. The second time I prayed for the one eye, his eyesight was totally restored and he wanted a Bible.

Oh yeah, the men that were with him, they were so impressed with what Jesus had done that each of them wanted a Bible too.

There are a couple of things to notice here. First, I did not even understand the language so it sure wasn't I who healed this man.

Also, **I took away from this experience that many times when praying for healing God wants us to be very specific about what we pray for.**

The man knew what he needed and what he wanted. And he made sure I knew exactly what he needed and what he wanted God to do. Notice the persistence of this man. He could have been satisfied seeing out of one eye, but he wanted all of what Jesus had to offer, and he wanted to see out of both eyes. Finally when he came back to give God the praise, **he did not come back alone.**

The next day we flew to Southern India where two brothers have established two orphanages. The brothers were also the head Pastors of a number of small churches.

A number of these churches began when New Harvest Ministries drilled and installed fresh water wells. We visited as many of these small churches as possible.

One afternoon when we were at a small village church, I went outside. In the open area in front of the church a woman was standing. She indicated she wished to talk to me. I found Pastor John to interpret what she was saying. She wanted to tell me how after she had had a child many years before, she had never stopped bleeding and would I pray for her.

I went inside to where Pastor Herb was talking with the local pastor and told him about the lady. Pastor Herb stopped talking long enough to look at me and he said, "Okay, so get out there and pray for her."

I now had the Pastor's blessing and out I went. I prayed with her for some time before she left for her home.

Two nights later at an evening meeting, this lady showed up and was as happy as she could be because the bleeding had stopped. Once again God had healed.

During another evening meeting an epileptic man had a seizure right in the middle of the meeting, and in the Name and power of Jesus we dealt with that. At the same meeting there was an eighteen year old girl who was mentally bound. Herb and I prayed with her and watched as Jesus put an end to that bondage.

As I was writing this section I reviewed my daily notes I had made during this trip to India. One of the many notes read and I quote, "So far I think we have seen everything ever recorded in the healing ministry of Jesus, except for raising someone from the dead."

There are many more stories that I could share with you where I was personally involved, and where God made it plain that He is still in the healing business today.

But don't just take my word for it. Go to any Christian bookstore and they will have for sale numerous books sharing stories of what God is doing in the healing ministry in this day and age.

Does Jesus heal today? You better believe He does, and it doesn't matter if it is within your own family, your church family, or way across the ocean.

God heals today.

SIX

Early on I indicated that this book is being written because of what God has done in my life, especially in the area of healing. I apologize again for the use of the personal pronoun and other references to my life, but I do not know how to tell this any other way.

I will be sharing some of the times where God has healed me. Having said that; let me make it very clear that **God is no respecter of persons**, and He has made this quite clear in His Word. What He has done for me, He will also do for you.

I also want to make it very clear that Father God is in the business of healing multitudes of people, not just me. A person can go on line with their computer, or to any Christian book store and purchase any number of books that tell stories of how God has healed them personally.

The answer to '**The Biggest Question'** includes a number of incidents where God healed me personally. Of course for God to heal me, I had to have a problem in my body that required healing. All the sicknesses, diseases and everything else that I have been inflicted with, God allowed for a reason.

As you read about the health problems that I have had, and how God through Jesus Christ has healed me, keep in mind God wants to do likewise for you.

It is always easier to tell a story when it is your story, and I believe that is what Father God had in mind with the health and healing that took place in my life over these past many years.

I am sharing my life's story with you as it relates to Father God's desire that His kids should not be sick, but if they do become sick, He is not only willing to heal, but that He has put things in place whereby they can be healed.

God is the Divine Healer and God has also outlined His health care plan in the Bible. He would prefer that His kids live in His Divine Health instead of needing Him in His Divine Healing function.

In an early chapter we went through the Bible and determined that in God's eyes, if you have believed in His Son Jesus Christ, then He considers you a saint.

I know from Bible passages God considers me a saint. But I can assure you that most of those who have made my acquaintance over the years, **would _not_ agree with that 'saint' description of myself.** When I look at my life, even though God says I am a saint, I have a hard time seeing myself as a saint.

I mention this because of the healings that have taken place in my body. If you trust and believe in Him through Jesus Christ, God will do the same for you also. **He is no respecter of persons** and God considers you a saint regardless of what you may or may not have done in your life.

One of the earliest recollections I have where God touched me personally took place in my late teens.

Linda and I were married quite young and we quickly had our five children. One evening there was a scheduled concert featuring Henry and Hazel Slaughter. I liked their singing and I really wanted to hear them sing. Linda agreed to stay home with our oldest son so that I could go.

Before Linda could change her mind, I quickly purchased a ticket for the concert and shortly thereafter took myself to the Grand Rapids Civic Center.

The music was all I had hoped for, but I got more than I had expected when I purchased my ticket. In the course of the evening Henry and Hazel talked about how God had healed teeth during some of their concerts.

That was extremely interesting to me because I had very poor teeth. From the time I was just a youngster; my mother had a problem when bringing her little boy to the dentist.

It would be an understatement to say that I did not like going to the dentist. I usually pitched a fit, and the nice old dentist in order to work on my teeth, had to give me gas and knock me out.

By the time I was a teenager, I had had a number of teeth pulled because my mouth just was not big enough for all the teeth.

For those of you who know me you probably will find it hard to believe that my mouth was not BIG enough. It seems that my big mouth has always been getting me into trouble.

In addition to the removal of a number of teeth, I had a mouth full of cavities that needed to be filled, or a bunch of teeth where the cavities had already been filled. My teeth were soft, and they were a mess as well.

As Henry and Hazel shared about teeth that had been miraculously filled, even some where the fillings had a cross etched on the top of the filling. I just sat and listened with wonder.

Then I began to wonder if God would do that for me. I am not sure I was looking for a miracle, but if this would keep me out of the dentist's chair, I wanted it, **and I wanted it badly.**

By the time Henry and Hazel prayed for the heeling of teeth, I was into it, and I claimed that healing for myself. Later when I had left the concert I did not feel any different, and I was not sure anything had happened.

It was only some time later that I realized I wasn't going to the dentist any more. I did not have the agony of tooth aches any more. Since that time, the only dental work, other than cleaning, that I have needed, was to fix some of the cavities that had been filled years earlier.

Fifty some years later, I still only go the dentist once every two or three years for cleaning. With the exception of an old filling falling out, or where some rot has occurred around the edge of an early filling I have not darkened the door of the dentist's office.

Often when brushing my teeth I thank God for the first miracle that took place in my life.

My first miracle had a unique twist to it because I was not in any special relationship with Father God at the time. In short, I had not yet asked Jesus into my life.

I had the privilege of being raised in a Christian home by Christian parents. I was raised when attendance at our local church twice every Sunday was not only the norm, but it was just something we did every Sunday. I attended a parochial school from the time I was in kindergarten, and every Wednesday after school, we went to catechism class.

After high school and a brief period in collage, Linda and I were married. We moved to Holland and joined a local church where I was involved in church activities such as teaching Sunday school.

As soon as the children were old enough we brought them to church with us. I always thought what a sight we must have created when we walked into church with five children aged so closely together that they looked like a step ladder.

You would think having grown up in a Christian home, having attended parochial schools, attended church faithfully, done the expected things one would expect of a Christian, that I should have been in the kingdom. But the truth was, from the time I was eighteen years old, I knew that if I were to die, I was not going to be going to be going to heaven.

What I want to point out here is that even though I was not where I should have been spiritually, **Father God is so gracious and loving, He healed me anyway.**

And He will heal you if you are willing to have the faith to believe that He not only can heal you, **but He also wants to heal you.**

That was my first real exposure to Father God's healing power and I had no idea what God had started in my life. In hindsight not knowing what was coming was probably a good thing.

I mentioned earlier that on my computer monitor I have a note that reads, 'God has a plan and a purpose for my life, **BUT** He only gives it to me on His installment plan, one installment at a time.'

How often I have been thankful that I can only see the current installment of God's plan for my life.

During the early years of our marriage my biggest concern was to make a living. Then, if there was any time left over I spent that with Linda and the kids.

In the course of earning a living, we moved around West Michigan to various places. I really don't remember having any thoughts, or even any serious health problems requiring the services of either a doctor, or of Father God.

I do remember attending a church in Holland, where our pastor had a heart attack and was told he needed to have by-pass surgery. I will never forget a comment he made to me at the time. He said that his greatest fear was to have the by-pass surgery.

At the time I did not think too much of the comment, and he died before he was able to have the necessary surgery. After he died, I often thought about his comment and wondered what part the 'fear' of the surgery played in his early death.

Many years later the Biblical significance of his comment registered with me. We will talk more on the 'fear-factor' later, but for now, ask yourself where fear comes from, and who it is that exploits the fear within our minds?

The church's new pastor became more than just a pastor to me. He became a very good friend as well. A few years after he took over the pastorate, he was diagnosed with Lupus disease.

I took it quite hard and I will never forget one evening after a board meeting. All the board members were sitting on the church floor in front of the pulpit, tears in our eyes praying and asking God to heal our pastor.

God heard and answered our prayers, even though we did not see the evidence at that time. Shortly after this late night prayer session the disease progressed to the point where our pastor had to resign. He moved out West where he was raised, intending to live until God either healed him, or took him home.

This pastor friend taught me much about faith for healing even though he was not aware of it. To make a long story short, God honored his faith, and a few years later he had the evidence that was not seen while he was with our church.

God restored him to health, restored him to the ministry, and now many years later he is still enjoying the health that came from this healing.

As I look back, I would have to say it was at this time that God began to expose me to faith messages and healing incidents. God started in small ways to open me up to what He could, and would do, if I would just believe and trust Him.

In the last chapter I shared the welding incident that occurred with our son and that it is my belief that it was Father God who healed him. Over those formative years, I had a number of what I would describe as minor health problems that I brought to God in prayer and faith.

Even though these were not life threatening situations, God healed me. For myself I think it was beneficial to have learned to trust and believe God for healing in smaller, non-life threatening health problems.

Later when it became necessary for me to believe for a healing that was more serious, I already had a foundation of trust and the faith to believe and to build on.

I also shared with you the story of our daughter-in-law and how God not only answered the prayer for healing our first 'not-yet-born' grandchild, but threw in a bonus as well by letting us raise him. God was working to build my faith to trust Him to heal, but also teaching me to let Him take charge and do it His way.

Do I think it makes any difference to God if you have put Him to the test in small occurrences before needing Him in a big way? No, I really don't think so. I do however; believe your faith can be built up through experience, to the point where it is easier for you to have the additional faith when needed.

When you have a problem or need that is greater than anything you have previously encountered, it helps if you know you can trust the Father at a time when you need Him in a more troubling situation.

The years passed, and about nineteen years ago I needed to increase my life insurance to cover a bank loan needed for the business. No big deal I thought, and made the appointment for a good physical and the resulting blood work.

When the results of the blood work came back to the doctor, I received a call to come in and talk with him. The blood work revealed that my PSA count was a bit disturbing. For you ladies, the PSA count is an early detection for a possible prostate cancer problem, similar to finding a lump in a breast.

My doctor explained the potential problem and suggested an appointment with an urologist. That visit was interesting, humiliating and hurtful, and the result was that yes, I had prostate cancer. That doctor wanted to operate immediately, but for some reason my spirit said no.

I scheduled an appointment with Mayo Clinic and a few weeks later I traveled to Rochester, MN. I went through all the tests and blood work. The doctors at Mayo Clinic confirmed what I had been told, but included the fact that there are four different kinds of prostate cancer; and you guessed it, I had not only the worst one of the four, but that was also the one that progressed the most rapidly.

The doctors at Mayo Clinic also wanted to schedule immediate surgery. Again, my spirit checked me, and I said no.

Given the test results, the doctors at the Mayo Clinic had in effect given me a death sentence.

I had heard the Spirit say no and I had heard the doctors say go. Now I found myself between the Rock and the hard place.

Over the next few years God gave me the grace to do it His way, but Satan made sure I had plenty of doubts along the way.

I knew in my spirit that God said no to surgery, but what did He want me to do? And even though I prayed and asked Him, I was not getting any answers.

On one side God had said no to surgery, and on the home front I was being encouraged to have the surgery. When you are pulled one way and then pulled the other way, a person can feel stretched pretty thin.

A few weeks after the visit to Mayo Clinic, my company had a trade show scheduled in San Francisco. The first day of the event, I was in our booth when I happened to look down the aisle and saw a distributor friend of mine from Toronto walking towards me.

Just that quick, the Holy Spirit brought to my mind a conversation I had had with him over dinner some eighteen to twenty months earlier. That evening before the meal he had ordered arrived, he took out a container with a number of pills; pills which turned out to be mostly vitamins.

When questioned, he told Linda and me that some years before his sister had been diagnosed with cancer and the cancer had progressed to the point where she had been sent home to die.

Instead of dying, his sister went to Dr. D'Adamo, a 'holistic' doctor in Toronto. Dr. D'Adamo had been instrumental in turning her health around. Seven years later she was not only still living, but enjoying life as well. Dr. D'Adamo had so impressed my friend that he also went to the doctor, and hence the pills.

I am going to inject something at this point. I had no idea why the Holy Spirit impressed me to say no to the doctors' recommendation. Everything I knew or had ever learned was not to disagree with the doctors. Just do it their way.

There was no question that in my spirit I heard the 'NO' very clearly. **Over the next three years I learned it was easier to hear the Holy Spirit, than it was to walk out what I knew I had heard.**

Only as I look back, can I see what the Lord wanted me to experience so that I could share it with others and for me to give Him all the glory.

Seeing my friend walk towards me that day in San Francisco, the Holy Spirit brought to mind that long-ago-evening's discussion. I asked my friend to sit down and told him what I had been told by the doctors at the Mayo Clinic.

I told my friend that I wanted him to arrange an appointment for me with this doctor in Toronto. That would be difficult I was told, as it usually took six months to schedule an appointment.

I told my friend that in a few weeks we had a trade show event scheduled in Toronto, and I did not care how he did it, but I wanted an appointment.

I do not know how he did it, but I got the appointment. This doctor took my pulse in seven different places, looked in my eyes and did some other weird things. But this doctor, who had never seen me before and did not have any of my medical records, then told me things that had occurred in my body that I had forgotten.

He also confirmed the prostate cancer. Dr. D'Adamo put me on a restricted eating regimen as what I was eating, given my blood type, was just feeding the cancer.

Back home, I followed Dr. D'Adamo's instructions, continued to pray and believe for God to heal me, but as you probably guessed, my situation just got worse.

I had learned at the Mayo Clinic there are seven different levels of prostate cancer, and I progressed upward, or downward, until I was in the seventh level. Normal PSA blood count is below four. When I was first diagnosed I was already at an eight. That count continued to go up until at one time I my PSA level was measured at sixty-four.

The church Linda and I were attending at the time was a charismatic church which taught and believed in healing. There were numerous times I was prayed over and anointed with oil. I was counseled by family members to have surgery, etc.

I checked into all the options, even while I continued to believe God would heal me with a miracle.

One of the options that appealed to me was known as cyro-surgery. I thought this was a door opening and made an appointment with the doctor in Rochester Michigan who had experience with this type of surgery.

When I checked with my health insurance I was told because the surgery was too new, they would not cover the costs. Later my insurance agent convinced the company to cover the costs, and surgery was scheduled. The door that appeared to have closed now seemed to be opening.

On the day of the surgery, I was prepped and lying on the gurney waiting to be wheeled into surgery. Just before I was to enter the surgery room the hospital administrator came into the room and informed me that he had just spoken with the insurance carrier. My insurance carrier had changed their mind and decided they would not cover the cost.

That news made me very angry and I got up off the gurney, dressed, and left. At the time I was not a happy camper, **but it seemed again God was trying to tell me that this was not to be His way.**

I went back to the doctor in Rochester and he proscribed an injection he said would slow the growth of the tumor until I could decide what I wanted to do.

Back to option # 1, praying to the Lord, and more waiting. I did not mind going back to the Lord; it was the waiting that I did not like.

It was now almost three years since I had first been told that I had prostate cancer. Three years of praying, listening, going though doors that appeared to be opening, only to close. As far as I could tell nothing was happening for the better.

About this time I got a call from the cancer doctor in Rochester. He told me he really thought we should go in and do an ultra scan of the cancerous tumor. So back to Rochester, up on the table, and expose myself to the indignities that take place in the doctor's office.

During the procedure, I kept hearing the doctor say, hmm, hmm, hmm, and to his nurse, 'look at that'. Needless to say my confidence level went the opposite way from up. Finally he said I could get dressed and in a couple of days he would let me know what was up.

I left, but because of the hmm's, I was not very confident and the devil had a heyday with me. My faith was at rock bottom, and I just knew what I was going to hear.

Two days came and went, three days, four days, and still no call. The person who said that the mind is the Devil's playground could not have had any idea how big that playground in my mind was.

I finally summoned up the courage to call the doctor's office. The doctor was busy, so I asked the nurse if she could fax me a copy of the report. The report arrived and I read it, but the report I was reading could not be right, I called the doctor's office again.

This time I reached the doctor. I told him I had reviewed the report but obviously I must be reading it incorrectly, because it appeared the cancerous tumor was no longer active.

I had read the report correctly, and after more than three years, God had healed me in His way, and in His time. The tumor was dead. Obviously I was a happy camper and had to share with everyone who would listen what God had done.

During my Bible research for this book I came across a verse in Galatians 6:9 that reads as follows:

let us not grow weary while doing good, for in due season we shall reap if we do not lose heart.

God showed me that this verse applied to my healing. Keep the faith, follow the path He directs you on, and when the time is right, we shall receive.

But, and there always seems to be a 'but'; we shall receive only if we do not lose heart.

Life was again great and I was riding high, but God was just getting started. Just a year later, I was having trouble breathing whenever doing anything strenuous. Back to our family doctor who sent me to a heart specialist. The heart specialist informed me my arteries were plugged up and I would need by-pass heart surgery.

Okay, now that I knew what was wrong, I also knew what to pray for. The heart doctors wanted to do the surgery as soon as possible. But I had signed up for a mission trip to Honduras and I really wanted to go. So you guessed it, I told the doctors I would schedule the surgery when I got back. I was told there was a very good chance I would die before I got back.

Our church pastor was also going on this trip and more than once he had said he would like to see someone raised from the dead. So I said to the doctor that if the worst happened, my pastor would get the opportunity to raise someone from the dead.

They thought I was crazy, but if I was not going to listen to them, then they would prescribe some nitro-glycerin tablets to take along. That was a good precaution and twice I needed to use them or I would have died.

The mission trip was a good trip, and one afternoon I was scheduled to teach the service as the pastor was meeting off-site with the village church pastors.

I loved to teach about the Bible passages that dealt with healing because the people in Honduras were so open to what God could do. That morning, before I worked on the message, I was praying, when the Lord showed me a vision of the people in the congregation laying hands on me and praying for me.

In the afternoon session at the conclusion of the teaching, I told the fellowship that after we had prayer for any of those who desired it, would they please return to their seats as I had something more I wished to say to them.

We concluded praying for those who came forward and the people returned to their seats. I shared with them my physical heart problem and how I was scheduled for surgery when I returned to the States.

I told them about the vision I had early that morning. I asked if they would be willing to lay their hands on me and to pray for me. I stepped off the platform and kneeled in front of the altar.

No one came forward it seemed like forever, and I thought once again I had really blown it. Then the elderly lady, who had been interpreting for me, came and laid her hands on my head.

At that moment it was like the entire audience came in mass. And man did they know how to pray. I think I experienced every feeling and emotion possible. When they finished praying for me, I just knew I had been healed.

The next morning, I was praising and thanking God for my healing, when I had another vision. I didn't like this vision as well as the one I had had the day before.

I saw myself being wheeled into the operating room, and knew it was God's plan for me to have the by-pass surgery.

Two days later, the day before leaving for home we had a little time for R&R. We traveled to a picturesque place at the bottom of a mountain with a small stream flowing down ending in a large pool.

I climbed up the mountain to sit beside the narrow stream that was tumbling down. It was so peaceful, but it looked like a nicer place to sit on the other side.

The stream was narrow and it should not have been a problem to jump to the other side, Wrong, I slipped, and went down that mountain on my back in the rapidly flowing stream.

I finally reached the large pool at the bottom of the stream. Members of the mission team along with others from the church, were splashing around in the pool. I tried to get out of the pool, but the large rocks where I was trying to get out were too slippery.

I was rapidly losing it, I could hardly breathe, and my strength was almost gone. One member from our group realized that I was not playing around and that I needed help. They pulled me out and grabbed a nitro-glycerin tablet for me. Satan almost got me, but not quite.

The next day we flew out of Honduras to Miami. I was not even able to carry my luggage. The plane arrived in Miami a bit late and we needed to move quickly and for some distance in order to catch our next plane.

Once again I just about did not make it. Thank the Lord for the foresight of the doctors and the nitro-glycerin tablets.

Within twenty-four hours I was being prepped for by-pass heart surgery. I asked the physician how long I was going to be in the hospital. I was told from five to seven days. I said that I would like to go home in three. I thought I was kidding him, but he thought I was serious.

I went home in three days, back to work a few days later, and driving within a week. The healing miracle was not what I thought it was going to be after the Honduran fellowship prayed for me.

The miracle actually took place after the successful surgery. I will interject here that it has been more than fifteen years since that quadruple by-pass surgery, and God has honored my healing all these years.

I went home on a Sunday and the home we were living in at the time had twenty-eight steps to reach our living quarters. You are not supposed to climb steps after this type of surgery, so my paramedic son and his friend planned to carry me up the stairs. They were not there when we arrived home, so I did what I was not supposed to do and walked up those 28 steps.

The next afternoon I was lying on the couch when Linda came home and I could see she had been crying. Linda finally told me that she had just been told by her doctor that she had breast cancer. I think that news hit me harder than when I learned that I had prostate cancer.

The doctor wanted to schedule immediate surgery, but after Linda and I talked about it, we decided a second opinion might be a good idea. Linda's sister-in-law knew this female doctor in Lansing, Michigan and called to see if she would see Linda.

The doctor agreed to see Linda and an appointment was scheduled. The doctor asked us to get the breast x-rays before coming for the appointment. We got those X-rays and before Linda went to Lansing, I read them.

I am not a doctor and I don't understand what doctors write, if I can even read it, but the Holy Spirit directed me to a certain area in the report summary. It seemed to me that when the local doctor had done the biopsy on the suspect tissue, the area that was removed was larger than the cancerous area.

I showed this to Linda and suggested she show this to the doctor in Lansing. Yes, the cancerous area had been completely removed during the biopsy and subsequent tests indicated that the cancer had not spread. As a preventive measure Linda had radiation treatments.

God proved again that he can heal in many different ways. We just need to be open to His direction.

It has been over fifteen years since Linda was told she had breast cancer. The breast cancer has never returned and no operation has ever been needed.

I like to paraphrase a verse found in Deuteronomy 7. If you look up this verse it will not read exactly the way I am writing it:

And I the Lord will take away from you all sickness, and I will not put on you any of the terrible diseases which you have known.

Where the terrible disease known as cancer came from in Linda's breast, we do not know. This is what we do know. The Lord, in answer to prayer took the cancerous cells away without removing the breast.

I really should have kept a daily diary as God has done so much in my life and allowed me to be used and tested in a number of ways. But I didn't so I can only relate the larger incidents that I remember.

Three years after I learned the cancerous prostate tumor was dead, blood tests indicated my PSA count was increasing. Back to the doctor's office where a scan of the prostate was again preformed.

This time I was positioned so that I could see the screen and could see what the doctor was seeing. He pointed out the tumor and showed me the green edges of the tumor where the cancer was coming back to life.

He suggested the Lupron shot I had had before to slow the growth. I had the shot, went back to 'directed' prayer and asked the Lord to kill the cancer again.

The first time my faith was tested and twisted for over three years. On this second go-around, God killed the cancer is less than a year.

For all intents and purposes, given the type of prostate cancer and the projected growth, long before now I should have been dead. But God had other plans in mind.

Again no surgery, so how did God heal me? We will cover this type of healing in greater depth in the chapter entitled the Ways in Which Father God Heals Today.

Five years later, and for the third time, the tumor again returned to life. Same procedure, a shot to slow the growth, a lot of directed prayer, and in six months, God killed the cancerous tumor again for the third time. God is faithful, but He will test a person to find out if we really trust Him.

Each time Satan has done his best to convince me that this time was the one, the party is over, and God would not heal me again, and so on. **But the party isn't over until the Father says it is over.**

The same year that the prostate cancer had surfaced for the third time and just before Christmas, I woke up early in the morning to go to the bathroom. I remember getting out of bed, but then I could not figure out what I was doing lying on the floor.

I pulled my self up and by holding onto the wall I made my way into the bathroom. I don't remember what happened next, or when it happened, I only know that I found myself lying on the floor by the toilet. I made my way back to bed and went to sleep.

I usually got up rather early and this morning was no exception. My office at home is a short distance from my bedroom and I went to the office to review the emails that usually arrived from China during the night. I went to respond to the emails, but I could not read my typing. Okay, I will write a couple of checks, but I could not sign my name. Oh well, must have been something I ate the night before, don't worry about it.

That was a Friday and by Sunday things had not really improved. Linda called our son who was working at Spectrum Hospital. He came over, made me do a couple of things, and told me to get in his car as we were going to the hospital.

You guessed it, I had had a stroke. I was not always very faithful in taking the daily pill for high blood pressure, and it caught up with me.

This was the first time that I ever thought I was going to die. I was convinced that there was going to be a second stroke and I would die. I don't think I have to tell you where those thoughts came from.

While waiting for the fatal stroke to come, Satan began playing with my mind asking me why I thought what I believed was correct. Was I really going to go to heaven? Was what I believed the only way, and on and on it went. I was a mess.

But in this age of computers there is a vast store of knowledge available to all. I started checking on other religions. I read what they believed and what they taught. I read the Koran and then compared what I had read with what I had been taught and what I believed.

There is much written in the Bible that I do not fully understand, but I came away with a peace that had been eluding me for some time. And I am happy to report; the second fatal stroke never came.

Once again God was good, and in answer to my prayers, He has restored me almost entirely. I think He left just enough areas un-restored to remind me who is in control.

Two years ago, and seventeen years after first being diagnosed with prostate cancer, the cancer reappeared for the fourth time. About this time the church we were attending had been studying the life of David. David had been king for a period of time and he wanted to bring the ark back to God's house.

Now on the surface this was a godly thing to want to do and it should have been a God-pleasing thing to do as well. The ark represented Yahweh and David wanted to bring the ark back where it belonged. And King David wanted to do it in style.

In First Chronicles 13:1-4 we read how King David started the process to bring the ark back from the country of the Philistines.

Then David consulted with the captains of thousands and hundreds, and with every leader. And David said to all the assembly of Israel, "If it seems good to you, and if it is of the Lord our God, let us send out to our brethren everywhere—and let us bring the ark of our God back to us." Then all the people said that they wanted to do so, for the thing was right in the eyes of all the people.

What the king wanted to do, he did not do until he had gotten the support of everybody in the kingdom that counted. Bringing the ark back to Jerusalem was the right thing to do, and David had the support of the entire land.

With all of the support that David garnered, it seems that someone forgot to get God's input on the move.

David started by building a good looking, sturdy cart; got a couple of the best looking and strongest oxen he could find, loaded up the ark, and the journey to bring the ark to the temple began.

The people with David were dancing and singing. It was a God-party atmosphere and God was getting the glory. Things were going pretty good, and the ark was moving in the right direction, when the cart hit some ruts in the road.

Now if you were Uzzah and you were driving the cart, when the cart hit some holes or some bumps in the road, what do you think you would have done? Probably you would have done the same thing the driver-priest Uzzah did. Grab onto the ark to keep it steady on the cart.

That was the wrong thing to do because just that quick God killed Uzzah the driver, and just that quick the party was over. David was not happy with God and he let God know it.

Bottom line was that David was doing a good thing, but doing the good thing in the wrong way. If David or the priests had checked with God, or even read the manual, the Torah, they would have known how to transport the ark.

Uzzah would not have died and David could have saved the price of the cart and oxen as well. King David made two mistakes. He did not ask the Lord, and he did not check the manual.

Now I am told my old cancer problem is back. Three times I had done what I believe God had directed me to do. Each time God honored His word with healing by killing the cancerous prostate tumor.

Now the question came up in my mind, did God want to do it the same way, or did He want to heal me in a different way. David was doing a good thing but he was doing it in the wrong way.

Trusting God for my healing was a good thing. But I wanted to be sure that my prayers and my faith were directed in the manner which God proscribed.

It is like taking medicine. If the doctor says to take it once a day, and you think once is good, three times should be better, you could be making a mistake.

Doing it your way could negate the good effects of the medicine, or even worse, doing it your way could bring your life to an early end.

Many years before the episode of bringing the ark back to the temple, Moses had followed God's direction to strike the rock and water would come out.

The next time the Israelites needed water Moses was instructed to speak to the rock. Moses did not listen to what God told him; he only remembered how God did it the first time. So Moses struck the rock.

God honored Moses before the people, but later God had a private 'time-out' with Moses.

The Lord wanted him to do something. Moses was told how to do what God wanted, but for whatever reason Moses elected not to listen to the God-given instructions.

David did not ask God for direction and Moses did not listen to the God-given instructions. Both Godly men made a mistake and both paid a price for their mistake.

Godly men in responsible God-placed-positions have a greater responsibility to ask God for instructions and to follow God's direction.

Now I found myself back in the situation of the cancerous tumor again flaring up. What should I do? Should I do what God had honored in the past, or did God want to do heal in a different way?

I spent a lot of time in prayer and in the Word before I was convinced to do it the same way as before. Three months later, the cancerous tumor was again dead.

It has been a few years since this fourth incident with the prostate cancer. As I am writing this chapter I have just learned the problem has surfaced once again. I can not tell you if I am to do the same as before or is God is going to instruct me to go in a different direction, or if I will be tested in a new way.

What ever direction it is be, for now it is back to James 1:5,
'if any man lack wisdom let him ask.'

I will again ask, listen, and wait. Hopefully, before this book is finished I will have an answer for you in regards to the Lord' direction **this time.**

There have been numerous other healing incidents over the years and we may touch on a few additional ones as the book progresses, but for now I wanted to answer the question of whether God will heal you by sharing some ways in which God had healed me.

I am no more worthy of being healed than you are, and if God would heal a sinner like me, He will also heal you.

Let's look at some Bible passages where He plainly says that He will heal, but to answer the Biggest Question, **will God heal you;** the answer is a resounding **YES**. There may be some reasons that God is delaying your healing, and we will look at those in a later chapter. But be assured; **He not only wants to heal you, but if you let Him, He will heal you.**

In chapter four we looked at the subject, 'Can God Heal?' The answer to that question was a simple and solid, **Yes He Can!**

In chapter five we examined the subject of whether God heals today. We started the search for the answer way back in the book of Genesis and continued right through the time when Jesus walked this earth. Then we picked up the healing reports after Jesus departed for heaven.

I shared some personal events that happened in my life and as I wrote, do not take my word for it. Go to any Christian bookstore and pick up one or more of the literally scores of books telling about the healings that Jesus is still doing in lives during this present day and age.

There should no doubt in your mind that God, either directly or indirectly, through the Name of Jesus or through other Christian disciples, does indeed heal in this day and age.

Remember, God is no respecter of persons. What He had done for me and so many others, **He will also do for you.**

Let's review these three chapters referencing the Word of God. Take these verses to heart, read and reread them, and then let the Holy Spirit drive these words deep into your very being.

Starting with a few verses addressing the question of whether God has the power to heal you.

- *"For with God nothing will be impossible."* Luke 1:37
- *"The things which are impossible with men are possible with God."* Luke 18:27
- *"Now to Him who is able to do exceedingly abundantly above all that we ask, or think, according to the power that works in us."* Ephesians 3:20

These three verses tell us there is nothing, absolutely nothing, impossible for God to handle. God is telling you that nothing is too big, or too small for Him to handle. Do not let Satan confuse you with any thoughts that do not line up with the Word of God.

The world may change around you, and circumstances may change in your life, but God the Father does not change. He is the same today as He was yesterday, and He will be the same for all eternity.

Father God is so 'cock-sure' of this fact that He had it written down where everyone can read it, stating this in the Old Testament book of Malachi for the Jewish nation and then bringing the Gentiles into the picture in the New Testament.

- *"For I am the Lord, I do not change."* Malachi 3:6
- *"Jesus Christ is the same yesterday, today, and forever."* Heb. 13:8
- *"Most assuredly, I say to you, before Abraham was, I AM."* John 8:58

According to the Bible, God and Jesus are one and the same. We also read that He never changes, and now we read in John that both God and His Son Jesus have also been around for quite some time.

That great little saying that we learned in Sunday school so many years ago sums it up so well. **God said it and I believe it and that settles it for me.**

GOD DOES NOT LIE, period. If in His book, He said it, then He will do it. God can heal so let's again take a look at some passages where that fact is covered.

- *"He sent His word and healed them, and delivered them from their destructions."* Psalm 107:20
- *"For I will restore health to you and heal you of your wounds," says the Lord.* Jeremiah 30:17
- *"O Lord my God, I cried out to You, and You have healed me."* Psalm 30:2

These are three additional verses affirming that God has not only promised to heal, but that He has healed and He will heal again.

We previously discussed that it is the will of God to heal you, so I am only going to list two passages that you should keep in mind.

In Matthew chapter 7 the seventh verse we read,

"Ask, and it will be given to you; seek, and you will find; knock, and it will be opened to you." and in James 4:2 we read,

"Yet you do not have because you do not ask."

Have you sought, and have you knocked? And then James calls us to task by reminding us that we often do not have because we never took the time to ask.

Ask specifically for what you need. Don't take it for granted that God will move without you asking Him.

Yes, God knows what you need before you even ask, but God still wants us to ask.

In addition to asking, Matthew is quite emphatic when he simply says, 'seek'. What is Matthew implying here and where does one seek? Seek, or look for God's answers in His book. When you have asked, you will find answers, or God will supply the answers through someone.

When you have looked and now that you have asked, and you know what God has promised, now you need to knock.

Knock in the original language really means to keep knocking until the door is opened. James just reinforces what Matthew has already told us; it all starts with you asking God for what you need as it relates to your healing.

Summing up these last three chapters is rather easy:

1. CAN GOD HEAL?
2. DOES GOD HEAL?
3. AND WILL GOD HEAL ME?

The answer to all three questions is a resounding YES!

SEVEN

What does a person do when they get a 'Terminal' diagnosis? Isn't that a great way to begin a chapter designated to the ways in which God heals today? Just take the worst possible situation and start there.

I owe a lot to Dr. Ed Dobson, the former senior pastor of Calvary Undenominational church for my understanding that Christians need a more balanced approach to Biblical healing.

Dr. Dobson preached a series of sermons on healing that included various ways he indentified in the Bible which Father God uses to heal.

With his permission I have borrowed many of the ideas and scriptures that Dr. Dobson identified in his sermons.

My thoughts and feelings when I received the news that I had cancer were much the same as those Dr. Dobson experienced when he was told he had ALS.

For me when I got the bad news that I had cancer, I did not at first want to believe it. How could I be sick when I felt so good? Then after realizing it was true, I had to adjust my thinking as well as my attitude.

That was not easy, and I had to learn to pray for the Lord to give me grace to accept the sickness and as Dr. Dobson said, to give me the grace every day just to keep on living.

As Dr. Dobson said in his message, 'He was ready to die, but He just did not want to die yet'.

And that is also how I felt. It would have been easy to just give in and to give up, but that was not the direction I was given when I prayed.

I related some of my God-given directions earlier, but for now, let's begin with a Bible experience of a king that received notice that the sickness he had was going to end in his death.

The story in the Bible begins when God sent a message which most of us would rather not hear; namely get ready, you are going to die and you are not going to get better.

In the book of Isaiah the thirty-eightieth chapter, we read the story of this king of Israel who was told he was going to die. The king did not even have the luxury of hearing the sentence of death from his own doctors, his diagnosis came straight from God.

In those days Hezekiah was sick and near unto death. And Isaiah went to him and said to him, "Thus says the Lord; set your house in order, for you shall die and not live.

Ouch, here Hezekiah was, at the top of the pecking order, he was the king. Things had been bad for him as king and if the chronological order of Isaiah is correct, Hezekiah had recently prayed and God had just provided a great deliverance for Israel by killing 185,000 Assyrian solders, and those that were left went back home.

This slaughter of 185,000 men of war all happened because Hezekiah fervently prayed and God moved. Now Hezekiah gets sick and according to the story, Hezekiah was not too happy with this message straight from God that he was going to die.

In fact if I read between the lines of the story, he goes straight to the Lord and let's God know he is very unhappy and then he reminds the Lord just how he has served God to the best of his ability.

Okay, so he was not happy, but he did the right thing, he went to God in prayer. I don't know if Hezekiah had been under his doctor's care for his sickness prior to the visit from Isaiah, nor do I know if he had been praying prior to the visit. What I do know is as soon as he received the message from God that Isaiah delivered, the first thing he did was pray.

I have not always remembered to pray as soon as I have a health problem. I have gotten a lot better and it does not take me as long anymore to get my priorities in the right order.

Prayer to God should come first before the visit to the doctor or the taking of medicine.

The second thing that got my attention was how Hezekiah prayed. He did not mess around before telling God that he thought this sentence of death was unfair. We are told that after Hezekiah got his feelings out in the open with God, he wept bitterly.

What happened next is really interesting. In this story found in the book of Second Kings, Hezekiah must have prayed immediately, and God answered quickly.

Isaiah the messenger had not even gotten out of the palace when God turned him around with a new message he needed to deliver:

"I have heard your prayer, I have seen your tears; I will heal you and in three days you will go up to the house of the Lord. And I will add to your days fifteen years." II Kings 20:5,6

Okay that was the good news, Hezekiah got a reprieve. But I have often wondered what Hezekiah's thoughts were as the end of the fifteen years started coming closer?

Did you catch the part that said in three days Hezekiah would go up to the house of the Lord? God said I will heal you, and just so you know that it is Me that is doing the healing, your healing will be complete in three days.

Just a little side note here; as you read about prayers in the Bible note how many of them include why God should do what the person praying is asking Him to do.

Back to the story where God had informed Hezekiah that he was going to die. We have read in Ecclesiastes that the cycle-of-life includes a time to be born and a time to die.

Hezekiah had been informed of his time-to-die, and he did not like it. He had a lot of things that he believed still needed to be done. Hezekiah was not willing to accept his sentence of death and he reacted by praying to God. We are told that God changed His mind regarding Hezekiah's time-to-die. It is true that God never changes, but it also true that God has the right to change his mind.

Specifically, **it also appears true that God's kids may play a part in the changing of His mind.** The fact there was a time-to-die for Hezekiah did not change, but God can, and in this case did, change when that was to be for Hezekiah.

The story continues; when Isaiah returned to Hezekiah's bedroom to deliver the newest message from God that he was going to live, Isaiah also told the king's doctors, to take a lump of figs and lay it on the boil. The seventh verse reads:

So they took the lump of figs and laid it on the boil, and he recovered.

Just a little aside here; why did it take more than one person to place the lump of figs on the boil? What is that old generic joke, how many people does it take to change a light bulb? The answer is five, one to hold the bulb and four to turn the stepladder. Same principal do you think?

The Bible does not condemn the use of medical remedies, but in this case it is doubtful if the medical remedy by itself would have healed Hezekiah. God alone can heal, and He can do so by miracle means, by natural means or by human means. A lump of medicinal figs may have helped, but it was God who did the healing.

I noticed three specific things in Hezekiah' prayer for healing:

1. His prayer was a focused prayer. Hezekiah zoomed in on the problem. God had said he was going to die.
2. Hezekiah looked at what he had done for the Lord and reminded God of this evaluation of his life. When we go to God asking for something, especially something that is life or death, look at your life and if sin has been a part of your life get rid of it. Or as Isaiah said, "Get your house in order."
3. Prayers for healing include pouring out our hearts to the Lord; 'Lord help me'! It is certainly in order to remind God of why He ought to heal us. If you can not remind God of why He ought to heal you, then ask Him for His love and mercy in your situation.

It may have occurred to you this story is about Hezekiah and not about your situation. Before I address your observation, bear with me while we take a look at the message God so quickly sent to Hezekiah.

First, God said,

"I have heard your prayer."

Then God said,

"I have seen your tears."

Reminded me of the passage in Revelations where we read;

"And God shall wipe away every tear from their eyes,"

God just never changes does He?

Third, God promises that He is going to give Hezekiah fifteen more years.

And finally God promised to deliver the city, but according to God this was as much for His benefit and glory as it was for Hezekiah.

Yes, the answer and the promises were specifically for Hezekiah, but my Lord is the same Lord as Hezekiah's and my God is full of love, mercy, and grace.

So Lord, if you did it for Hezekiah, won't You do it for me as well?

Father God is no respecter of persons, and if He did this for Hezekiah, He will also do it for you and for me.

We will bring this story of Hezekiah to a close by reminding you that as we started this chapter, this Biblical story is a story for healing that starts with a prayer.

If you want God to heal you, it is always the right order of things if you start your request with prayer.

Going first to Father God when you are sick is the proper order. **Far too often we go to God as the last resort**, and usually after we have tried everything else.

That is not the way of the Bible; **we should go to God first**. Listen to what He tells you to do, and if that includes the medical profession, then go that direction.

My experience over the years is Christians are often guilty of what I call **'reverse'** thinking. What should be first we do last, and what we should do last we do first.

Keep in mind the basic principal found in the Bible when reviewing the ways in which God heals.

The principal is simply this; **ALL HEALING IS SOURCED, OR ORIGINATES FROM GOD**. No matter how your healing comes, it always comes from Father God.

In Acts 17:24-28 we again read that God made the world and everything in it. He is Lord of heaven and earth and He does not live in temples made with human hands.

While you should find God in your religious buildings, the temple where God wants to establish Himself is the temple that is you and I.

We are the church that Father God is interested in, not the building where we meet for group worship. He wants a personal, Father-to-child relationship, so go to Him first, tell him your problem, and ask Him what He wants you to do about it.

We have read and discussed the fact that God made this world and everything in it. If you were asked the question, "are you a part of this world" you would wonder at the stupidity of that question, because of course you are in this world.

God is not confined by our limited capabilities such as our human thinking or understanding. God really does not need us for anything except to give Him glory. And if His chosen ones do not give Him glory, the very rocks will cry out.

Paul speaking in Athens before the altar **'To the Unknown God'**, was telling the Athenians about this God. Paul had just told them that this God was not far from them. It was this God who has given us life, breath, and everything else. In Him we live, we move, and have our very being.

for in Him we live and move and have our being, as also some of your poets have said, "For we are also His offspring."
Acts 17:28

It is from this God where all kinds of healing are sourced or come from; miracles, medicine, surgery, and natural healing. And our healing goes way beyond just the physical healing of the body. Father God includes the healing of the body as well as soul, mind, and spirit. He heals our emotions, our mind, our relationships, and everything else that needs to be healed. God's healing is holistic because it involves the whole entire person,

Ten Biblical Ways in Which God Heals:

ONE | The Body is Programmed to Heal:

In Psalm 139 verse fourteen we read:
I will praise You, for I am fearfully and wonderfully made; marvelous are Your works.
Those are nice words but what does that passage mean for you and me?

When you examine the human body, you should be awed at what you find.

Your mind is more complex than a Cray computer with miles of tubing that carry blood throughout your body. You have ears that can hear, eyes that can see, a nose that smells, a heart that pumps gallons of blood every minute, and the list continues.

The human body is awesome, and with the exception of the mind and spirit, the animal creation is just as fearfully and wonderfully made.

God made the human body as the most complex and unique organism in the world. The word 'fearfully' in the Hebrew text means that the body was made with great reverence, heart-felt interest and respect. The word 'wonderfully' means: unique, set apart and uniquely marvelous.

God thought of all the problems the body, soul and mind could possibly encounter, and then God designed His human creation to heal itself.

God put a healing power into our bodies when He created man. The body will fight sickness and disease in its effort to restore you and I back to health.

The common cold is a simple example. When you get a cold you can go to the doctor, get a shot or some medicine, and in about seven days you will be better. Or you can put up with the cold and in about seven days the cold will be gone. The body heals itself.

Cut yourself and unless the cut becomes infected, the cut will heal itself. Fall and scrape up an arm or leg, the body scabs over and in a short time you find yourself healed. Break an arm or leg and after the limb is set, the body will heal itself.

There are between 50 and 75 million cells in our bodies. The cells in our bodies are dying at the rate of millions per second and they are replaced at a similar rate. Your skin is constantly flaking off and every week or so we literately get a new skin.

When I was diagnosed with prostate cancer the Holy Spirit directed me not to submit to surgery and/or radiation. The doctor suggested a shot of Lupron would slow the growth of the disease until I could decide what action I wished to take.

In this case, God used the time gained from the injection to allow the body to heal itself. The same course of action is what God used the next three times the disease again manifested itself.

All healing is sourced in God, and in this instance He used what He had designed in my body at the time of creation.

If you are diagnosed with prostate cancer, should you do what I did? I don't know as God uses many different ways to heal.

What I do know, is when you have a need; **ask God for His direction, and** when He provides the way in which you should go, **trust what He tells you**.

I have had a few faith-healing, Bible believing friends over the years that even after I shared how God had killed the prostate cancer in my case, they elected to have prostate surgery and be done with it.

Those friends have been dead for some time. Would they have lived if they did what I did? That I can not say, but **what I do know, they did not ask God what they should do, or if they did, they did not trust what God told them.**

I was following God's direction after the prostate cancer had reappeared the fourth time. I returned to the doctor's office for a follow up shot of Lupron.

Shortly after I had received the second shot I noticed a slight swelling where the shot had been administered, namely the right buttock. The swelling kept getting bigger and the pain kept getting greater.

Prayer did not solve my problem, so I went back to the urologist and I was given a prescription for the infection. I was told not to cover the site and of course the swelling became raw and then broke open, causing even more pain.

Over time the swelling went down, only to leave a gaping one inch in diameter and about a half-inch deep hole in my buttock. The doctor said there was nothing more he could do for me.

Eventually after 12-14 weeks the wound healed up. The body had again healed itself.

I believe in prayer and I believe that God heals, but sometimes the healing comes because of the natural healing God had already built into every one's body. The doctors did not have a remedy and the body eventually healed itself.

That was the healing God chose to do that time. Without medicine and without a miracle the healing occurred. **But who was still responsible for the healing?**

In I Corinthians the sixth chapter we read that our bodies are made to be the temple of the Lord. Our body is not our own but belongs to God the Father. One way in which we honor God is with our body.

He who is joined to the Lord is one spirit with Him. Do you not know that your body is the temple of the Holy Spirit, who is in you, whom you have from God, and you are not your own?
I Corinthians 6:17,19

We need to take care of our bodies. One way we can do that is to follow the command for a day of rest. If one does not rest, the body will sooner or later rebel and shut down.

That same passage addresses the subject of not abusing our bodies. Such abuse includes not only a lack of rest but includes substance abuse, sexual immorality and (the one least addressed) overeating or obesity. We need to take care of our bodies for the very reason that they do not belong to us.

The other 'built-in' reason why we need to take care of our bodies is also simple. **How can the body repair and renew itself if we are abusing it with the use of drugs, alcohol, improper sexual activities, smoking, lack of proper rest, and of course excessive food intake.**

Abuse of the body violates God's principal. Added to the above list we have Paul's words regarding exercise. Paul wrote, 'bodily exercise profits little', which really should read, bodily exercise profits a little but when it is compared with Spiritual exercise, it will not profit as much. **But we need to exercise.**

In summary of the first way in which God heals, we note that the body was created in such a marvelous way that it will heal itself **if we give it an opportunity.**

TWO | God Heals Through Medicine:

In first Timothy 5 we are told that Paul instructed Timothy to take a little wine as medicine because his stomach was giving him trouble. Red wine in those days was considered to have medicinal qualities.

Wait a minute here, Paul many times had exercised the gifts of healing? Couldn't Paul have just laid hands on Timothy and claimed healing for him in Jesus' name?

If the problem was demon related couldn't Paul in Jesus' name told the demon to leave? What is going on here?

I would not be surprised to learn Paul had already done all the things he knew to do. And if Paul had taught Timothy, then Timothy also knew about personal faith for healing. Apparently God had a different purpose for Timothy at this time.

Nor do I think this was an isolated incident during Paul's ministry, as Paul did not seem too concerned that Timothy was not instantly healed by God. Paul knew Timothy would be healed, but in God's timing.

I mentioned before, we need to be open to hearing from God, and that certainly applies to healing. In my case the doctors wanted to operate on the prostate cancer, but God restrained me until He could direct me in the way in which He wanted to heal me.

I had thought maybe cyro surgery was the way to go, and I went in that direction. God put the kabash on that as well.

Sometimes God may take a period of time, and for me the first go-around with the cancer took three years.

Can you imagine going forward in a healing service for prayer and being told to come back in three years, as that would give God enough time to heal you?

There have been other times of sickness in my life, where my prayers for healing did not appear to be getting an answer.

Sometimes I assumed the sickness was then demonic related, prayed the prayer of deliverance, commanded the devil in the Name of Jesus to leave, also to no avail.

I remember one time when I was suffering severe shoulder pain, and believe me it was so severe that not only could I not use the arm, I had to sleep at night sitting up.

I had tried everything spiritual that I knew to do and finally hollered out to God, '**What do You want me to do?**' I do not normally holler at God, but I was frustrated and I let it out.

God directed me to go to the doctor where he evaluated the problem and just gave me a shot of something. The pain went away, and so did the problem.

I had learned another lesson. **I should have asked God first what He wanted me to do.** Instead I went through all the God-given things for healing that I knew to do.

I did all the things which my faith-healing friends would have one believe should be all that would be necessary. I went that route first and was not successful. When I listened to God and did it His way, the problem was solved.

Please do not hear me incorrectly. I initiated every God given healing thing that I had ever learned; all to no avail.

What I had failed to do was to ask God what He wanted me to do in that situation.

Was my faith inadequate? Was my belief and understanding in the promise of the stripes that Jesus bore on His body incorrect? Did I really not have the authority over the devil that Jesus said He had transferred to His kids?

No, all of those things were still in effect, **but I had failed to ask God what He wanted me to do in this particular situation.**

We started this chapter with the story of Hezekiah. He was sick and if I read his character correctly, he had been praying. You remember the answer that God gave him was not the answer Hezekiah was hoping to hear.

Then God reversed the original message and Isaiah was instructed to have a lump of figs to be placed on the boil.

In both Timothy and Hezekiah's case, as well as with my shoulder problem, **medicine was the directed course of action.**

God can and will use medicine to heal. I only suggest that you make sure you are hearing from God, directly or through His intermediaries. Listen for what He wants **you** to do, when He wants you to do it, and then do it.

THREE | A Positive Attitude:

Proverbs 15:13 reads:
A merry heart makes a cheerful countenance, but by sorrow of the heart the spirit is broken.
And Proverbs 15:30 reads:
The light of the eyes rejoices the heart, and a good report makes the bones healthy.

If your reaction is the same as mine when I was first made aware of a positive attitude as a Biblical way for God to heal, you probably said, **'You have got to be kidding?'**

When a person gets a bad diagnosis it is not easy to get a handle on one's emotions. After all, how can you look and act cheerful when you are faced with a hurtful sickness, or a terminally ill situation. How does one act and look happy when you are full of pain.

Laughing is not what you feel like doing when you wake up and think about your sickness. Looking happy, laughing, and acting cheerful is usually not what you do when you are suffering with pain or looking death in the face.

Dr. Dobson relates the story that occurred a few months after he had been given the ALS sentence of death. He went to his office and there in front of his office door was a large, beautiful Poinsettia plant. He thought that was really nice for someone in the congregation to care so much to have sent such a beautiful plant to cheer him up.

He opened the card and saw the plant had come from a local mortuary. He said He laughed and laughed and laughed, but he felt really good after laughing so hard.

But is that Biblical? Let's read what the Word has to say.
Proverbs 17:22 reads:
A merry heart does good like medicine, but a broken spirit dries the bones,
And Proverbs 16:24 reads:
Pleasant words are like a honeycomb, sweetness to the soul and health to the bones.

The medical profession has proven that laughing improves a sick person's health and quickens the recovery. I suppose we could say that we can laugh our way back to health.

This morning as I was leaving church, it had started to snow again. I said to the lady walking towards me that I had hoped we were done with the snow. Without missing a beat she said, "Rejoice in the Lord always." Without thinking I replied, "Sometimes it is easier to do that than at other times."

When I got into my car I realized our weather communication was indicative of our humanness when we are sick.

The Word tells us to rejoice always no matter what circumstances we find ourselves in.

Rejoicing is easier when we are not sick, but we are told to rejoice always.

From experience I will share with you that moving from a negative attitude to a positive attitude is not easy. Disease is definitely a negative. It is necessary to focus on the positive. When someone tells you that you look great, hang on to those words and focus on them. If you feel better than you have, thank God and hang onto that positive.

Look for the positive in what you hear and even in what you say.

Focusing on a positive attitude is one of the most important things you can do.

FOUR | God Heals Through His Word:

He sent His Word (Jesus) and healed them, and delivered them from their destructions.
Psalm 107:20

For those of you who will read this passage in its entirety, the sickness was punishment for transgressions? Sometimes the Lord allows, or even sends difficulty or sickness to get our attention.

However, we are not discussing the 'why' possibility here. We are looking at another way in which Father God heals.

The Word and Jesus can be used interchangeably. God can send Jesus the Word, or you can refer directly to the Word known as the Bible.

You are reading the Word in this book. God uses His written word to carry out His promises. Focus on the Word and what it says, as these are the written words of God's direct promises to you.

When you find yourself in a health related situation that is serious you will learn it is a struggle to just get through the day and to just keep on living. You may find you can only take little bits of God's word at a time. Dr. Dobson said even though he is a pastor he found this to be true. I am not an ordained pastor but I found those words to be right on.

I am going to make an observation. It helps if you know the Word before you find yourself in a position where you really need it.

Spend time in the Book before you find yourself in a situation where you really need to know what God has said, and what God has promised.

Let's take a look at some additional scriptures that can help, comfort, and give a person hope in the time of trouble.

Hebrews 13:5b –
For He Himself has said, "I will never leave you nor forsake you."
II Corinthians 1:3,4 –
Blessed be the God and Father of our Lord Jesus Christ, the Father of mercies and God of all comfort, who comforts us in ALL our tribulations.

Praise God and rely on Him, as ultimately it is God who provides your healing. It is God who is the Father of compassion and the passage goes on to tell us to comfort others.

I read Dodie Osteen's book, 'Healed of Cancer', where she wrote how she took James 5:16 to heart.

Pray for one another, that you may be healed,

and Luke 6:38 says we are to:

Give and it will be given to you.

Dodie Osteen even when she was sick went out and prayed with others who were sick. She said that this not only strengthened her, but actually made her feel better.

According to the passage we are to have patience and endurance, and we are not to rely on ourselves. God will deliver you so set your hope on Him.

James in the first chapter says:

Every good gift and every perfect gift is from above, and comes down from the Father of lights, with whom there is no variation or shadow of turning.

Good gifts and the perfect gifts come from the Father, and we can rest in assurance that He never changes, **not even a little bit.** Spend time in the Word, know what God promises, and then hang onto the promises for yourself.

God may use different healing time schedules, and God can use extended periods of time for your healing, BUT it is God who promises your healing, it is God who has offered atonement for your healing, and it is God from whom all healing comes.

FIVE | God heals through Healthy Relationships:

Family relationships can operate in different directions. For example, the husband to wife relationship can be in opposition to what God requires of the husband Biblically. A husband is to love his wife in the same manner as Christ loves His church.

The wife may not be living as wives are instructed in the word of God. In Proverbs 12 and verse four we read:

An excellent wife is the crown of her husband, but she who causes shame is like rottenness in his bones.

Rottenness in his bones is an issue of health, so an excellent wife can help her husband stay healthy.

In Exodus there is a passage that reads,

Honor your father and your mother, so that you may live long where the Lord, your God has put you.

I took the liberty to paraphrase a few words to make it easier to understand in today's vernacular. Bottom line is that according to this passage in Exodus, lack of honor for your parents may well shorten your life.

The interpretation of what it means to honor your father and your mother I leave you to work out in your relationship.

Remember the passage in James where we are told if anyone lacks wisdom let him or her ask and it will be given.

If in doubt, ask, and when you get the answer should it not agree with what you are thinking, be very careful before you disregard your God given answer.

As for parents, the word tells us not to provoke our children to the point where they get angry. Instead we are to raise them up to fear the Lord. I will go out on a limb here; if your children are angry with you, take a look at your reactions and inter-actions with them. It may be that you need to ask them to forgive you.

Living outside of a healthy family relationship will (not can) bring sickness and disease.

Deuteronomy 30 verses 15 through 20 make this very clear and I will quote the pertinent parts of this passage:

See, I have set before you today life and good, death and evil. I command you to walk in the ways of the Lord your God, and to keep His commandments, statutes, and judgments. But if you turn away you will surely perish and not prolong your life. I, God, have set before you life and death, blessing and cursing; choose life that you and your family may live. For He, God, is your life and the length of your days.

Again in Proverbs 3:1,2 we read:

My son (or daughter), do not forget my law, but let your heart keep my commands; for length of days and long life and peace they will add to you.

Simply put, God is saying that we can make the choice as to how we want to live. We can make the choice to obey what He has commanded or we can choose to be stubborn and disobey, the choice is ours.

But keep this in mind; the commandments are given to us by the God of love. If we want to enjoy life to the fullest, this can only happen if we live as God has outlined in His word. Proverbs 1:25 and 26 express it so well.

Because you have disdained (held in contempt) all My counsel, and would have none of My rebuke; I (God) will laugh at your calamity: I will mock when your terror comes.

God in His Word has made it clear what He expects of us in family relationships. If we choose to hold His counsel in contempt, God makes it very clear that He will laugh at our problems, including sickness and disease.

The quickest way to shorten one's life span is to get sick or contract a fatal disease. And when a person elects to disobey the Father's statues or commandments regarding the body, believe me sickness will have a very adverse effect on the family relationship.

When the wife elects to live in the marriage state in a manner other than God has lain out, there will be disharmony, opening up an opportunity for the devil to move in.

And the devil loves to put a sickness or disease on a person whenever he finds a weak spot or opening.

Husbands, when you elect not to love your wives in the way in which Christ has commanded, the same opportunity for the devil is opened up.

And rest assured the devil will not miss a golden opportunity like that.

Children, God's command to you is to honor your parents. You can take the time to figure out what that means for you. Some of you will have a hard time to honor your parents given how they may have abused you.

There are books written on that subject, and there are Christian counselors who can help you, but the command of God does not change.

One other note-worthy observation I would like to share is this: Sickness and disease will most often bring out the best or the worst in any family relationship. If the situation brings out the best, thank God, but if it brings out the worst, go to God for help.

Remember, you can choose life and blessing, or you can choose death and cursing. Choose life and God's way and you will find yourself blessing and praising Him.

The alternative is to be rebellious and choose to have it your way which will lead to cursing God and the death will be eternity without Him.

EIGHT

SIX | God Heals through Faith:

Finally, I can hear some of you saying we get to faith. Let's review again what faith is according to the Bible.

The Biblical verse quoted so often in describing faith is found in Hebrews 11 the first verse:

Now faith is the substance of things hoped for, the evidence of things not seen.

These words certainly sound pious, but do they really tell us anything?

When one reads the entire passage, Paul is not providing a definition of faith, but instead provides a description of how faith works. It is by reading the description of how faith works that we can get a better idea of what faith is.

Read the rest of the chapter to see how Paul defines faith. He starts with Abel, then Enoch, Noah, and starting with verse eight Paul talks about Abraham and Sarah. These all had one thing in common, they moved out in the promise that God had given. Some even died before seeing the entire promises of God come to completion.

Faith is when a person puts his trust in the God of the promise, without seeing any evidence of the promise coming into existence.

Paul interjects something here in the sixth verse of the eleventh chapter that I would like to share with you.

without faith it is impossible to please God, for he who comes to God must believe that He is, and that He is a re-warder of those who diligently seek Him.

There are two things that jump out at me when discussing faith. First, the persons mentioned in Hebrews 11 never put their faith or trust on themselves, but on the God who made the promise, or promises.

The second thing that I noticed is no matter what we do in our Christian walk, it is of benefit only if we use our faith in God for our walk with Him.

If a Christian does not use his or her faith to trust in God, He is not going to be pleased with us no matter how many boards we serve on, mission trips we go on, or how many pulpits we occupy.

Faith is the need to put our dreams, our hopes, and everything else in the God of promise, trusting Him to see us through. Even if what we hope and pray for does not come to pass as we wanted, when we wanted, or how we wanted.

Okay, it is time to address how faith for healing was used in the Bible. There are many instances in the Bible starting way back in the Old Testament and moving on into the New Testament where faith is involved in a person's healing. However we will only touch on a few in this section.

There will be a detailed listing of various faith Scriptures in the appendix at the back of the book, and I invite you to look them up at your leisure. We are gong to take most of our examples for this section from the writings of Luke, because Luke was a doctor and he saw healings from more of a medical perspective.

I am going to take a bit of a side journey to shortly before Jesus began His stated goal of bringing the Kingdom of Heaven to the people.

This little side trip is found in the fourth chapter of Luke and I am going to list some of what took place as I think it has a bearing on the healing ministry of Jesus.

Then Jesus, being filled with the Holy Spirit was led by the Spirit into the wilderness, and was tempted for forty days by the devil.

Jesus had received the Holy Spirit when He was baptized by John. This is a special filling of the Holy Spirit for what was to come. Following the leading of the Holy Spirit, Jesus goes into the wilderness. Did Jesus know what was coming with the Devil? I don't think so, but God did and God sent the Holy Spirit to provide what would be needed.

Jesus is now in the wilderness and Satan shows up. In response to a seemingly innocent suggestion by the devil Jesus answered,

It is written, Man shall not live by bread alone, but by every word of God. Jesus went on to say, Get behind Me, Satan! For it is written, You shall worship the Lord your God and Him only you shall serve.

When the devil's temptations were completed we read that the devil departed until an opportune time. **The devil was coming back again and that is also true for us.** The devil may depart, but you can count on the fact that he will be back to try again.

Notice that Jesus started His ministry with a special filling of the Holy Spirit. When we do the work of Jesus, we also need special fillings of the Holy Spirit, whether it is in the healing ministry, the deliverance ministry, the teaching ministry, the preaching ministry, or any other ministry.

There is a Holy Spirit filling for a full time vocation of serving God. However it has been my experience that God sends special fillings of the Holy Spirit **as needed for special times**; be it faith for healing, faith to operate in the gifts of healing, faith to teach, faith to pray and believe with someone, and the list continues.

These special Holy Spirit fillings are available for all Christians, not just for those in a position of leadership. **And let me add that God sends the Holy Spirit with what is needed at just the right time.**

Jesus started His public ministry by reading the Scripture taken from Isaiah. Jesus read the passage and tells the people He has been sent to heal the brokenhearted, to free the captives (if you are sick you are a captive), give sight to the blind, and kick the devil out of people when they are oppressed.

What a way to start a ministry by stating that which had been promised by Father God so many years before was now going to be fulfilled. Let's go on and see how Jesus went about bringing the Kingdom of God to those on this earth.

Luke 4:38 reads:

Now He arose from the synagogue and entered Simon's house. Simon's wife's mother was sick with a high fever and they made a request of Him concerning her. So He stood over her and rebuked the fever, and it left her. And immediately she arose and served them.

Peter's mother-in-law did not ask to be healed. Second, notice how Jesus healed her. He rebuked the fever, and rebuking would seem to indicate this fever was not the result of a sickness but of the devil.

It is obvious that this fever was not a serious sickness or disease, but Jesus did not flinch from doing what was needed. How often do you think that the small problems we have are the result of harassment from the enemy?

And finally notice the result of the healing. She arose and served them. **I think she was healed to serve but what do you think?** This healing was the result of the faith of others that Jesus could heal.

Later that same day Luke records:

'as the sun was setting, all those who had any that were sick with various diseases were brought to Him, and He laid hands on every one of them and healed them.'

Again the faith of others led to the bringing of those that needed and/or wanted to be healed.

In the next chapter a man who had a serious case of leprosy begged Jesus saying,

Lord, if You are willing, You can make me clean. Jesus put out His hand and touched him saying, "I am willing, be cleansed", and immediately the leprosy left him.

Here we have the faith of the man with the leprosy which resulted in his healing. Notice the leper came to Jesus with what seems to be very little faith because he said if you are willing, not if you are able.

I think he knew Jesus was able, but being a leper, he was not too sure if Jesus was going to be willing. I have never found anyone that Jesus was not willing to heal, or to make whole and clean.

Moving on we come to the story of four men with their paralyzed friend who could not get into the house to see Jesus. They were not to be deterred by a simple problem of too many people around. They simply climbed up on the flat roof, removed part of the roof, and lowered their friend in front of Jesus.

I have already included a healing incident where the faith to be healed was the faith of someone other than the person who needed the healing. In the case of the leper, faith for healing did not seem to be the issue, but there was doubt if Jesus would be willing.

This healing was different because of the manner, or the how-and-why in which Jesus healed. Luke 5:20

When He saw their faith, 'He said to him (the paralyzed man) Man, your sins are forgiven you.'

Not all sickness and afflictions are the result of a specific sin; in this case sin appears to be the cause. In many cases prayer for healing should begin with the confession of sin and the repentance of same. Read James 5:16 and I John 1:8,9

In this healing incident the faith included both the cure for the paralyzed limbs, as well as forgiveness of the man's sin. In this healing, the **paralyzed man was both physically cured and spiritually healed.**

As I was re-reading this scripture passage a question rose up in my spirit that I will have to address at a later time. Could it be that just putting your faith in Jesus Christ for something like healing be enough to get a person saved?

There will be times when a person is involved in the ministry of the 'gifts of healing' where the word of knowledge is very helpful. The Word of Knowledge was active in Jesus' life as He knew the problem that caused this man's sickness.

Jesus used the word of knowledge that comes from the Holy Spirit not only to cure the paralyzed man, but also to heal him spiritually. Without the working of this spiritual gift the man may have been cured, but his healing may not have happened.

Jesus' linking of healing with forgiveness of sin is evidence that human wholeness in every area is of concern to Father God. **Jesus knew what this man needed was not only physical but spiritual.**

In the passage found in Luke 7 we read of a woman who knew she was a sinner, but came and anointed, or washed, Jesus' feet with oil. She did not have a mental or physical ailment, but she knew she was sick spiritually. She came and sought Jesus for healing, but of a different sort. Verse 40-50:

Then Jesus said to her, "Your sins are forgiven', your faith has saved you. Go in peace."

This woman was saved because of her personal faith, and this healing was eternal, not just temporary as a physical healing would be.

Again in this passage, I do not read where this woman came to Jesus and asked Him to forgive her sins. She came, used her tears to wash the feet of Jesus. She showed her love by continuously kissing the feet of Jesus. And Jesus response to Simon the homeowner whose house He was at:

"Therefore I say to you, her sins, which are many, are forgiven, for she loved much. But to whom little is forgiven, the same loves little."

This is another subject, but could the denominational church be a bit to dogmatic on how a person's sins may be forgiven?

Luke 8:40-56 we read of two healing incidents that are very different in nature. There was an important church ruler who had a problem. His twelve year old daughter was not only sick, she was dying.

This important man came as a father and fell down in front of Jesus, and begged Jesus to come to his house and heal her. Jesus agreed to do so and while they were walking to his house, the people around Him tried to get even closer to Him.

One lady in the crowd had been suffering with a flowing blood problem for twelve years. According to the Jewish tradition she was considered unclean.

Probably because she was considered unclean she did not even dare to ask Jesus to heal her. She just hoped if she could get close enough to touch the robe of Jesus just maybe that would be enough and she would be healed.

Well she got close enough and you guessed it, she was healed because we read the blood stopped flowing immediately. Now the story gets interesting.

Jesus knew that healing power had flowed outward and wanted to know who had enough faith to believe that by just touching His clothes that would be enough to be healed. When the lady finally confessed, Jesus response was one of love and mercy. Jesus told her:

"Daughter, be of good cheer; your faith has made you well. Go in peace".

Two things here; the first being the woman's faith generated her healing. And second, when you come to Jesus for healing, **you will not be denied.**

Okay, back to where this story started. Jesus is still on the way to the house of Jairus to heal his daughter. Jesus doesn't even get finished telling the woman that her faith has made her well, when the message arrives that the young girl had died, and it was no longer necessary to bother Jesus.

Apparently the father gave Jesus the message because Jesus responded directly to the father. Jesus said,

"Do not be afraid; only believe, and she will be made well."

They all keep walking until they get to the house of Jairus where they find everyone weeping. Jesus basically said to knock it off as the girl was not dead, but sleeping.

Those present thought Jesus was a bit touched in the head. Maybe the sun had been too hot for Jesus on the walk down, because these people all knew the young girl was dead. What they thought did not bother Jesus. He just took her by the hand and said,

"Little girl, get up," and she did. All Jesus said was to give her something to eat.

It was the faith of the father as head of his house that caused Jesus to move, and in this case the father had to hang onto his faith even when it seemed to be too late for his daughter to be healed.

How long should you hold onto faith for your healing? Dr. Dobson said, "He was going to believe for God to heal him until either God healed him, or told him something different."

Believe, trust, and listen, seems to sum it up nicely.

I am going to insert a passage from Mark relating the story of a healing that involved a 'little' faith and a father who knew his faith was doubtful. In the ninth chapter of Mark a father brought his son who had a demonic problem that the disciples were not able to handle. The father said to Jesus:

'If You can do anything, have compassion on us and help us.'
Jesus said to him, "If you can believe, all things are possible to him who believes."

The father responded, in tears probably, because he knew his faith was small by saying, 'Lord, I believe, help my 'little' faith and give me unquestioning faith.

When you find yourself in a situation where your faith may be small, Jesus will hear you anyway, and if you ask, the Holy Spirit will increase your faith.

Remember, your faith is in the giver of faith, God Himself. And your faith is not in the amount of your faith, **but in the amount of your trust.**

So far we have seen a number of different faiths being put into action. We have seen 'little faith', 'medium faith' and 'large faith'. We have seen personal faith, faith of friends and faith by the head of the household.

Healing can be manifested or come in different ways, but in every case when a person came to Jesus, and they or someone else believed, **Jesus always healed.** No one who came to Jesus was ever denied. Jesus heals all who come by, or in faith.

Jesus also healed for reasons that had nothing to do with the 'receivers' faith. If Jesus needed to make a point, to get their attention, or even to start an argument, many times He did so by healing without being asked.

From the few stories I have chosen, plus all the additional stories I have not referenced, **God is a God of healing.** When Jesus came to announce that the Kingdom of God had arrived, He did so in a rather dramatic manner. **He healed and He set free**. Healing is just a part of the gospel of the good-news that the Kingdom of God has arrived.

I have on my computer a sign that reads: Preach the Gospel at all times, and if necessary use words. **Healing is that part of preaching the 'Good-News' which does not require words.**

We started this section on faith by saying that faith is not really a word definition, but a description of how faith works. Which brings up the question of why does faith work?

Remember, our efforts will not get us healed. Faith, prayer, and the right people can not heal us.

Prayer and faith may open the door to healing, but God does not heal because we pray. God heals because He is the God of love and grace. He heals so that He may get the glory.

When you pray, fix your focus not on your illness or on your healing, but on the God who heals.

What is Faith, or more importantly, who can I trust in the midst of my tough situation?

- **When sickness overwhelms me, who can I trust?**
- **When I have no control over the disease, who can I trust?**
- **When the doctors really have no control over the sickness, who can I trust?**

Faith is putting your trust in God, and **not putting your trust in your faith**. We can not control or manipulate God, nor can we force God to act.

A few years ago I thought it would be interesting to sky-dive. I made the arrangements, got all suited up, put on my parachute, climbed into the plane and took off headed upwards.

Putting my faith in the plane was not as hard as it was to put my trust in that pack on my back. When we reached 10,000 feet up from the ground it sure looked like a long way down to where I had started.

Once I gathered up enough courage to jump, all my trust was in that thing on my back, and if it did not do what it was designed to do, it was going to be a long, quick fall, with a sudden and hurtful stop.

I jumped a few times after that first time and the parachute never failed. Putting your trust in God is similar to my putting my trust in the parachute.

Except for one thing, **when you put your trust in God, He never fails, but parachutes sometimes don't open**.

When you are in a tough situation and God tells you to jump, it is nice to know that God is not only trust-worthy, but He has never said anything that was not true.

We can rest assured in His promises because He does not lie. Your assurance rests on the promises of God, a God who is capable of only telling the truth.

Faith is not 'rooted' in what I see, but in whom, I choose to trust.

For instance, if your doctor says to do this or that and you will get well and you trust him or her, then your faith is rooted in your doctor. If on the other hand God says to do this or that and you will recover, then if you are willing to trust God, you faith is rooted in Him.

Please understand I am not saying that you should not trust your doctor. **Just remember that ALL healing is sourced in God. Trust in God first and your doctor after that.**

Dr. Dobsen indentified five reasons why we can trust God.

- Trust in the **Providence** of God no matter where the sickness came from.
- Trust in the **Purpose** of God as found in Romans 8:28, because sometimes it is hard to take input from someone who has not walked the same road as you are walking.
- Trust in the **Power** of God. Cancer, ALS, bad relationships, no big deal to God. You name it; it is not too big for God.
- Trust in the **Provision** of God. Paul's thorn in the flesh is an example. God's grace was sufficient and God's grace is always sufficient for us no matter what state we find ourselves in. We can trust God in any situation, but God does not usually give us the grace we need, **until we need it.**
- Trust in the **Passion,** or love of God for us. He is the Father of compassion and the Father of all comfort. We can get lost in the wonder of God as this is faith in God.

Faith is not the absence of doubt; faith simply trusts God and NOT your own faith. Who you place your trust in is what matters.

One last thing, God heals because of faith or trust in Him, and faith is a gift from God. Just as salvation is a gift from God and you must ask for it, even so for the faith to be healed God expects us to pray and ask for it.

<u>Do not take faith for granted</u>.

<u>Faith Thought:</u>

It is far easier to have faith when you are in the palace than it is to have faith when you are in the valley.

SEVEN | God heals through Confession of Known Sin or Sins.

James in the fifth chapter addresses this issue and he makes it very clear that he is talking to those who are sick.

Is any among you sick? Let him (or her) call for the elders of the church, and let them pray over him, anointing him with oil in the name of the Lord, and the prayer of faith will save the sick, and the Lord will raise him up. And if he has committed sins, he will be forgiven. Confess your sins to one another, and pray for one another, that you may be healed. The effective, fervent prayer of a righteous man avails much.

Man-oh-Man, there is so much contained in this single passage that it is hard to know where to begin. Let's start with the obvious, and that is the beginning.

A sick person who calls for the elders is most likely a Christian. Obviously if you are sick, somebody has to pass the word. We have seen that when a sick person came to Jesus for healing, they were never turned away. So call for the elders of your church or fellowship and they are to take action.

The action the elders are to take is the anointing of oil. Today most often oil will be applied to the fingertips of those doing the praying and touched to the head of the sick person.

The anointing of oil is a symbol of the work of the Holy Spirit who is present in these situations to glorify Jesus in healing works.

Following the anointing of oil, the elders are instructed to pray for the sick person. But how are they to pray? The elders have to pray the prayer of faith for the sick person to recover.

Here are a couple of really big questions. What if the elders do not recognize the healing power of Jesus, or the love of God that wants to heal the person? What if the elders who come to anoint and pray, are not able to pray the 'prayer of faith.' What if the elders who come are not able to pray effectively or fervently?

Think about that for a moment and we will come back to these questions.

Then we are told to 'confess your (known) sins' to one another and pray together, that you may be healed. This is another aspect to the healing of the sick person. Not all the sick persons that call for the elders fall into this category.

Sometimes sickness is the result of sin, and if that is the case, the sin must be confessed. **There are times God will allow sickness to get your attention because of a particular sin.**

It should be obvious here, the elders need to be elders above reproach and they must be able to keep their mouths shut as to what they hear.

A second observation is that it would be very helpful if some of the gifts of the Spirit were in operation within the group of the elders.

Gifts such as the Word of Knowledge, the Word of Wisdom, and the Healing gift of Faith, often are of great help.

There will be times when the sick person may not be aware of the sin and the word of knowledge can enlighten the sick person. The word of wisdom many times provides the supernatural perspective to know the divine means for accomplishing God's will. And of course the gift of faith is the supernatural ability to believe the promises of God without doubt.

I said we would get back to the question of elders who are not sure enough in their belief of who God is, and cannot espouse the promises that God has placed in His word.

First of all, I really would rather not have elders come and pray with me that do not believe what God says He can and will do. Second, please don't send me any elders who pray, 'God if it is your will, heal so-and-so.

No, send me elders who know God's will and can pray and act accordingly. I don't think elders always have to mean those serving in the church with the 'official' title.

Elders can also mean those spiritual persons that are Spirit filled for special needs.

Just so you know it is Biblical that sickness can be the result of sin, I will add one additional passage of scripture and then we will move on. Psalm 38:3-5:

There is no soundness in my flesh, or body, because of Your anger, nor any health in my bones because of my sin. For my iniquities (or sins) have gone over my head: like a heavy burden they are too heavy for me. My wounds are foul and festering because of my foolishness.

Many sins can result in a sickness that produces foulness and festering sores? I am sure you can think of sins that can result in sickness or disease? Sexual sins for example can result in sickness that produces foul and festering sores.

Smoking may not be considered a sin by some, but your body would argue other wise. If you have ever seen a loved one suffering with lung cancer you know what I am saying.

Addiction to substance abusing drugs or alcohol often results in sickness because the body loses the capacity to heal itself.

I have talked to many people who think they can sin without suffering any ill effects. Aside from the obvious eternal consequences, the writer of Proverbs sums it up so well in the 3rd chapter the 7th and 8th verses:

Do not be wise in your own eyes; fear the Lord and depart from evil. It will be health to your flesh and strength to your bones.

There is no question that God is a God of love and mercy. When you come to Him, He will heal you if for no other reason than to glorify Himself. But you should also be aware of what was said earlier, you are the one who can choose life or death. God's will is for you to choose life and health, not death and sickness.

EIGHT | God not only heals, He also keeps sickness from us .

It is well and good to know that God can heal, wants to heal and does indeed heal. But other than the fact God should get the glory when He heals, it is far better if we did not get sick in the first place?

Keeping sickness away in the first place needs to be added to the list of the ways God heals. If I can be kept from getting sick and not have to go through the pain and emotional suffering, I think I would move not getting sick to 'number-one' in the ways in which God heals.

There are three parts to God's Health Care Plan and this is the best of the three parts. **It is far better not to need God's healing touch. And if the Christian never got sick, he or she would never have to be healed.**

Earlier we discussed it was the fall of man that triggered sin which opened mankind up to sickness. Now we are stating that God not only wants to heal, but He wants to prevent sickness.

Starting early in the Bible, way back in Deuteronomy 30 verses 15-16 we read that God gives His kids a choice.

See I have set before you today life and good, death and evil. In that I command you today to love the Lord your God, to walk in His ways, and to keep His commandments, His statures, and His judgments, that you may live and multiple; and the Lord your God will bless you in the land.

A casual reading would support the word that God is giving His kids a choice. Live a good life by choosing God and His ways, or choose an evil way which will include sickness and disease which will surely lead to death, physically and eternally.

Let's look at another Biblical passage and this one is found in Exodus 15 the 26th verse:

God, tested them and said, "If you diligently heed the voice of the Lord your God and do what is right in His sight, give ear to His commandments and keep all His statutes, I will put none of the diseases on you which I have brought on the Egyptians.

For I am the Lord who heals you.

God Himself says that He will heal by bringing none of the diseases upon you, and He also points out that He is the God who heals us. It seems obvious that God equates keeping sickness away from us as a form of healing.

The reference to Egyptians in this passage is to those outside of the chosen ones or in less tactful terms, those who are not willing to accept the gift of salvation and eternal life that the Father has made available.

There is no question that God can heal, cure, repair, mend, and restore health. But how much better it is for us if we do not need to avail ourselves of the healing atonement God has instituted for us through His son Jesus Christ.

God is a good God and He desires only His best for you, including health. In this promise of His continued healing presence, God puts two conditions before us.

First, God tells us to heed Him, or listen for His voice, and if we will have a hearing ear He will speak to us. God speaks in many ways including through His word, through servants He has anointed, and through your inner man. God is a spirit and He will speak to us through our spirit. **We need only to cultivate a hearing attitude.**

Second, God asks us to do what is right in His sight. God wants people that not only hear His words, but take them to heart and act on them. As James says, 'be doers of the word and not hearers only'.

God's nature is that of the Healer to those who obey His word, not only to recover health, but also to sustain in health. Sin and disobedience are not always the direct causes of sickness, but man's disobedience, rebellion, and the subsequent fall into sin is the original and underlying cause of sickness and disease.

Let's look at a few more verses found in God's word that addresses His desire to keep sickness and disease from us.

Exodus 23:20-26 covers a lot of ground and I will select only passages that pertain to the subject of God keeping His kids from sickness, and in this case even giving them long life.

Behold, I send an Angel before you to keep you in the way – Obey His voice and do not provoke Him and if you obey His voice, I will be an enemy to your enemies. The Lord will bless your bread (food) and your water. And I will take sickness away from you. No one shall suffer miscarriage or be barren: I will fulfill the number of your days.
Proverbs 3:1,2:
My son do not forget my law, but let your heart keep My commands; for the length of days and long life and peace will they add to you.

God is the Divine Healer, but God is also the giver of Divine Health. If Christians will live according to the plan of God found in His Holy Word, they will not need God in His divine healing role. They will be living under the divine health section of God's Health Care Plan.

God seems to be very clear that if we will listen and obey what He tells us, it will directly reflect on our enjoyment during this life as well as our enjoyment in the life to come.

If we obey, He will bless what we eat and drink. He will keep sickness away from us, and if you are into having kids, He will even take care of that for you.

Finally, God sums it all up and says that if we live in obedience, He will add to our days, let us live longer, and in the process let us live in peace.

God goes on to offer strength and peace to us, but in the passage **He also cautions us that He can take it away from us as well.**

I would suspect that along about here some will be saying that now that Christ has come, we live under the law of God's grace and mercy and those verses are no longer in effect for God's kids.

Yes, you are correct, we do live under God's grace and mercy, but also remember, (1) God never changes, and (2) obedience to what God requires also never changes.

Father God seems to be quite clear in Psalm 29:11 when he says,

"The Lord will give strength to His peoples; the Lord will bless His people with peace or Shalom."

Strength is lack of sickness or disease, and Shalom is the peace we enjoy when we are healthy and not in need.

The opposite is also true and this is recorded for us in Leviticus 26:16.

"I, God, will also do this to you; I will appoint terror over you, wasting disease and fever which shall consume your eyes and cause sorrow of heart.'

God also promises vitality of life if we elect to live in obedience and I would like to do a father Boyd paraphrase on Psalm 36:5-9 –

Your mercy, Your faithfulness, and Your righteousness, O Lord, reach from the top of the mountain to the very heavens. But Your judgments are a great deep O Lord, and You preserve man. How precious is Your loving kindness, therefore we can put our trust even

in the shadow of Your wings. We can be satisfied with the fullness of Your house and we can drink from the river of Your pleasure.

You can read this passage in your Bible, but in the paraphrase it is easier to get a handle on just how great and full of life God's promises are for us; **but only if we will be obedient to His commandments**.

The writer of Ecclesiastes says it so well in the second chapter the 24th verse:

Nothing is better for a man than that he should eat and drink, and that his soul should enjoy the good in his labor. This also, I saw was from the hand of God.

Finally healing is the righteousness of God. In Romans the fifth chapter the first verse we read:

therefore, having been justified by faith, we have peace with God through our Lord, Jesus Christ.

A quick summary of the verses we have examined should make it clear that Father God requires obedience to His commandments, but Father God loves us so much that He promises His kids health, peace, and spiritual prosperity in return.

<u>As parents we have to punish a child who is disobedient. Why would you think that God will not punish His kids if they are disobedient?</u>

There are laws of the land which the citizens are expected to obey. If the law is broken there will be punishment that follows. Would you expect God to react differently?

As I read the scriptures it would seem to me that the choice of obedience or disobedience rests solely on us. At the beginning I stated one of the purposes of this book is to being a balance to the healing ministry. There are Christians that produce Bible texts to support their belief that it is God's will to heal everyone, if only they have enough faith.

Many Biblical texts can be produced to support that belief. But God is a God of balance, and balance also includes the other side of the coin so-to- speak.

Listen to this passage found in Proverbs 1:24-28:

I have called and you refused. I have stretched out My hand and no one regarded. Because you have disdained all My counsel, <u>and would have none of My rebuke,</u> I also will laugh at your calamity; I will mock when your terror comes. – Then they will call on Me, but I *will not answer; They will seek me diligently, but they will not find Me.*

Food for Thought:
If God were to make it too easy for Christians to be kept from sickness, or healed every time we asked, could that encourage Christians to be lazy?

NINE | God heals through Prayer.

I do not intend to go deeply into the definition of prayer, why we should pray or how we should pray. There are countless books and articles available to the Christian who wants to delve more deeply into this subject. We will just touch a bit on prayer as it relates to healing.

Prayer in the English is considered a noun. To the Christian, prayer is a request for help or an expression of thanks addressed to God. Prayer should be a place where pride is abandoned, hopes are lifted up and requests are made.

Prayer is the privilege of touching the heart of the Father through the Son of God, Christ Jesus.

Prayer is the outpouring of the heart, and to a loving God, prayer is accepted from everyone who comes to the Father without pride and in a humble attitude of hope and expectation.

James 4:8 tells us,

'draw near to God and He will draw near to you.'

and in verse ten we read,

Humble yourselves in the sight of the Lord and He will lift you up.'

In the context James is referring to Christians who are having problems and why they are having problems. But when you isolate the text, it would appear that anyone who humbles themselves and goes to God with a request; **will be lifted up**.

That should give all of us a great measure of comfort. Even when we Christians are messing up, there is a way to God. **And if you are not a child of God but having problems, He wants you to come to Him also.**

Dr. Dobson identified five kinds of prayer that I want to share with you. The first prayer we will look at is a personal prayer and found in Isaiah 38:2.

Then Hezekiah turned his face to the wall, and prayed to the Lord.

Simply put, personal prayer is your concern, or praise, that you personally bring directly to Father God.

This story of personal prayer reminds me of a humorous story I once heard. It seems that a priest, a minister, and a guru sat discussing the best position for prayer while a telephone repair man worked nearby.

Kneeling is definitely the best way to pray the priest said. No the minister replied, the best results I get are by standing with my hands outstretched to Heaven. You are both wrong the guru said. The most effective prayer position is lying down on the floor.

The repairman who had been listening to the discussion could not contain himself any longer. 'Hey fellas' he interrupted, 'the best praying I ever did was when I was hanging upside down from a telephone pole.'

The position of prayer really does not matter, but with both the telephone repairman and king Hezekiah, the fervency was what counted with God.

A second type of prayer is called intercessory prayer, where as a child of God you find yourself praying for someone else. An example of this can be found in Genesis 20 the seventeenth verse where we read,

So Abraham prayed to God and God healed Abimelech, his wife, and his female servants. Then they bore children.

In the book of James we find an experience of 'community' intercessory prayer where the collective elders were to pray.

Is any among you sick? Let him call for the elders of the church, and let them pray over him,

A fourth kind of prayer, and one which could open up a can-of-worms if we let it, is found in Romans 8:26,27.

Likewise the Spirit also helps in our weaknesses. For we do not know what we should pray for as we ought, but the Spirit Himself makes intercession for us with groanings which cannot be uttered. Now He who searches the hearts knows what the mind of the Spirit is, because He makes intercession for saints according to the will of God.

When you find yourself in a place where you do not know how to pray for something, or how to pray properly and effectively, we are told by Paul we can bring it to the Holy Spirit and He will take over for us.

I believe this verse can be used both for those who do not practice praying-in-tongues and by those who do. Either way, the Holy Spirit will help us pray and ask for God's help and intervention **when we find ourselves in a situation where we do not know how to pray.**

The final form of prayer that I am going to touch on is found in Romans 8:34 and Hebrews 7:25 where we are told that,

It is Jesus Christ who sits at the right hand of God, who also makes intersession for us.

and

Therefore He is also able to save to the uttermost those who come to God through Him, since He always lives to make intercession for them.

Man-of-man, it does not get much more personal or powerful than that. Jesus, Himself, goes to bat for us directly with Father God.

TEN | **God heals through Worship:**

True worship has no selfishness in it. True worship forgets about getting; only about giving.

Worship gets the focus off ourselves and unto God, or to put it another way, worship is not about us nor is it about our needs. **Worship will have an impact on healing and disease simply because we are putting all of our focus on God the giver.**

One of the best ways I have found for me to worship God is by singing or listening to songs. I was surprised when I began looking, at how many songs deal with sickness and disease.

And finally, worship will lift us into the very presence of God.

A Quick Summary of the ten Biblical Ways in Which God Heals:

These are ten Biblical ways in which God uses to heal. It would be wrong to put God in a box and say that this or that is the only way in which God will heal us.

God may choose any one or more of these ways to heal you, or even keep you from getting sick.

<u>**Always Remember, no matter how God heals you.
it is He who gets the Glory!**</u>

Before we move on, I would like to take a look at three things:
Healed & Cured, Cured but not Healed,
and Healed but not Cured

What in the world am I talking about, you are either healed or you are not, right? No, according to the Word that is not correct and please let me explain.

<u>Healed and cured</u> is the one that I would always want for myself, and is also the one which I would choose for you.

In Luke 17 there is a story of ten lepers who came to Jesus and asked Jesus to have mercy on them.

These lepers according to the story did not even ask Jesus to heal them, just to show mercy.

Jesus never touched them nor did He say to them to be healed. Jesus only said that they were to go to the priests and show themselves.

A leper only did that when he no longer had leprosy. They went, and **as they went,** they were declared clean, or healed.

All ten were cured of leprosy. One of the ten returned to Jesus and glorified God. Jesus asked him a question as to whether all ten were cured, and if so where were the other nine?

The answer was obvious, but Jesus' response to the one who returned was simply this:

'Your faith has made you well.'

The other nine did not return and they were cured of leprosy, but were they healed spiritually?

It is interesting that numerous times the only thing required of a person was to have faith and they were healed, and they were also assured of eternal life.

To be cured relates to the body, to be healed or made well is a right relationship with Jesus Christ.

This one former leper was both cured and made right with Jesus Christ.

Cured, but not Healed can be shown using the same passage.

'And Jesus answered and said, "Where there not ten cleansed? But where are the nine?"

I found it interesting that the nine that did not return to give thanks were Jews, God's chosen. They were cured but they were not healed spiritually.

I often wonder is this could be true today with those who consider themselves to be Christians.

Can they too be cured, but never healed? Could we get so caught up in the curing, that we miss the healing?

Healed, but not Cured is an interesting concept for the Christian and we can find the Biblical support for this in II Corinthians 4:16.

Therefore we do not lose heart, even though our outward man is perishing, yet the inward man is being renewed day-by-day.

And in II John the second verse,

Beloved, I pray that you may prosper in all things and be in health just as your soul prospers.

In the Corinthians passage we are told that we are getting older and our body is deteriorating normally, but on the inside, the spiritual part of us is being transformed into something that is more Christ like on a daily basis.

In Second John it would also appear that those to whom he is writing are not enjoying good health or John would not have contrasted their health physically with their prosperous spiritual health.

I suspect that if you or I have a choice, we would prefer to be healed and cured. **But if that is not God's plan, then I personally want to make sure that I am healed spiritually.**

God can cure a person of sickness, and if you are willing to trust God to cure you He will do so.

But often God will cure you to get your attention so He can get you to focus on being healed Spiritually.

NINE

Is a Christian healed every time?

Is a Christian cured every time they come to God for healing? If the Biblical answer is no, then the question is, why not?

In the last chapter we touched on the difference between being cured and in being healed. Unless noted differently, when we use the word 'healed' we are generally referring to being cured in the entire body, as that is the way in which healing is more commonly understood.

We have previously noticed Timothy had a stomach problem that Paul recommended taking a little wine for. We have also touched on Trophimus who was left behind because he was sick.

Now we come to II Corinthians 12:7-9 where it is written,

And lest I should be exalted above measure by the abundance of revelations, a thorn in the flesh was given to me, a messenger of Satan to buffet me, lest I be exalted above measure. Concerning this thing I pleaded with the Lord three times that it might depart from me. And He said to me, "My grace is sufficient for you, for My strength is made perfect in weakness."

Obviously Paul is being afflicted by something. Some interpret this passage as a physical ailment, and some interpret this passage as a person. But it really doesn't matter as we have defined healing to include the entire body.

If this relates to a sickness of the eyes, or some other physical problem, or if this relates to a person that is irritating Paul, it doesn't matter. **What does matter is that Paul is very much aware that this particular problem originated from the devil. Paul is also aware of how this problem is affecting him and Paul uses the word buffet to describe what he is experiencing.**

The use of the word 'buffet' in this application is defined by Webster's as, 'to drive, force, move or attack by, as with repeated blows. What ever Paul was experiencing was not a one time deal. It kept coming and coming, and what ever this was, it was striking Paul with telling force. And Paul was not happy with whatever the problem was.

We know that Jesus Christ paid the atonement at Calvary for our sicknesses and diseases. Paul had been used in the gifts of healing since the beginning of his ministry. He believed in the power of Jesus to heal and to kick out the devil when needed.

Yet this time when Paul really needed to be healed or delivered, God did not heal or deliver him of this 'thorn-in-the-flesh?'

Paul had confronted the devil many times and probably did so here as well, but the result this time was different.

Was Paul's faith too weak? Was the power residing in the use of the Name of Jesus not strong enough? Was there sin or lack of forgiveness in Paul's life at this time?

No, this time God said that healing was not in the cards because even though this abnormality in Paul's life may have originated with Satan, God was allowing this for a purpose.

Notice how Paul went to the Lord three times and pleaded (which is not the same as asking,) but the problem did not disappear. God did however give Paul an answer. Paul wanted the problem to go away but God said no. Instead He would provide Paul with enough grace to see this thing through.

God's grace has often been the answer for Christians down through the ages. If God's answer to your prayer is not the answer you wanted to hear, it could be because He has something better in mind for you.

I know when you are hurting you would rather be healed than given grace, but again, **in whom is your trust?**

Paul did not give up when God did not heal him. When God does not heal you when you ask, regardless of how you have Biblically attacked the problem, don't give up but go directly to the Father to find the reason.

The passage tells us that Paul did not get God's answer until he had earnestly gone to God three times.

Do not give up on your healing until God tells you He has something else in mind.

In all three Biblical cases I have mentioned, we are never told that God did not provide healing at a later time. Given the fact that we never read of the problems again, I would venture a guess that God had a purpose for the sicknesses, attacks or problems that Timothy, Trophimus and Paul suffered at that particular time.

Personally I think God did in fact cure Timothy's stomach, and Trophimus did in fact recover and Paul's 'thorn-in-the-flesh' was indeed later removed.

In Hebrews 13:23, Paul writes:

--know that our brother Timothy has been set free.

Paul does not specify what Timothy was set free from. It could have been a physical prison or the prison of sickness, we are just not told.

If God has a reason or purpose for the sickness in your life, your healing may be delayed for a season. In this case Paul learned how effective the power of God's grace is in a bad situation.

In any of the incidents mentioned here there is nothing said that would change the fact that God's will for His kids is health. Father God would prefer that His kids live under His divine health plan, but if necessary God will heal you when you get sick or have a disease.

I am going to inject an observation here. What is most important; instant earthly gratification for your healing, or your spiritual healing which is eternal? How much are you willing to trust God in what He has planned for you?

Some years ago a very good friend of mine was told that he had pancreatic cancer. Both of us were attending a Charismatic church at the time.

We regularly heard messages on healing preached and we believed in the power of Jesus to heal. I visited my friend at his home and I asked my friend how he wanted me to pray for him.

He told me that I should just pray for his peace as he knew he was going home. Could I have prayed for his healing? Did I believe that Jesus could and would heal?

Yes, I could have, and yes I believed God could and would have healed him. **But God had told him otherwise, and had I assumed, I would have prayed incorrectly.**

If I had just taken over and prayed for my friend's healing, we would have both been out of God's will. He for not telling me what God had told him; and me for not asking.

My friend had done things correctly when he was diagnosed with pancreatic cancer. As soon as he knew the nature of the physical problem he told the pastor. Collectively and in smaller groups, he had healing prayed into his life.

My friend also talked privately with Father God about his healing. Just as Paul was told no when he asked, my friend was told he was coming home.

Prayer and faith may open the door to healing, but God doesn't heal because we pray. When God heals it is either for His glory, or to bring glory to Him.

Christians can not control or manipulate God by using words or scriptures. We can remind God of His word and promises, but we can not force God to act.

God's words and promises as found in the Bible are all true, but when the promises are manifested that is entirely up to God. Claim your healing whether you see your healing manifested now or in eternity.

In Exodus 15:26 the Bible says it so very clearly:

I am the Lord who heals you.

Your prayers should be fixed not on your illness or your healing; but on the God who heals.

Why was my friend not healed before he went home I do not know? Was it because his faith was not strong enough, I don't think so. Was it because the church had not prayed healing over him; no it was not.

God had given my friend the answer to his prayers. God then gave him the grace to accept the answer to his prayers and it was a peaceful visit every time I went to see him in the time before his death.

My friend may not have received his physical healing in this life, but he did receive God's ultimate healing.

I lost a friend for a short time, but as King David said when Bathsheba's son died, "he can not come to me, but I will go to him."

When you are sick, God can, and He may, heal you when you ask and believe. But no matter how many times God may heal you; God still has a time-to-die scheduled for all of us.

I am reminded of a story I read some time ago where a woman had been praying for her son's healing. He was only 10 years old when he came down with an incurable disease and was only given a short amount of time to live. The mother prayed to God for her son to be healed.

God kept telling her that He did not want to heal her son and that she was to let the matter go. The woman would not take no for an answer and kept pressing in to God that He heal her son. **Due to her continued persistence, God finally healed the woman's son.**

The mother lived long enough to watch her son hanged as a criminal for a murder he committed when he was forty-one years old.

God's knows the future and we do not. **We need to line up our wants with the will of God.** In the story related above, there is no question the mother believed if she was persistent, God could and would heal her son. Of course we have the story Jesus told of the woman and the unjust judge. How her persistence finally got her justice because she just kept on asking. Yes Jesus taught that we should be persistent, but we also need to listen to God and hear what He wants in any given situation.

God had repeatedly told the mother, **no**, but she refused to listen to what God told her. The Bible tells us that God will give us what we want, but the same passage continues with the words that He will also send leanness of spirit.

And they tested God in the wilderness. And He gave them their request, but sent leanness into their soul. Psalm 106:14,15

This mother's son probably did not one day decide to commit murder. There was more than likely a long period of time leading up to the final act of murder. The mother probably had plenty of time to reflect on her persistent prayers for God to heal her son.

In a previous chapter we spent some time with the story of King Hezekiah, how he prayed to God and God healed him, then gave him an additional 15 years of life.

At the time king Hezekiah prayed, he did not have a son to take over the kingdom upon his death. Hezekiah, we are told had a son after God had granted him an additional 15 years of life. We also read that this son was the most ungodly king that ever ruled Judah.

Both the mother and the king loved God. Do you think they would have wanted their prayer(s) answered if they knew what the future held?

God never says NO without promising so much more. Just don't box God in, and let God do His thing in your life. In other words, go with God's flow in any given situation because sometimes what appears to be God's **NO** to your request is no more than a **NOT NOW**.

Sometimes God's NO also means NO, and that can include your healing.

If your healing is delayed, ask God if He has another purpose in mind that takes precedence over an immediate response to your prayer for healing. If we miss what is God's purpose for the sickness or disease, we could end up going to heaven without ever being cured from the sickness or disease. Or we could also go to heaven cured, but have missed a lot of Spiritual blessings that God had for us.

I am going off on a tangent here but I do have a purpose in mind, so please bear with me.

Let's backtrack to the time Jesus was walking around in Israel and look at a passage found in John the fifth chapter.

In these five porches lay a great multitude of sick people waiting for the moving of the water.

Jesus had undoubtedly walked this path numerous times so why didn't Jesus heal all those waiting there for the water to move?

The first thing that pops out to me from this passage was they had never asked. I am sure with the pool being a part of the temple complex, those waiting by the pool had heard of the miracle healings preformed by Jesus. And yet it appears they themselves never asked Jesus to heal them.

This seems to be another example of a situation where Jesus did not 'heal everyone'.

Could those sick people waiting by the pool have placed their faith and trust on the moving water, and not on the One who moved the water? That could have been the reason they did not ask Jesus to heal them. But the one lame person that Jesus healed had not asked either, and Jesus healed him.

We are never told why Jesus healed some but not all. When they came asking and expecting, scriptures indicate He healed all.

But what about the sick people that were in attendance at the occasions where the Bible says that Jesus healed all who came and asked, that did not ask. Where they healed as well?

In the Old Testament book of II Chronicles the 16 chapter the 12th verse we are told of what may happen if we do not seek the Lord when we have a sickness or disease.

And Asa became diseased in his feet, and his sickness was severe; yet in his disease he did not seek the Lord, but the doctors. So Asa died.

Asa was a good king and we read he did the things that the Lord showed him. But just as those lying in the temple area never asked Jesus to heal them, Asa also never sought the Lord for his healing.

The other principal I picked up is, while it may not be wrong for a Christian to go to a doctor; **God wants us to seek Him first**. Putting their trust to be healed in the moving water is a case of misplaced trust. Asa, putting his trust in his doctors was also a case in misplaced trust.

Where a Christian puts his or her trust will make a huge difference.

We told the story of a Sunday school teacher who wanted his class to memorize Psalm 23. He gave them a month to do so.

Little Ricky was excited about the task, but he just could not remember the words of the Psalm. Finally the month was up and the children were scheduled to one-by-one recite the Psalm in front of the congregation.

Ricky was nervous and finally it was his turn. He stepped up to the microphone and loudly recited, **"The Lord is my Shepherd, and that's all I need to know."**

Ricky was so right, the Lord will take care of you, but Jesus also wants and expects us to ask for our healing. Ask Him and He will take care of you. And ask Him first before seeking other means. **But listen for His answer.**

When I first read the story of the moving water in the pool, I was struck by the fact that God loved His people so much that He had provided a way for them to be healed.

Even before Jesus paid the price for the healing atonement, people were being healed. Jesus healed before the atonement, how much more so today when Christians are covered by the healing atonement.

Jesus has come ushering in the kingdom of God, and healing has been transferred to Jesus the Living water. Put your faith, or trust directly in the God who heals and the Son who paid the price.

Finally we come to the end of the passage where this man who was healed meets Jesus in the temple. Jesus did not ask him about what had just transpired, Jesus simply said,

"See, you have been made well. Sin no more, lest a worse thing come upon you." John 5:14

Jesus in effect told this man that he had been cured, but Jesus did not stop there, He also told the man to sin no more or a worse thing could happen. I take what Jesus said to mean the man could miss eternity. He would have been cured, but not healed spiritually.

This is also another incident where Jesus healed a person that had not asked. But as one reads the story in its entirety the reason becomes obvious. Jesus healed this man on the Sabbath to upset the religious leaders. The man was cured, but Jesus warned him not to miss the spiritual healing which would result in a future that would be far worse that not being able to walk.

Let me summarize where we are so far. First your delay, or even a NO in your healing could be because God has a plan and purpose for you that can preempt your healing at this time.

It could also mean that God wants you to ask Him directly why your healing is delayed. A third reason a person is not healed could be because their faith or trust is misplaced.

There is another reason given us by Paul in the eleventh chapter of I Corinthians which reads,

> But let a man examine himself, and so let him eat of the bread and drink of the cup. For he who eats and drinks in an unworthy manner eats and drinks judgment to himself, not discerning the Lord's body. For this reason many are weak and sick among you, and many sleep. (or have died)

This Biblical passage zeros in on the need to ask forgiveness of a Christian brother before we engage in communion. Paul picked out one area of examination, but there are other areas we need to examine as well.

If we do not ask the forgiveness of a brother, **or of God if we are blaming Him for something**, in effect we are making a choice that is going to come back to bite us in the butt.

Not forgiving and taking communion was a choice that had resulted in the death of a number of Christians, and this could result in our premature death as well.

Not forgiving someone as we are commanded to can certainly hinder a person's healing, even to being the cause of your premature death.

I have been in many communion services where everyone who knows the Lord Jesus personally are invited to take of the communion. **But never have I heard the warning of an early death mentioned.**

Yet Paul is very clear that many have died prematurely if the Christian partakes of communion when he or she is not in a right relationship.

I have not read anywhere in the New Testament where this warning by the apostle Paul came to an end. If this warning of a premature death was in effect then, it is still in effect today; every time we take communion.

In the Old Testament book of Deuteronomy there is a passage I think directly relates to what Paul is telling us can happen if we eat and drink communion in what Paul refers to as an 'unworthy' manner.

If you do not carefully observe the words of these laws that are written in this Book, and reverence the Lord your God, then God will send plagues, serious and prolonged sickness, all manner of diseases, and God Himself will increase trials, troubles, sicknesses, etc. Until you are destroyed. Deuteronomy 28:58,59

Granted this Scripture was given directly to the nation of Israel as a whole, but it is also applicable for the individual Christian as well.

Whoa, what is this, God will send plagues (like AIDS for example) serious and prolonged sickness, disease, trials and tribulations.

How do we equate this with a God of love and a Jesus who paid the price for sickness and disease?

Maybe we better see if there are additional passages in the Bible that support this passage found in Deuteronomy 28.

In Exodus 15:26 we again take note of who can send disease upon God's people:

If you diligently heed the voice of the Lord your God and do what is right in His sight, obey God's commandments and keep His laws, (then) I, God, will put none of the diseases on you which I, God, have brought on the Egyptians. For I am the Lord WHO HEALS YOU.

I understand this passage to clearly say God can and will send sickness and disease when necessary, but He will also keep you from sickness and disease, as well as healing you when you need it.

In Exodus 23:25& 26, God also promises the opposite of sickness and disease for His children if they will obey and serve Him.

So you shall serve the Lord your God, and He will bless your bread and your water. And I, God, will take sickness away from the midst of you. No one shall suffer miscarriage or be barren; I will fulfill the number of your days.

For every warning or condition, God also has a promised reward for those who listen to what He commands.

However, the healing atonement at the cross does not cancel out what God has said He would do if we are found in willful rebellion to Him.

Remember we stated that God is a God of balance. Yes God is a God of love, grace, and mercy, but God also is a God of justice and responsibility. The Old Testament laws did not go away when Jesus came to usher in the kingdom.

There are those who say that now that Jesus has come, God has changed and is now a God of love and mercy. This is incorrect theology as the Bible tells us that God has always been a God of Love and Mercy, but do not forget God is also a God of balance.

Leviticus 26:15-16, again tells us that God can and will send sickness and disease to His children.

And if you despise My statues, or if your soul abhors My judgments, so that you do not perform all My commandments, but break My covenant, I will do this to you: I will appoint terror over you, wasting disease and fever which shall consume the eyes and cause sorrow of heart.

Again in Numbers 21:6 we are told:

So the Lord sent fiery serpents among the people, and they bit the people, and many of the people of the Lord died.

Absolutely, Jesus has paid the price of atonement for our healing, but that atonement does not negate what God requires of His children. Again God is always a God of balance.

In summary of this short chapter and keeping in mind the preceding chapters, it should be apparent that sickness and disease can be part of the normal cycle-of-life caused by the fall. Sickness and disease can also come from Satan. Sickness and disease can also be the result of our sin.

And sickness and disease may also be directly attributed to improper taking of communion. From the passage in Deuteronomy it is also apparent that sickness and disease can come directly from God Himself as punishment, chastening, or reproof.

Dr. Dobson said that we are to always remember that when God permits sickness, He will not allow it without passing through His heart, His mind, His will and His purpose.

No matter what the situation, God is not surprised, nor is He uninvolved in what is happening in your body. **And nothing happens for a Christian that is outside of Father God's permission.**

God always uses sickness for a purpose, a purpose in which He will use to accomplish something in your life. **But you have a free will and you can defeat God's purpose or accomplishment.**

- God can **Permit** sickness,
- God can **Send** sickness,
- God can **Prevent** sickness,
- God can **Heal** sickness,
- God can **Use** sickness,
- God can **Get-Rid** of sickness.

The answer to 'Does God heal every time' is both a NO, but then again, YES He Does.

God can Permit, Send, Prevent, Heal, Use, and Get-Rid of sickness, but the bottom line is:

ALL HEALING ON EARTH IS BUT TEMPORARY!!

Thank you God, for everything You gave me, and
thank You God for everything You took!

Food for Thought:
Many people want the promised results; without
any responsible commitment.

TEN

Faith, Doubt, Unbelief & Fear
Faith:

In the previous chapter we touched just briefly on 'faith-to-believe' as it relates to healing. Now let's take a look at faith in a deeper sense, then take a brief look at doubt, unbelief, and fear as they relate, not only to our own healing or moving in the gifts of healing, but also how doubt and unbelief can have a negative affect on our faith.

Most studies on the subject of faith start with the well recognized passage written by the apostle Paul in the eleventh chapter of Hebrews, and again that seems like a good place to begin; Hebrews 11:1:

Now faith is the substance of things hoped for, the evidence of things not seen.

I am not a theologian, but my simple understanding of this faith verse is that I am supposed to believe I have something because I have either asked for it, or God has promised it.

Oh, and just to make it interesting, I have to believe that I have what I have been promised, **without any indication that I have it, will have it, or even that I will receive what it is I am expecting.**

Then Paul lists a number of examples of those who believed what they had been promised, and goes on to tell us these heroes of faith sometimes took their belief of what they had been promised to their graves, **without ever seeing the promise fulfilled in their life.**

Paul further complicates the issue with the sixth verse of Hebrews 11:

Without faith it is impossible to please God, for he who comes to God must believe that He is, and that He is a rewarder of those who diligently seek Him.

There seems to be a number of things in this verse.

1. No faith, unhappy God.
2. If I do not believe that God is, and by inference that He is not the great I AM, **then don't come to God asking for anything.**
3. But if we have faith, and **if we come to God asking, He will reward** those who earnestly seek Him.

If I am reading these verses correctly, it would appear that if a person has faith, then he or she has a title deed for whatever they have asked for, or for what has been promised.

We have not yet seen any of the things we are to believe for, and **maybe we never will**. But, only if we have this kind of faith can we have any expectation that God will reward us with what we believe Him for.

This explanation could result in a person just throwing up his hands in exasperation, but really faith is not that complicated. Just as that young Sunday school student summarized the 23rd Psalm by saying, "The Lord is my Sheppard and that is all I need to know," even so faith can be explained with the simple words, **'my trust is in my God and I have faith in Him to do what He promises',** even if that means we need to wait for awhile.

To put it in simple words: '**I trust God to do what He has promised, and that is all I need to know.**

Mark 11:22-24 -- Jesus is telling us what we can have, if we put our faith or trust in God:

Jesus said to them, "Have faith (or trust) in God, for I say to you, whatever things you ask for when you pray, believe that you receive them and you will have them."

Faith is the conviction, the confidence, the trust, the belief, and the reliance that a person puts in God. When you are willing to put your confidence and your trust in God, and you are willing to rely on the trustworthiness of God, **then you have faith.** If you have to see it, it is not faith.

Quite often Christians can mouth the words, but '**Faith in God' is not a trick performed with our lips**. Faith is a spoken expression that springs from the conviction of our heart. In other words, you can not trick God by just mouthing some words in order to get what you want. **What you speak better be what you believe, because you can not fool God.**

Long ago I read a book, the name and author I can not recall, but I remember the author said that far too often people are looking for a '**short-cut**' to healing. Please pray for me using your faith and I will be cured. However, **I am really relying on your faith** to be cured because I do not have much faith.

There is a time when someone else's faith is needed, but if you are a Bible believing Christian, then God wants you to use your faith.

And as Christians we need to make sure that what we speak, and what we believe, is personal. God may sometimes cure, but are you willing to settle for just being cured? The 'cure' is temporary but the 'healing' is forever.

Herb Stewart in his book the Mighty Hand of God said, "When a person is given something that costs them nothing, then the gift is often treated as worthless."

You may have no problem with accepting the healing in your body that you need, **but are you then willing to both thank God for your healing and willing to live in service to Him?**

Let me add something here for you to think about. Have you come to the point in your sickness, disease, or any other troubling problem, where you can thank God for the problem?

This is Biblical and here are a few of the scriptures to support the fact that you need to thank God for what, or where, you find yourself:

I Thessalonians 5:18

In everything give thanks; for this is the will of God in Christ Jesus for you.

Ephesians 5:20,

giving thanks always for all things to God your Father in the name of our Lord Jesus Christ.

And also in Philippians 4:4 were it is written:

Rejoice in the Lords always. Again I say, rejoice!

When you receive a bad report from the doctor it should force you to look, not only at your life, but as a Christian it should also cause you to look at your faith and in what you believe.

Dr. Ed Dobson said that after he had received the diagnosis of ALS he wanted to ask God to keep him shallow and healthy, rather than sick and spiritual. Not real shallow, but healthy.

I know how Dr. Dobson felt, because when I learned what type of prostate cancer I had and how quickly it could grow, I was much more interested in being healed that I was in being spiritual.

Those feelings are really an oxy-moron. I really needed to be more spiritual and exercise my faith as it pertained to my healing if I wanted God to heal me, and yet that was not what I wanted to do.

Read Romans 12:3 where Paul informs us that God has given to each of us a measure of faith. Initially that small measure of faith is needed to even believe God for our salvation. That little measure of faith then needs to be cultivated and watered in order for it to come alive in each Christian.

We need to trust God to meet our daily needs. We also have to trust God when our need is greater than just the everyday needs of life.

Paul tells us in Romans 10:17 that faith comes by hearing, and hearing by the word of God. Paul is telling us we need to increase or build up our faith level, and to do that we need to **hear the word** of God as well as to **read the word** of God.

We are told that faith is like the mustard seed which is a very, very, small seed. God will take this tiny 'mustard-seed-size' of faith and make it grow, and grow, and grow.

In Philippians 3:16 we are told we need to walk, and move out in the little bit of faith we have, but we are always to strive for a higher level of faith.

Nevertheless, to the degree that we have already attained, let us walk by the same--

Remember the incident with our youngest son and his welding without the use of a mask. I had a minimal amount of Biblical healing knowledge, limited experience with healing in the Name of Jesus, and not very much Biblical understanding regarding either.

But I moved and prayed with the knowledge and faith that I did have. The same is true with the prayer for the health of our unborn first grandchild.

The first time I moved out in faith and trust, the result of my 'faith prayer' was answered quickly. The next time it took some months to see God's answer to my prayer of faith.

Later when I was first diagnosed with the fast growing, and life threatening, prostate cancer, the God-given healing took over three years.

This growth of our faith happens in two ways; one by moving out in the level of faith we currently have, and second by allowing God through His word to increase our faith.

This has been true in my experiences with the gifts of healing. I trusted God even though I understood only in limited amounts. But as I trusted and walked out my little faith, God through His written and taught word has added to my faith, as well as increasing my knowledge.

And as my faith has been increased, I have been able to believe and trust God quicker, more often, and for greater miracles, both for my self and for others.

When I first started to pray for the healing of others and began to exercise the gifts of healing, God gave me easy ones at first. My faith in what God could and would do, grew until the time came when God restored the eyesight of the blind man in India.

I don't think God would have performed the healing of the blinded eyes if my faith had not grown to a level where God could work this through me. I believe it took a number of healing incidents and a number of years for me to reach this level.

But again, never put God in a box. If there had been the need earlier, God would have provided regardless of the level of my faith at the time.

We could spend more time on what faith is, but again you can find numerous books written on the subject, or you can use your search engine and check 'faith' out on your internet computer.

I am going to move on to some examples of what faith can do, will do, and has done.

Galatians 3:11 reads:

'the just shall live by faith'.

The first question is, 'who are the just?' The just are those who have put their trust in God, for salvation of course, but also for everything else, including healing.

Before we get into a number of Biblical stories of faith that worked, I want to share a story I read about a woman during the depression that experienced how God worked when she put her trust in Him.

A poorly dressed lady with a look of defeat on her face walked into the small neighborhood grocery store.

She approached the owner of the store, and in a humble manner asked if he would let her charge a few groceries. She softly explained that her husband was very ill and unable to look for work; they had seven children, and they needed food.

The grocer scoffed at her and requested that she leave his store.

Visualizing the family need, she said, "Please sir! I will bring you the money just as soon as I can."

The grocer told her he could not give her credit, since she did not have a charge account at his store.

Standing beside the counter was a customer who overheard the conversation between the two. The customer walked forward and told the grocer that he would stand good for whatever the lady needed for her family.

Reluctantly the grocer asked the lady if she had a grocery list.

The lady replied that she had a grocery list, and the grocer said she should put her list on the scales, and she could have as many groceries as her list weighed.

The lady hesitated a moment and with a bowed head, she reached into her purse and took out a piece of paper and scribbled something on it. She then laid the piece of paper carefully on the scales with her head still bowed.

The eyes of the grocer and the customer showed amazement when the scales went down; and then stayed down.

The grocer said that he could not believe it, but began putting groceries on the other side of the scales. The scales did not balance and he continued to put more groceries on them until the scales would hold no more.

The grocer stood there in utter disgust, and finally he grabbed the piece of paper from the scales and looked at it in utter amazement.

It was not a grocery list; it was a prayer which simply said: 'Dear Lord, you know my needs and I am leaving this in Your hands.'

The grocer gave her the groceries that he had gathered and stood in stunned silence.

The lady thanked him and left the store. The other customer handed a fifty-dollar bill to the grocer and said that it was worth every penny of it to see how much a prayer weighs.

I have left out the names, but this is a real story. The question for you and for me, as it was for this lady: **How much do we trust God, as that will determine how much faith we have?**

This previous story is not about physical healing, but we have stated Father God is interested in healing our entire being, and that includes the mental and emotional needs this wife and mother was experiencing

THIS LADY WAS IN CHARGE OF HER FAITH, BUT GOD WAS IN CHARGE OF THE RESULTS!

The level of a person's faith is based upon the **knowledge** of God's Word, as well as an **understanding** of His character.

The spirit-of-this-world is Satan, and everything he does in this world is in opposition to everything God has promised, or would like to do in our lives. When we stand against the spirit-of-this-world in faith, Satan loses his controlling influence over us.

God does not always promise immediate results, but God's grace is so great that He will always give immediate assurance to us.

Would you allow me to digress for a bit? I am getting closer to the end of my life as I have passed the Biblical age of three score and ten. I reflect more on what is to come next than I used to. There are times when Satan will try very hard to plant seeds of doubt as to my eternal destiny.

Personally I believe it was easier for me to accept the gift of salvation and eternal life, than it has been to believe God for His gifts of healing.

I have spent a lot of time thinking about this. I have come to the conclusion that for me the gifts of healing, especially the physical ones God has given; occur in a shorter time frame, and I receive them while I am yet alive.

The gift of a life after death will not be realized until I die, even though the Bible says that eternal life begins the moment I put my trust in God through Jesus Christ.

When I am healed I can see and experience this in the here-and-now. Heaven will not be seen or realized until I leave this present life; and as far as I know no one has come back to earth to tell us about heaven.

The gifts of healing have to be believed for; and the gifts are received now, right here, and for the most part while I am living.

This takes a lot more **'present-day'** faith, than the faith to believe for the eternal part of life that continues after I take my final breath.

The gift of faith for eternal life, this life after death, is a gift I will not really realize until I die.

Some years ago, I was involved in a telephone calling campaign where we called various phone numbers and asked the person who answered this simple question, "If you were to die tonight, do you know where you will be spending eternity."

I will never forget the response I received from a gentleman, who after further conversation shared he was a retired pastor. He said, and I quote, "I don't think we can know the answer to your question until we die." The words of that retired pastor were technically correct as we will not experience the evidence of our faith until we die. But he did not mean it that way. This retired pastor had no real personal assurance of eternal life.

This retired pastor may have prayed and asked God to forgive him of his sins. He may have received eternal life because of his actions.

But he never trusted God's promises, nor did he allow the Holy Spirit to provide the assurance of eternal life.

I don't want to live without knowing the assurance that Father God has promised. I sincerely hope that you my brothers and sisters don't want to live without the assurance that the Holy Spirit wants to impart in you either.

John 3:16 may have been a reality in his life, but because he had never fully accepted the gift of faith God had offered, he never got the God given assurance from God's promises that 'whosoever' believes in His Son will have eternal life.

It is my belief that Jesus Christ **suffered** for my sicknesses and diseases just as He **died** for my sins. God is not a respecter-of-persons, and just as Jesus suffered for my sicknesses and diseases, He suffered for your sickness and disease as well.

I also believe God has a two-fold purpose in mind for me and you with the atonement of Jesus at the cross of Calvary.

The Bible tells us that God sent His Son to die and to cover the penalty for our sins. The Word of God also told us many years in advance that Jesus was to die on the cross. The two thieves that were crucified next to Jesus were not tortured before being nailed to the cross like Jesus was.

Jesus' death to cover our sins could have been accomplished without the additional torture and humiliation. Except, according to Isaiah, the stripes, the suffering, and the humiliations, were a payment to cover the atonement for our healing needs.

The first purpose in the healing atonement of Jesus is for our **'present-day'** existence, or our needs in everyday living.

These individual gifts of healing by faith need to be accepted and claimed just as we need to accept and claim the gift of eternal life.

Accepting God's 'gifts-of-healing' offers us a present-day glimpse and experience into the power of Jesus Christ right now and before we leave this planet called earth.

Second, a person's faith for the longer term promise of life eternal can be greatly increased if we can believe, claim, and accept that which Father God, through Jesus Christ, has offered us for the short term.

As a Christian if you are <u>unwilling</u> to take advantage of what God offers for the here-and-now in the healing of your mind, soul, and body; you will have missed a fantastic opportunity to experience and build up your faith and your assurance of salvation for a life that will continue after leaving this planet.

Remember the Bible story of the Israelites wandering in the wilderness for 40 years? They had failed the first test of their faith regarding the land God promised them? They failed to take advantage of what God had promised them.

An entire generation missed the opportunity to enjoy and experience that which God had promised them. Reading between the lines, it is safe to say that many of the Israelites living during this time also died prematurely.

The same is true for mainstream Christians today. Jesus Christ has paid the price for our sickness and diseases. The Holy Spirit is willing to provide the faith and the power to both claim and to move in the gifts of the Holy Spirit.

But we have failed to move out in His Name. And many Christians will die prematurely because we have not been willing to move out.

Have you traveled in the wilderness of sickness and disease long enough? Has you family been sick long enough? Would you like to be used in the healing of others?

If your answer to any or all of these questions is a YES, then are you willing to step out in faith and claim and accept what the Father has offered?

Isn't it time you step-up-to-the-plate, not only for yourself, but for your family as well?

As Christians, isn't it time for us to again implement all of the Great Commission?

You have the promise of eternal life because you have used your faith in the death and resurrection of Jesus Christ to claim the forgiveness of your sins. God did not lie when He promised us this free gift of eternal life.

God also does not lie when He offers you the gifts of healing through the stripes, the suffering and the humiliation borne by His Son. It is no harder to claim the gifts of healing for yourself, than it was for you to lay claim to the gift of salvation.

Each gift is offered and each gift is accepted by faith. **The two do not come as a package deal; you have to believe and accept each gift individually.**

What we have been discussing could be described as 'The Law of Faith' because faith is an unchangeable fact. God Himself instituted this unchangeable law which will never change, and this law of faith will work for anyone.

God's laws have always been there but they have not always been discovered. **Sometimes they have been discovered but not always appropriated**. An example of this would be the law of aerodynamics.

The law of aerodynamics allowed the first airplane to get off the ground and fly. God had put this law into place at the time of creation, it had always been there, but it was many years before the law was discovered.

The law of aerodynamics was first experienced by the Wright brothers. Then those that followed this first flight of a man-in-a-machine, built on the principal. Today we have planes that fly faster than the speed of sound, and are able to carry large numbers of passengers and/or cargo.

Even as God placed into being the law of aerodynamics at creation, God also placed the gift of faith into existence at the time of creation. **His created human life forms practiced faith long before Jesus came to earth.**

When Jesus left this earth following His resurrection, the gifts, fruits and miracles that followed were directly related to an increase in faith and power now available through the use of His name and His gift of the Holy Spirit.

Even as the use of the law of aerodynamics grew since that first airplane flight, **just so the use of the 'law of faith' should have grown 'exponentially' following the coming of the Kingdom of God.**

The miracles related to faith in and through Jesus Christ should have greatly multiplied in number; because that same law of faith was totally unleashed through the power of the Holy Spirit and became available to every Christian.

Laws and principals never change, but attitudes about them can change. I go back to what Billy Graham said in his book, **'Whenever Christians lose sight of a gift from God, they dishonor Him'.**

I am going to do what I said earlier we must be careful not to do; I am going to take a verse out to its immediate context. However, I believe the verse fits into the overall context of the law of healing, and fits what Billy Graham said regarding how Christians can dishonor God.

Mark in the 12 chapter and the 24th verse said it this way:

Jesus answered and said to them, "Are you not therefore mistaken, because you do not know the Scriptures nor the power of God?"

God gave us the law of faith, and the gifts of healing should be used to build upon that law. As Christians, by-and-large we have disdained the law of faith for the gifts of healing; either for ourselves or to use in the healing of others. **And as such we are dishonoring Him.**

The Bible says that we can NOT please God without faith. Assuming this is a true understanding of God's word as it relates to faith; then the opposite would also be true. **We make God very happy when by faith we accept the promises He has given us.**

Think for a minute about what I just stated. God does not lie and God wants you to have and to exercise faith.

Then why not please Him by having the trust in Him and using your faith to be healed? Why not have faith for your family to be healed? Why not have faith that He will use you to heal others?

Christians have grown lazy and no longer know the Scriptures, nor are they following the Great Commandment of Christ. Far too many of the messages from the pulpit are do-good, feel-good messages instead of the Word of God found in the Bible.

If Christians were casting out demons, healing the sick and being healed of sickness and disease, the churches would not be able to contain those who would believe.

What is involved on our part as God's kids in using the gift of faith in receiving the gifts of healing?

- First we need to believe the words and promises that God has given us in His book, the Bible.
- Then we need to believe that the promises God has made; He is fully capable of providing.
- Just as God has made the promises, believe that Jesus' suffering installed the provision for atonement.
- Finally, allow the Holy Spirit to provide the faith needed for the promises to be fulfilled in your life.

In a recent Sunday morning service, Pastor Brian made the following statement: **"To be a follower of Jesus is not just what you believe, but it is also how you behave."**

If you know Jesus Christ personally, you are on the road to eternal life. As a follower of Jesus Christ you need to move beyond what you believe now. You need to walk out your faith in Jesus Christ as it relates to your healing.

Now move out in your circle of influence in the healing of others. Jesus Christ ushered in the Kingdom of God with His teaching, His preaching, and His good-works. **Jesus then told us to go and do likewise.**

The apostle James has said it so well in the short book of the Bible that bears his name. My paraphrase of the words found in the book of James goes like this:

He who is not a forgetful hearer but a doer of the word; this person will be blessed in what he does. God has chosen the poor of this world to be rich in faith, and if we show any partiality of person we commit a sin. And what does it profit, if someone says he has faith but does not have works. Faith by itself will prove to be a dead faith if a person does not do works. I will show you the depth of my faith by the works that I do. Faith in Jesus Christ will save you, but <u>*faith working together with the Holy Spirit in works will result in a faith*</u> *made perfect.*

God expects people to believe because of what He has shown and done through His people. **'People-to-People'** is God's designed way!

People who have seen and experienced God's healings, must show and tell others how they can see and experience God's grace in healing as well.

I am going to list just a few of the many Bible verses relating to faith and of healing resulting from faith.

- *Daniel 6:22 -"My God sent His angel and shut the lions' mouth, so that they have not hurt me... So Daniel was taken out of the den, and no injury whatever was found on him, because he believed in his God.*

- Matthew 9:28 – *the blind men came to Him. And Jesus said to them, "Do you believe that I am able to do this? They said to Him, "Yes, Lord." Then He touched their eyes, saying, "According to your faith let it be to you." And their eyes were opened.*

- Matthew 15:28 – *Then Jesus answered and said to her, "O woman, great is your faith! Let it be as you desire." And her daughter was healed that very hour.*
- Matthew 9:21 – *for she said to herself, "If only I may touch His garment, I shall be made well." But Jesus turned around, and when He saw her He said, "Be of good cheer, daughter; your faith has made you well."*

These are just a few of the verses where faith in God resulted in restoration of health, or the return and/or saving from death. In the appendix you will find a more complete and detailed list of scriptures relating to faith and the results of faith or trusting in God.

Thought for the Day:
Faith is not the means by which we get God to work in our lives;
Faith is the means by which we enter into His will for our lives.

Doubt & Unbelief:
Before we get into what the Scriptures have to say about doubt and unbelief I am going to re-share my prostate cancer story with you, from the first diagnosis right up to the present time.

Eighteen or nineteen years ago I was told that I had prostate cancer. A short time later I learned this type of prostate cancer was the most severe type of the four possible. My local urologist and Mayo Clinic both recommended immediate surgery, but I was sure that Father God had said this was not direction I was to take.

God told me what He did not want me to do, but He did not bother to tell me what He wanted me to do, so I waited.

As I look back I am amazed at how many of my Christian family and friends, both directly and indirectly, were telling me how stupid I was not to listen to the doctors.

Fortunately God did not keep me in suspense too long. A few weeks after my visit to Mayo Clinic I was at an industry trade show in San Francisco, California. I happened to look down the aisle and saw a friend from Toronto, Canada walking towards me. God immediately brought to my mind an incident that had taken place in Toronto a few years earlier.

Linda and I were visiting this business friend and his wife. We went out for an evening meal, but before the food arrived, my friend opened a small bottle and shook out a number of pills. When asked about all the pills, I learned they were vitamins, and my friend then told us an incredible story. Seven years previously his sister had a severe case of cancer; so severe the doctors had sent her home to die.

Someone told her about Dr. D'Adamo, this 'holistic' doctor in Toronto. She went to his clinic and Dr. D'Adamo placed her on a restricted food diet, along with various vitamins. My friend said that seven years after she had been given up for dead, she not only was alive, but vitally alive as well.

I recalled that evening's discussion as my friend walked to the booth where I was waiting. I asked him to sit down and told him what was happening in my life.

I said to him that in two weeks we had a trade show event scheduled in Toronto and I wanted an appointment with this holistic doctor. My friend said this would not be possible as the doctor was scheduled out at least six months in advance.

I told him I did not care how he did it, but get me an appointment. I got the appointment and learned what I thought was God now directing me in the way in which I was supposed to go.

Was the visit Linda and I made to Toronto, the evening meal, and the pill episode a coincident, or had God known I would need this years' later? Was it a coincident the incident came into my memory the instant I saw my friend?

Following my visit to the Toronto clinic, I put into practice what I had been instructed to do. Wouldn't you think now that I knew what God was directing me to do, my health would improve and I would be healed of the cancer?

Wrong, my test reports continued to get worse, the cancer continued to grow, and the opposition to what I knew was God's leading also increased.

As I look back on this time, I realized that this was just one of the waiting times God would have for me. God was putting my faith and trust in Him to the test. **This was an open door, but it was not the completed picture.**

My stubbornness in following the direction I knew was from God, led the company's management team to put together a plan to oust me from the company; and shortly thereafter I was out.

I now had the problem with the cancer that was getting more severe. I no longer had the company that I had started. And I had alienated family and friends with my refusal to listen to their advice.

If that was not enough, I was diagnosed with a heart problem and told I needed quadruple-bypass-surgery.

Previously in the book I shared with you my heart by-pass story so I won't repeat it, but you may remember, the same time as the bypass surgery, my wife Linda was told she had breast cancer.

It was an interesting few years to say the least. The direction with the Canadian holistic doctor; and later what appeared to be an open door leading towards Cryo surgery for the prostate cancer; were simply diversionary steps God allowed me to go through until His perfect plan for my life was worked out.

I really thought that God had opened a door for the Cryo surgery. And to tell the truth I was a bit annoyed with God when that door closed while I was on the gurney waiting to be wheeled into surgery.

But again, God had His plan for my life. I know now His plan for me was to experience Him in new ways, and then to share these experiences with others.

I honestly do not know how my faith held up during these years. Satan certainly used these incidents to undermine my trust in God, and to question the direction God was leading me.

These installments in God's plan for my life were such that I am glad I was not aware of what they would entail beforehand.

The health issues with my heart and God's subsequent miracles, plus the breast cancer with Linda, and God's handling of that, helped me to stay the course.

Every time I really needed it, God sent His grace to see me through.

It was more than three years after I first learned I had prostate cancer, before I learned God had killed the tumor. God did not remove the tumor, He just killed it. God had rewarded my trust and my faith.

A few years later I learned why God had not removed the tumor. He had further use for what looked like a black, golf-ball size, round object below my bladder.

Three years later blood work indicated my PSA count was on the rise. I was given an ultra scan of the area and on the monitor I could see some of the edges around the 'once-dead' tumor were now glowing green, indicating the tumor was coming back to life.

God directed me to take the same action as He had laid out the first time, and again God honored my faith and the cancerous tumor died. A few years later for the third time the PSA number started to climb. Once again the same course of action. I was good to go, but only for a time.

The fourth time the tumor came back to life; I really questioned God about the direction I had taken the first three times. I did not want to take the same direction if God had something else in mind.

Once again, after much prayer, I was led to do the same things I had done before, and you guessed it, God was faithful again.

The prostate cancer has now come and gone four times. Statistically I have been told I have been dead for some years. Between you and me, I am glad God doesn't go by statistics.

I have shared this lengthy and personal story with you for a purpose. Twice a year I have blood work done and two weeks ago I learned my PSA count is again on the increase, suggesting the cancerous tumor is reactivating.

The last few days I have been praying and asking God what to do, hoping He would just tell me to do again what He had previously directed. Not this time; this go around God has something else in mind. What I do not know, but He has made it clear to me, and then reinforced what I heard Him telling me, with various scriptures.

This time I am to place my trust for healing entirely in Him and in Him alone.

As my pastor friend with Lupus said when he left the pastorate, "I am going back home until God heals me or takes me home." Or as Dr. Dobson said, "I am going to believe for my healing until God shows me He has something else in mind."

Father God has assured me that He will not take me until I finish this book. I am asking Him for an additional time period as I would like to also teach others what I am sharing in this book, but that is up to Him.

Keep in mind a couple of things I have already shared. The first one is '**all healing is but temporary**' and the second was found in Ecclesiastes where we read there is **a time to be born and a time to die**, and we do not control either one.

Now you now know why I started this section of doubt and unbelief with my personal journey with cancer. Once again my trust and belief in Father God will more than likely be put to the test.

I have shared a number of scripture verses on faith, and my understanding of these God-given passages will now have new meaning for me personally.

As we take a look at what the Word has to say regarding doubt and unbelief, keep in mind these warnings will have a special meaning for me as well. I am not preaching words that have never been put to the test personally.

God is no respecter of persons, what He has done, what He is doing, and what He will do for me; He will also do for you, and by that I do not mean the sickness, **but I do mean the healings.**

Unbelieving Believers:

Faith unlocks the storehouse of God' blessings, but doubt and unbelief will lock you out of the storehouse of blessings. Faith results when God's spirit communes with our spirit. Faith also comes from knowing what God says in His word, the Bible. Faith will be increased when we hear and listen to the preached and taught Word of God. And faith will unlock the storehouse of God's blessings, **but only when we put into practice what we have heard from God.**

At the beginning I stated this book is being written primarily to my Christian brothers and sisters. The question each of us must ask is this: Am I a Bible believing, faith-based, Father trusting, child of God, or am I an **'unbelieving' believer**?

Are you going to have just enough faith to guarantee your entrance into heaven? If so, will you miss out on the blessings God has for you right now before you get to heaven?

Father God has His perfect plan for each of our lives, but He loves us so much that if we choose **not to allow His perfect plan in our life,** He will let us live out our lives in His **permissive will.**

We can miss the blessings He has for us in this life, but He will not deny heaven to anyone who comes to Him through His son Jesus Christ.

No one is immune to doubt. It can, it will, and it does happen to us all. As one writer put it, "You just have to know how to handle doubt when it comes."

Doubt is not unique to you or I. Some of the greatest men and women in the Bible had to deal with doubt. We will take a look at some of these great heroes of faith who had moments of doubt.

One of the heroes of faith mentioned in Hebrews 11 was Abraham. The writer of Hebrews mentions Abraham and Sarah, both as heroes of faith. Yet Abraham doubted the promise of God to provide him and Sarah a son when he married Sarah's handmaid.

The result of Abraham's small period of doubt in God's promise was the beginning of the Middle East problems the world has today. Even though Abraham had doubts regarding the promise of a son, God provided the promised son anyway.

Thank goodness God did provide this promised son to Abraham and Sarah because through that son Jesus Christ came.

I could also mention the times when Abraham, worried for his safety, passed Sarah off as his sister. You think maybe Abraham had a lack of faith in God's protection?

Sarah was listed as a hero of faith and yet when God said she was to bear a son in her old age, she literally laughed at what God had said.

Moses is listed in this passage also and yet when God told him to speak to the rock, Moses instead relied on what God had done the first time, and he struck the rock. Moses paid the price for not doing it God's way. Once again we read of a lack of faith by one who is listed as a hero of faith.

And the Old Testament list goes on. We could list Joseph, David, Job, and a multitude of other well known men and women of God who had periods of doubt crop up in their life.

Oh, you say, "it is all different now that we have the Holy Spirit operating in our lives." **Are you sure about that?**

What about John the Baptist? The Bible tells us that He was separated unto God and filled with the Holy Spirit while he was still in his mother's womb.

We never read where Jesus was filled with the Holy Spirit in the womb. The first time we read where Jesus received the Holy Spirit was at His baptism by John.

In addition to being filled with the Holy Spirit at a young age, John also lived a separated life that was dedicated to God and preparing for a ministry that would only last six months.

John is the one who saw Jesus coming for baptism and said, in John 1:29, and John 1:34:

"Behold the Lamb of God, which takes away the sin of the world."

"I saw, and bare record that this is the son of God."

"One mightier than I cometh, the latchet of whose shoes I am not worthy to unloose."

The anointing on John had to be exceptionally strong and powerful because logic could not have defined his ministry. Thousands of people had come to hear John preach the gospel of repentance.

God had revealed to him that a visible sign from heaven would tell him who the Messiah was. John baptized the Messiah and John saw the dove descend to the head of Jesus.

John heard the booming voice from heaven telling him and everyone there at the time, that Jesus was the Son of God.

And yet John after being imprisoned for a short period of time began to doubt. Two things stood out to me when I read the story of John sending his disciples to ask Jesus if He really was the Messiah.

If this man of God, anointed with the Holy Spirit even before he was born, and was told by God Himself who Jesus was, could have doubts, then should we be surprised that we also can have doubts?

The second thing that got my attention was the response of Jesus. In Luke 7:22 we have a record of the answer Jesus sent back to John.

Jesus answered and said to them, 'Go and tell John the things you have seen and heard; that the blind see, the lame walk, the lepers are cleansed, the deaf hear, the dead are raised;, the poor have the gospel preached to them. And blessed is he who is not offended of me."

Jesus reassured John by quoting a passage of Scripture found in the Old Testament book of Isaiah 35:5 where it reads:

Then the eyes of the blind shall be opened, and the ears of the deaf shall be unstopped. Then the lame shall leap like a deer, and the tongue of the dumb sing."

Jesus virtually repeated the passage in Isaiah, added a couple of additional healings and sent the disciples of John back to John.

I would think John would have deserved more than that from Jesus. Jesus could have said, 'Tell John not to lose heart, keep the faith, I will see you soon in heaven', or something along those lines.

But what did Jesus do? He just quoted a simple passage from the prophecy of Isaiah.

To counter the doubts that had surfaced in John's mind, Jesus simply reminded John of what was written in the Scriptures. This is exactly the method Jesus wants us to use when we need to deal with our doubts.

It is not that Jesus did not care about John's feelings, the opposite is true. **Jesus cared so much that He sent His very best. Jesus gave John the written Word of God.**

Many of us have Bibles lying around gathering dust, and maybe we even carry them with us when we go to church. But when doubt and unbelief come along, we don't want a scripture; we want something tangible or emotional that we can feel.

Our prayers and thoughts can go something like this: 'Please Jesus just put your arm around me and tell me everything will be all right'. Or Jesus, 'Send the pastor over to pray with me and assure me.'

But overcoming doubt is not just about feeling better; it is about getting the kind of faith that only comes from the word of God.

Romans 10:17 puts it as simply as it can be said:

So then, faith comes by hearing and hearing from the word of God.

It is this word of God the Holy Spirit will quicken to you that provides the faith to trust what God has said.

John was looking for reassurance from Jesus for his weakened faith, but what did Jesus send back to John? Jesus just sent the Word.

When you are having some doubts as to whether Jesus will heal you, check the Word and find out what God has promised. The Holy Spirit will take it from there.

Just as Jesus loved John so much He sent the very best, even so Jesus loves us so much He just sends us back to the promises written in the Word of God.

We will talk more on the enemy later, but keep in mind where doubt and unbelief come from. Satan got to John during a point of weakness. John had been in prison for a time. He was probably tired, hungry, cold and wet. John knew Herod could have him killed at any time. John was probably worried that all the effort he had put into his ministry was going to be worth nothing.

It was in this time of vulnerability that Satan snuck into the mind of John and started planting the seeds of doubt.

When you are sick, tired, grieving, or in a moment of weakness, Satan will be right there to plant the seeds of doubt in your mind. **If you then allow those seeds to linger he will help the seeds to grow, and to grow quickly**.

Jesus overcame and defeated the devil; then Jesus passed this same resurrection authority on to each of us. Use His name, use His words, and trust the Holy Spirit to provide the gunpowder to kick those satanic-inspired seeds of doubt out of your mind.

Before you allow thoughts of doubt and unbelief to get from your mind into your heart, take the authority that Jesus has given to all of His disciples. Use His Name, and the power of His name, to order Satan to take all of the doubts and fears running loose about in your mind and to get out.

I promise you the devil will have to leave and take these doubting thoughts with him.

Doubt and unbelief starts in the mind, but the progression of doubt and unbelief will move both the doubt and the unbelief into the heart. The heart is the center of our being and out of which are the very issues of life.

The heroes of faith in the Bible had their times of doubt. What made them heroes of faith rather than defeated children of God, was the fact that those doubts never got beyond their mind. And when they did they asked Father God for forgiveness and relief.

When you are facing doubts about the trust-worthiness of God, recognize your doubt for what it is and where it is coming from. Take care of it then and there; do not let the doubt form unbelief in your heart.

In the first chapter of James, directly after the verse where we are told to ask for wisdom from God, James goes on to tell us how to use that God-given wisdom:

"But let him ask in faith, with no doubting, for he who doubts is like a wave of the sea driven and tossed by the wind. For let not that man suppose that he will receive anything from the Lord: he is a double-minded man, unstable in all his ways."

When I read that passage found in James, I realized James was not pulling any punches. Once you have asked God for something in faith and then you start to doubt, you will not receive that which you have asked for. From that point forward, you will feel tossed and driven; **shalom or peace will no longer be yours.**

There is good news however. God is a God of grace and mercy. Get back on track, kick the devil out if necessary, ask God to forgive you of your doubts, and let the Holy Spirit once again fill you with faith.

I could list more Bible versus that pertain to doubt, but that is a Biblical exercise and with the help of a Bible concordance, or by using a search engine on your computer, you can identify these verses and passages for yourself.

When the Holy Spirit quickens your spirit as you read a verse that applies to your situation, then do not harden your heart, but let God's words strengthen your faith and move you into a closer relationship with your heavenly Father.

FEAR:

Webster defines fear as 'an unpleasant emotion caused by a belief that someone or something is dangerous, likely to cause pain, or is a threat'.

Fear of the unknown could certainly be considered an unpleasant emotion. Fear of a sickness and where it could end up is certainly an unpleasant emotion as well.

The word "fear" in my King James Bible has two meanings. One is an unhealthy fear and the other is a healthy fear. When we are told to fear God, it has a different connotation. That type of fear is really reverence and is a healthy fear. This is the type of fear that leads to peace or Shalom.

The other type of fear will lead to unhealthy emotions, unsettled mind, tossing and turning at night, worry about the future, and the list continues.

We have touched on how doubt can often lead to unbelief when a Christian allows doubt to linger and grow. Doubt and unbelief will displace your faith, but doubt and unbelief will not stop by just replacing your faith. Satan first tries to move your God-given faith out of the way. Once your faith has been moved to the side, his next step is to slowly begin to fill you with fear.

Fear takes a number of different avenues in a person's life. One can literally move into the fear realm regarding sickness. A person can have a fear of failure that can translate into inaction, or no action. Let's take a look at how fear of failure can affect the Christian.

Andy Stanley in his book, 'The Next Generation Leader', stated that the reason so many current disciples of Jesus do not embrace and enter into doing the things that Jesus did is because of the fear of failure.

Stanley goes on to say that if we wait for our fear to subside before we take the plunge into believing action, we will be left standing on the sidelines for a long time.

The Christian who refuses to move until the fear is gone will never move. Without the courage to move, we will simply accumulate knowledge of God's word that will never be put into practice.

In the area of healing, both the one who should have stepped out in faith, and the person who would have been the recipient of that faith will lose out on what God would have had for them.

Max DePree the founder of Herman Miller has said that, "An unwillingness to accept risk has doomed more leaders than anything he could think of."

This is so very true within the Church of Jesus Christ. Stepping out in faith is the mark of a leader. Yes, there is a risk of failure but then again if God is really in control in your life, is stepping out in faith really a risk?

A Christian rooted and grounded in Jesus Christ and with the knowledge of God's word, should view failure differently. A Christian that has knowledge of the Bible will not fear failure in the eyes of man because his or her faith is rooted in Jesus Christ and the Word. Instead of being afraid of failure, the Christian needs to move out.

But move out in the Name of Jesus, trusting in the Father's promises and provisions, and with the ammunition supplied by the Holy Spirit.

If the Christian moves out in faith and the move looks like it is not working, then go to the Father and ask Him what is wrong. And just maybe you will learn that it had nothing to do with your faith at all.

Whenever there is fear, there is opportunity. Wherever there is great fear, there is great opportunity.

The person who is afraid to trust Jesus Christ for their healing misses a great opportunity. The Christian pastor, teacher, or lay person, who fails to honor the commandment of Christ and the Word of God to move out into the area of healing of others; **not only fails God and misses great opportunities, but they fail to help others receive what Jesus had for them.**

Isaiah 42:10 should be written into the heart of every Christian who moves out in faith:

Do not fear, for I am with you; do not anxiously look about you, for I am your God, I will strengthen you, surely I will help you, surely I will uphold you with My righteous right hand.

It is easy to be paralyzed if you are consumed by thoughts such as these:

- What if it does not work?
- What if I am wrong?
- What if my faith is not strong enough?
- If it does not work, what will others think of me?

David Turner professor from GRTS in teaching a class on Bible Study 101 stated there are four indentified, or specific, things involved in Bible study. I would suggest these same four principles apply to the healing ministry.

First would be observation; what do the healing passages found in Bible teach us?

Second is the interpretation; or what do these passages mean in the current situation?

Then follows correlation; how does it fit into this situation or need?

Finally number four the application; how should I respond to this situation or need?

Know the Word, understand the Word, use the understood Word for the need, and then respond as the Holy Spirit tells you.

Faith is measured by your trust in God, His Son and His promises.
Your level of faith is a sign of your spiritual maturity.

Just a quick review:

The initial gift of the Holy Spirit differs from the Gifts of the Holy Spirit. When a person invites Jesus Christ into their life they are given the Holy Spirit as a gift from Father God.

It is the initial gift of the person of the Holy Spirit that provides the increase in your level of faith needed to accept the special Gifs, which include the gifs of healing.

Doubt is <u>not</u> a sign of your lack of spiritually, **what you do with doubt is.**

Fear can be healthy or unhealthy, that is up to you. Fear needs to be dealt with or the result will be inaction, worry, lack of peace, and instability in your mind.

> *There is no fear in love. Perfect love drives away fear, for fear has to do with punishment; those who fear do not know perfect love.*
> I John 4:18

ELEVEN

For me this will be the most difficult chapter to write in this book. Why do I say that? Every thing that I have written to this point has been in a way, very personal. I have experienced sickness, disease, personal healings, and healings of others. I have experienced doubts, temptations, bitterness, and lack of forgiveness.

But when it comes to depression I thank God that I have not experienced this first hand. I have seen it in my family, friends, acquaintances, and fellow church members; but other than some thoughts bordering on depression that quickly passed, I can not write about this from a personal experience.

Depression has often been referred to as the 'common cold' of mental illness or mental problems. It has been estimated that mental depression effects 30-40 million Americans.

The World Health Organization defines health this way:

‘Health is a complete physical, mental, and social well-being; and not merely the absence of disease or infirmity.

Depression certainly fits within this definition and as such, mental illness is a sickness and certainly comes within the guidelines of God's Health Care Plan.

While depression has not been an illness experienced, I have learned how Christians, including myself, can be oppressed by the enemy. How the enemy gets a foot hold and then digs himself in deeper, often to the Christian's dismay.

I have no idea how often depression in the lives of Christians effects various other issues. Or how these other issues such as grief, troubles, sickness and related problems allow Satan to waltz right in and make a bad situation even worse. I do not even know how often depression is directly demonic in its origin.

All the problems that result from chronic depression may not be demonic in nature, but the enemy will sure try to make any depression in a person worse if he can.

There are cases where depression is related to things like generational, physical or verbal abuse, biological problems, etc. but when Satan moves in, all of these can then become demonic in nature.

A full gospel Christian physiologist who has studied depression from the Biblical and the sinful human nature viewpoint might have an idea as to the percentage of depression cases that arise from demonic oppression, or how many are directly related to other issues.

From a detached view it would seem that most bouts of depression are not demonic in origin but can quickly move in that direction.

Many times the Christian just has not put on the Biblical armor, or the Christian has Biblical issues that need to be dealt with for the God provided armor to be effective.

Depression may be described as feeling sad, blue, unhappy, miserable, or down in the dumps. Most of us have felt this way at some time in our life, but usually it is only for short periods.

True depression is better described as a mood or lifestyle disorder in which feelings of sadness, loss, anger or frustration interfere with everyday life for weeks or longer.

To be depressed in itself is not a sin! Let me say that again. Depression in itself is not a sin, but it must be dealt with. If depression is not checked, it can come to control one's actions and thinking, and when that happens most often the devil has snuck in.

In many cases this original depression is an issue within the control of the Christian. But once depression settles in, the depressed person may need medical help for a time to get control of the depression.

It will take time for the promises found in the Bible to be absorbed, and faith often has to be built up to claim the promises.

The help of other Christians may be needed to discuss the Biblical passages and to pray with the depressed person. Other Christians may well be required to use the authoritative power of Jesus Christ in taking back control.

The depressed Christian must learn the Biblical understanding of how the devil operates in a person's life. Jesus Christ has defeated Satan at Calvary and that is a done deal. Jesus has told the Christian that He has done His part in defeating the devil and **now it is our job to use that God-given power to kick the snot out of the devil.**

Chronic depression often causes an unreal view of the world and people. Chronic depressed Christians can have a strong desire to withdraw or a strong desire to escape.

This often results in over eating, excessive shopping, drugs, alcohol, various binges, and in spending an inordinate amount of spare time on recreation.

Regardless if it is a physical sickness or the sickness of depression, Jesus Christ has paid the price of atonement for healing both. He has paid the price both for healing the mind and restoration from depression.

God has pleaded with us to ask Him for wisdom regarding healing for the depressed state of mind.

Listen for His answer and allow Him to restore you to health or move you out of your depressed state.

The Bible has much to say regarding guilt and how this can affect the daily life of a Christian. Dr. Charles Stanley in a recent Sunday morning TV broadcast put it this way, **"Unresolved guilt often leads to depression."**

Dr. Stanley went on to say that everyone experiences guilt now and then, but for some people it is a constant companion. A sense of condemnation robs them of their joy, assurance, and confidence. He went on to say, "Remember, **Jesus is not in the business of condemning you**." Discover the root of your guilt feelings and find freedom in forgiveness through Jesus. Simply confess the cause of your guilt feelings, and ask God for forgiveness.

Just an aside here; when you ask the Lord to forgive your guilt feelings, then leave these feelings with Him. **If you are not willing to trust His forgiveness, don't bother asking.**

In John 8:11 Jesus told the woman taken in the very act of adultery that her sin was not going to result in condemnation:

And Jesus said to her, "Neither do I condemn you;
go and sin no more."

Dr. Stanley said, "As believers we do not have to live with guilt. It really does not matter if the guilt is true or false. Guilt and guilt feelings in our life must be dealt with."

Guilt that has fueled, or is fueling depression often results in a hindered prayer life, poor relationships with others, **suffering from physical illness,** or just missing the will of God. **Christians in order to be healed must deal with the guilt issue.**

I have studied what the Bible has to say about depression, even though the word is never used. I will share some of these Scriptures with you of Biblical Christians who seemingly suffered with depression, or harbored thoughts related to this emotional state.

My experiences with depression and with those suffering from depression have led me to conclude that more often than not, **the root causes may be; lack of forgiveness, depression that is generational in nature, feelings of guilt, biological problems, abuse that is often sexual in nature, substance abuse, parental rejection, anger, fear, or intolerable and/or grieving situations**

The opposite of chronic depression is what is known as manic depression. A manic depressed person instead of withdrawing and doing nothing, will switch to being ego driven, know everything, be correct on everything, feel that they know things no one else knows, not listen to anything that does not agree with whatever they currently believe, and is in every respect the direct opposite of the state of chronic depression.

Often a manic depressed person will believe that he or she is being led and directed by God Himself, but their actions are the direct opposite of what the Bible teaches.

As one person said; God expects spiritual fruit and not religious nuts. In Galatians 5:22 and 23 we are told what the fruit of the Spirit is:

-- *the fruit of the Spirit is love, joy, peace, longsuffering, kindness, goodness, faithfulness, gentleness, self-control.*

Regardless of what the manic depressed person says or claims, if he or she is not displaying the fruits of the spirit; and in most cases they will display everything but; **then the person is being led by the enemy and not by the Holy Spirit.**

I have listed ten things that I know can, or have, caused depression in people. Any of these factors by themselves can bring on depression. When these depression-inducing-factors are present, Satan has long known how to use these unprotected areas to sneak into a person's mind.

Satan would like to overcome a person's thought process and through the thought process take over control of all or a part of a person's life. When that is not possible, Satan will settle for oppressing and harassing both the Christian and the non-Christian alike.

I will give you my opinion on how a person can determine if the enemy is involved and what to do about it, but first let's see if we can make some Biblical sense out of this particular sickness.

.We read in I Peter the fifth chapter and the eighth verse the following: *Be sober, be vigilant, because your adversary the devil walks about like a roaring lion, seeking whom he may devour.*

I don't know about you but if I encountered a lion that was not behind the bars of a cage and he started to roar, I just might soil my underwear. But if I knew that the lion no longer had any teeth, had his claws removed, and was behind bars, I don't think I would have any problem if the lion were to roar at me.

And that is exactly what has happened. Jesus has defeated our prime enemy, Satan. Jesus pulled his teeth, cut off his claws and placed him behind bars.

We no longer have to give Satan the time of day, nor do we have to put up with his shenanigans.

My experience has been that Satan has his greatest success in messing me up if I allow him to play in my mind.

Our mind is the door to our spirit and the only way the devil can get to us is through our mind.

One of Satan's greatest weapons is the power of suggestion. It starts with a thought that if I dealt with immediately would stop right there. Fear, anger, bitterness, immoral thoughts, or any other improper thoughts should not be entertained by a Christian.

For me, if I allow those thoughts to continue I will soon find these thoughts becoming an action on my part.

We cannot help who may knock on our front door, but we can help who we invite into our house.

If the Christian, and that includes myself, were to take the apostle Paul's warning found in II Corinthians 10 to heart, the problem would no longer be a problem. The apostle writes:

For though we walk in the flesh, we do not war according to the flesh. For the weapons of our warfare are not carnal but mighty in God for pulling down strongholds, casting down arguments and every high thing that exalts itself against the knowledge of God, bringing every thought into captivity to the obedience of Christ.

In plain language Paul is telling the Christian that we walk in the flesh, but we do not have to withstand and confront Satan in our human flesh.

We have God on our side, and if our knowledge of God is sufficient, we will know what thoughts are not God-thoughts.

It is these thoughts that Paul tells us we need to bring into captivity, and we need to control these thoughts before the thoughts grow and become a sin.

We can not control what thoughts enter our mind, but with the help of Jesus Christ we can get rid of those thoughts.

Jesus said He had defeated the devil. He then transferred His authority over Satan to us via what is known in the legal field as the "power of attorney".

We can use the Name of Jesus and tell Satan to take that thought, or thoughts, and to get out, and to do it right now.

The Bible is quite clear that Jesus defeated the devil and then provided the Christian with His authority and power to carry on the fight.

The Bible is also clear that Jesus is all done taking on the devil. Now it is our responsibility to carry on the fight in His name.

When it comes to our thought process there is one problem. **You and I have got to want to rid ourselves of those thoughts**.

So often I have found that I really like the thought or mental images that are playing around in my mind. Even though I know they are wrong, and even though I know I have the power to use the Name of Jesus to rid myself of those thoughts or images, **I really do not want to let them go.**

That is when the thoughts become sin. Often what a Christian has been thinking about in his or her mind will stay there for a time. But these sinful thoughts many times do not stay in the mind. Satan will make sure that you have an opportunity to move them beyond the thought stage into actuality.

I said I would tell you how I think if you are suffering depression you can determine if the devil is a part, or all of the problem, so let's give it a layman's shot.

Start by taking a spiritual assessment of your current walk with the Lord.

- Are you having trouble in concentrating on reading the Word of God? When you read your Bible is what you are reading confusing and not making much sense?
- How about your prayer life? When you pray do your prayers get through, or are they hitting the ceiling and falling back?
- Are you constantly living in fear of something?
- Physically are you always tired and fighting sickness or disease?
- If you are a male, are you able to love your wife in the manner in which Christ loves you?
- If you are a female, are you able to Biblically see your husband as Christ sees him?
- Are the fruits of the Spirit as found in Galatians operating in your life?

If you have prayed and sought Father God regarding the problems to no avail; I would take a hard look to see if Satan is the root of the problem. If you think Satan is the cause of the problem either deal with him yourself, or get other Christians experienced in deliverance to work with you.

Many Christians will read these signs and say, "Wait a minute, I have one or more of these problems in my life, but I am not depressed." And you are correct as these problems can also be the result of our sinful human nature.

There may be sin in a Christian's life that results in manifestation of any of these warning signs. If as a Christian you find any of these problems in your life, repent of the sin and get rid of the problem.

If after repenting and asking God for forgiveness, the problem does not go away, it probably is a demonic problem.

This is a poor analogy, but the Holy Spirit can own and have the title to your home, but others can also live in it. Spirits do not need very much room and there may be several spirits living in the house, along with the Holy Spirit.

As a child of God Jesus holds the title to your home, but you are the landlord. You have the choice who inhabits all, or parts of your house.

You can pick and you can choose what tenants you allow to live there with you.

If you are depressed and these warning signs are weighing you down deeper and deeper, then maybe you need to look at the problem from a different perspective. If somewhere you have given Satan an inch, he will do his best to take a foot. If you give him a foot, he will grab for a yard.

Jesus in John 10:10 said it so well:

The thief does not come except to steal, and to kill, and to destroy. I have come that they may have life, and that they may have it more abundantly.

In this passage it is clear that the thief, which is Satan, has his plan for your life and that plan is in stark contrast to the plan for your life that Jesus offers. Satan will steal your joy and anything else that you do not have securely fastened down.

But Satan will not stop there because he wants to completely destroy you if possible. Satan is willing to kill you figuratively, as well as your eternal life in Christ Jesus.

Jesus on the other hand said that He has come so that you may have life, and not just life; but life abundantly. Jesus came that you might have life, eternal life starting in this world. By giving all sickness and disease unto Him, you have the opportunity to live your life abundantly.

Two specific plans are offered for each of our lives, but we get to choose which one we want to live.

<u>Words to Live By</u>

<u>Thoughts may come and thoughts may go; but thoughts that are not put into actions or words, will die unborn.</u>

Biblical examples of depression:

Beginning in the book of Genesis it is likely that the first persons to experience depression were Adam and Eve after they sinned against God. Their feelings of guilt caused them to hide from God, and guilt is one of the major causes that pushes a person into a depressed state of mind.

When a person, especially a Christian, commits a sin against God, if forgiveness from God is not asked for, guilt feelings can quickly surface.

Fear, including fear of God, is another area that can cause depression. When the Bible says that we are to fear God, it means awe or reverence and not the afraid kind of fear.

The fearful kind of fear starts in a person's mind and if not dealt with Biblically, and immediately, **Satan will move in and he will enlarge the original fear thoughts until those fears become irrational.**

The Bible says that perfect love will cast out fear. If a Christian puts God first, the Holy Spirit will move fear out of the picture. If you are having a hard time overcoming fear in your mind, you can be quite sure this is the devil using your mind as a playground.

When you notice this happening, use the Name of Jesus and the power He has given to every Christian to command that demon of fear to get out of your life.

Let me give you a word of caution. When the demon leaves **as he has to**, then fill that void with God's Word.

The Bible makes it very clear that un-forgiveness with anyone, but especially un-forgiveness of a brother or sister in Christ, family members, or of yourself, opens to the door to satanic oppression.

In addition to those human members that you have not been willing to forgive, can be God Himself.

You may have been blaming God for allowing some unpleasant things or happenings in your life.

You may be blaming God for not giving you the mate or career that you thought you should have. Just as you have to forgive others, you must also forgive God.

Please note that I have not said possession, but oppression, as the Bible is quite clear that Satan cannot possess a Christian with the Holy Spirit in residence.

Satan may not be able to own, or totally possess, a house occupied by the Holy Spirit, but there are a lot of rooms in a large house that he can hide in and oppress the home owner.

The ten causes I listed are just the most common areas. If the demonic is allowed to get past the thought stage, Satan will use the confusion in your mind to sneak in and move a person along toward depression.

Satan will take advantage of the cause that allowed him to get his nose under your tent flap. Once inside he will steal your joy and do his best to lead a person into a depressed state. Both the root cause and Satan need to be dealt with quickly and decisively.

In Genesis 15, Abraham following his victory over the kings that had abducted Lot and his family, and after receiving the blessing from Melchizedek, apparently went into a depression.

In the first verse of chapter 15 God came to Abram in a vision telling him not to be afraid. One of the torments of depression is fear, and Abram was fearful of something.

Reading the entire passage, it would appear that Abram was depressed because he had no son to pass on all that God had blessed him with, or that which God had promised. So even this great hero of faith knew what it was to be depressed.

In the book of Jonah the fourth chapter we read that Jonah was depressed to the point where he asked God to take his life. This feeling of depression followed right after God had used his preaching to create a revival in Nineveh. In Jonah's words to God:

"-- it is right for me to be angry, even to death."

Jonah was not only depressed, he was angry at God. Very often when a person is depressed they blame God for the reason they are depressed.

Sometimes a Christian in the state of depression is actually angry with God but they are afraid to address the issue because they are afraid of what God will think.

When this is the case, the person that is angry at God will need to face the truth and ask God to forgive him or her for blaming Him for whatever it is that they blame God for doing to them. (You may have to read that through more than once, but I can not think of a clearer way to say it.)

In this case Jonah had finally agreed to do what God told him to do. But the last thing Jonah wanted, was to be successful and have the citizens of Nineveh repent. Jonah blamed the repentance of Nineveh on God and became depressed because of it.

The book of Job starting with the third chapter makes it clear that Job not only suffered from depression, doubt and guilt, but Job sums it up in the 25th and 26th verses:

For the thing I greatly feared has come upon me, and what I dreaded has happened to me. I am not at ease, nor am I quiet; I have no rest, for trouble comes.

Apparently Job had been entertaining some fears in his mind and Job's thoughts apparently came to pass. But notice how Job's depression affected him; he was not at ease, his mind was in turmoil, he could not sleep, and trouble just seemed to keep on coming. I have talked to people in depression and they indentify with the feelings that Job expressed.

They don't come a whole lot more spiritual in God's eyes than Elijah was, and yet Satan got his nose under the tent flap and caused depression. Elijah was exhausted both spiritually and physically to the point where he wanted to die and just get away from it all.

We are told the story in First Kings 19 were we read:

Elijah arose and ran for his life - and sat down under a broom tree. And he prayed that he might die, and said, "It is enough! Now, Lord, take my life, for I am no better than my fathers.

God had just worked a miracle through Elijah, and Elijah had caused the death of 400 of Jezebel's evil prophets. Jezebel was peeved and threatened to kill Elijah and he ran, and then Satan moved in.

I wonder how often after a Christian has a mountain top experience that Satan finds a hole in the spiritual armor, sneaks in, and causes depression.

The more I read about depression, the more I believe depression can be satanic in its origin, if the depressing thoughts start in the mind. I am certain that depression is often satanic in the depth or degree of a person's depression.

The more I learn, the more I can understand how depression can lead a person to commit suicide.

Can a Christian in depression commit suicide? <u>Yes they can</u>. Will a Christian that commits suicide still go to heaven? If I understand the Bible correctly, **yes they will go to heaven**.

Depression if not caused by the devil, will always be made worse by the devil.

Starting with the mind, the devil plants the seeds of destructive thoughts and then works to enlarge these thoughts until he has more than a foothold.

Here is where I may get in trouble.

If the church had not abandoned the teaching of Jesus regarding casting out demons, or taking authority over them, a **large number of**

Christians would never get to the point where they consider and/or commit suicide.

Christians by-and-large have allowed the devil free-rein in driving fellow brothers and sisters in Christ right into committing suicide. And if the depression does not lead to suicide, **depression will certainly steal the joy of a Christian.**

Depression will open up a Christian for additional attacks and oppression by the very enemy that Christ defeated at the Cross.

Maybe as brothers and sisters in Christ we share some of the blame, and if so, we need to ask God to forgive us for not doing as He has commanded us to do.

Many well meaning theologians, preachers and teachers have long taught that the demons were active when Christ was on this earth. But with the death of Jesus on the cross Satan was defeated and Christians no longer need to be concerned with the devil.

But if that is the case, how is the Christian supposed to understand Ephesians 6:11-12 where we read:

Put on the whole armor of God that you may be able to stand against the wiles of the devil. For we do not wrestle against flesh and blood, but against principalities, against powers, against the rulers of the darkness of this age, and against spiritual host of wickedness in heavenly places.

Paul doesn't seem to think that just because Jesus Christ defeated the devil that His brothers and sisters in Christ could forget about him.

When I read this passage, Paul seems to make it quite clear that as Christians we will be involved in spiritual warfare that will come against us daily.

If spiritual warfare in the life of a Christian is not the case, why would Paul tell us to pray against this always?

I stated earlier, if a Christian cannot fight off depression; if it seems your prayers hit an eight foot ceiling and stop; or if you find it impossible in your day-to-day living to live in accordance with the fruit of the Spirit indentified by Paul in Galatians, then it is very probable that there is demonic activity involved.

What the early church called demonic activity we are told is mental illness. Terms such as schizophrenia, paranoia, psychosis, are merely labels classifying various symptoms.

When all the fancy names of the symptoms are removed through counseling or dealt with using drugs, **the basic problem still remains.** The medical profession can only provide a bandage to hide or cover over the real problem.

Medical help and counseling can help get a person through the problem, but a depressed person can not solve the problem by dealing with its symptoms.

The cause behind the problem must be dealt with. If the depression problem is demonic in nature and not just our sinful human nature, then the solution will also be different.

There are some Christians who try to cover up or hide from the problem of depression by becoming super-spiritual, spout Biblical verses, and become involved in the church or church related activities; instead of going to Father God and dealing with the root cause.

When the church by-and-large quit teaching that the devil could harass and oppress the children of God, and how to Biblically handle the devil; the devil then had free reign in the life of the Christian.

And Satan has made the most of this freedom from exposure as a dispassionate look inside the church pews will quickly confirm.

Again just a word of caution; many times depression can be traced to the demonic realm, one must also be very much aware of 'sin-caused-depression' that is directly related to the individual's sinful human nature. Anger for example that is allowed to fester and turn inward, according to the Bible is a sin. **In addition to being considered a sin, anger often leads to depression.**

Get rid of the anger issue; ask God to forgive you for your anger, and if necessary ask forgiveness from the party that has caused you to harbor anger.

Anger is just one example of the man's sinful human nature. If in doubt as to whether depression involves man's arch enemy or man's sinful nature, **ask God to reveal this to you.**

First Samuel 16 makes interesting reading as it relates to depression. We read that the Spirit of the Lord departed from Saul, and was replaced by a **distressing spirit** from the Lord that troubled him. It is interesting to note that the Spirit of the Lord left Saul, or to put it in a different way, the anointing left Saul.

Whether the devil filled the void that was left with a distressing spirit, or whether God told Satan to send a distressing spirit to trouble Saul is a distinction I am not going to address.

Suffice it to say, that when a person rebels against God, and God removes His protective hand, bad things can happen quickly as King Saul found out.

When God's spirit left, Saul went into a depression. I find it interesting that music was used to lift the spirit of depression. In an early chapter I mentioned that Christian music was one thing that no other religion practices. It would appear that at least in this case music was what lifted Saul out of his depression.

Christian music will often lift a depressed person out of depression. However, some of what is considered Christian music today may in fact not qualify as music that will lift the spirit of depression.

Jeremiah was a prophet anointed and sent out by God. He became discouraged when his ministry went south and he was persecuted for doing what God told him to do, and to say.

Starting with the seventh verse of the twentieth chapter we read how discouraged Jeremiah became.

O Lord, You induced me, and I was persuaded; You are stronger than I and have prevailed. I am in derision daily; everyone mocks me. – Because the word of the Lord was made to me a reproach and a derision daily. Then I said, 'I will not make mention of Him, nor speak anymore in His name.

Jeremiah was called and anointed by God for a purpose. Jeremiah is unhappy with the results of his ministry and blames God for seducing him; until he was persuaded to do what he was commanded to do by a God that was stronger than he was.

Unhappy with being mocked daily he had decided to bug out; but fortunately for him, God had him on a short leash.

Further on we read how God picked him up and drove out the depression. In this case Jeremiah was doing God's will for his life when he became depressed, but God was faithful and picked him up out of his depression.

If you have become depressed doing God's will, go directly to God and tell Him you are ticked off and why. Let God be the one to guide you out of your depression and get you back on track.

If you have allowed Satan to get a foothold, take authority over that spirit and kick it out using the power and authority given you in the Name of Jesus. Then let the Holy Spirit refill you so that you can have life abundantly as promised by Jesus in John 10:10.

David is known as a man-after-God's-own-heart yet he often suffered depression during his life. We read in Psalm 38:5a, 6-8 the following:

Because of my foolishness, I am troubled, I am bowed down greatly: I go mourning all the day long. For my loins are full of inflammation, and there is no soundness in my flesh. I am feeble and severely broken; I groan because of the turmoil in my heart.

There doesn't seem to be any question that David is suffering with depression. When one reads the fifth verse it would appear that the depression came because David did something foolish. Reading the entire passage David was being chastised by the Lord for a sin that he had committed.

Sin can bring on depression until we ask God for forgiveness. Satan will do his best to convince us that the sin we have committed is so bad that God will not forgive us.

Tell that lying spirit in Jesus Name to get lost and then ask for and receive God's forgiveness.

Something else you may have noticed in the scripture is David's sin not only resulted in depressing his spirit, **but this sin caused some pretty hefty sickness.**

When the area around the base of the spinal column gets inflamed you will have a problem with movement, ache in every bone in your body, and you will be affected even to turmoil in your very being.

Christian Answers has identified 46 different Psalms where David is dealing with bouts of depression.

If David, a man after God's own heart could suffer depression to this extent, is it any wonder that Christians today can also have periods of depression?

But let me tell you what excites me when I read of David's struggles in the area of depression. Every time I read where David has a problem, I also read where God pulls him back from the black hole of depression. If he sinned, he asked forgiveness. If it was something else that caused the problem, he brought it to God and got it taken care of.

We can do likewise today as Christ not only died for our sins; he also suffered for our sicknesses. But Jesus did not stop there; Jesus also defeated the devil and then He passed on His authority over Satan and his demons to us.

We have God's word, along with Jesus' authority, plus faith provided by the Holy Spirit to overcome any depression. The way to defeat depression in our life has been provided.

However, it is up to each of us to believe the Word, use the faith God provides, and then act in the God-Given, Holy Spirit Power that Jesus gives to each Christian.

It is your choice to live with depression or to get rid of it. When you are depressed, place your hope in God.

James has said it perfectly, if any man lacks wisdom, let him ask of God. If you do not know how to proceed, ask God to direct you using His God-given wisdom. Let the Holy Spirit guide you to the Scriptures that can help you.

If you know that guilt or sin is the cause of your depression, ask God to forgive you of the sin. If it is guilt, take it to God and have Him release you from this guilt, **especially if you are feeling guilty for blaming Him for the something that has led to your depression.**

And remember it is often easier to accept the fact that someone else is being oppressed by the devil than it is for you to admit that maybe the same oppression is true for you.

Even Paul in second Corinthians eleven found himself facing a period of depression. Read the chapter and experience what Paul was going through and how he dealt with it.

Remember, it is Biblical to experience depression. Great men and women of faith have had the problem long before you came along. It is what you do with depression that will make the difference.

It is not wrong to use drugs to control depression, but drugs will only mask the symptom. Drugs will not deal with the problem that caused the depression, so use this period of relief to learn the real cause, and then allow God to guide and direct you into properly dealing with the root cause.

When God removes your depression, do not allow a vacuum to occur. Feed your spirit with the Word, or depression could return; and return leaving you in a worse condition.

Remember the passage where the demon left and the house was swept out. The devil returned and found a nice clean, but empty house, so he moved back in with some of his friends that were more depraved than he was.

In the appendix there are a number of scriptures that will speak into your heart and mind if you will let them. These Scriptures will build up your faith so God can bring you out of the miry clay that the feelings of depression wrap around you.

In my Biblical research on the topic of depression I have come to the conclusion that regardless of the initial root cause of depression, it is Satan who moves in and makes what was initially a minor problem into a very major problem.

There are many knowledgeable books available on how the Christian can deal with the devil and I urge the reader who is suffering under the cloud of depression to beg, borrow, or purchase these. Learn how you can deal with the Christian's greatest enemy.

Jesus Christ defeated the devil and then passed His authority over the devil to us. **You do not have to allow the devil to continue to cause you or your family problems with depression**.

I am going to leave you with this final thought. **There are many Christians who are building up their spiritual muscles, but they never put those muscles into use.**

James put it a bit differently when he says your faith, and that includes your spiritual knowledge, by itself without works is dead.

It does not matter how much scripture you can quote, or how many times you have read the Bible; if you do not put that Biblical knowledge into works by kicking out Satan, it is a dead or meaningless faith.

When James the Lord's brother references faith without works as being dead, he is not just referring to preaching, teaching, serving on the church board, handing out food, or taking care of the widows. These are all good works and we should do them.

James refers to putting your faith to work and one of the ways to put your faith to work is to rebuke the devil using your faith in the power of Jesus' Name.

James is also making reference to the faith that results in healing of the mind, body and soul.

If you are suffering from sickness that has resulted in depression, read the Biblical passages that relate to depression. Then read God's promises and His Biblical solutions for getting out of depression.

If you are not in depression, learn from the stories of some of the great Biblical heroes **as you may not be always be on the outside of depression**. Learn how to deal with depression before you find yourself or someone you love in a depressed state of mind.

Neal Anderson in his book the Bondage Breaker says there is no inner conflict for the Christian which is not psychological, because there is never a time when your mind, emotions, and will are not involved.

Likewise there is no mental or physical problem which is not spiritual because there is no time when God is not present in the life of the Christian.

In summing up this section on depression, the Christian needs to be reminded that God has made every provision for you to be alive and free through His son Jesus Christ.

If you are a Christian who lives in bondage to fear, depression, habits you can not break, thoughts you can not get rid of, or sinful behaviors that you can not escape, then Satan has gotten into your life and you need to be set free from his oppression.

A Christian's mind should not be filled with confusion to the point where their daily walk with Christ is unfulfilling and unproductive. A Christian according to the Word should be victorious, productive, and joy-filled.

A Christian trudging through life, hanging on until Jesus comes, or they go to Him, is not living the life God has promised.

Nor are they living the life God longs to provide for His children.

Scripture points to many issues where sin, guilt, human nature and even satanic involvement can lead to depression. If a person asks God for forgiveness and then continues to have feelings of guilt or depression over what God had been asked to forgive; **this refusal to receive your God-given forgiveness then becomes sin.**

I have mentioned the devil and demonic activity often during the subject on depression. The Bible is quite clear that Satan goes about as a roaring lion. A roaring lion can not hurt you, but if you let it the roaring lion will certainly fill you with fear.

God is a God who can and wants to heal you. If depression has moved into your life, why not let God remove it?

Before a Christian gets too caught up in the demonic, keep in mind that many times the believer does not need a spirit cast out; often it is a sin that **they just need to rise up against.**

TWELVE

Addiction:

The word definition of addiction according to Webster's is, **"to surrender oneself to something obsessively or habitually.** Characteristics of an addiction can be compulsive in nature and can be described as 'must have, want more, not a problem, and cannot stop'.

I f a person is addicted to anything, and that includes a religious truth, they will find it almost impossible to admit that they have a problem.

I probably shocked some of you readers when I said that a religious person can be addicted to a religious truth. But if you have ever known a religious leader, pastor or lay person that is totally hung up on one truth found in the Bible, you will know what I am saying is true. Everything else found in the Bible takes a distant second place, and there is nothing that will change their mind about what they believe and feel passionate about.

If the religious person has obsessively surrendered themselves to this one Biblical truth they are addicted, **as the Bible is very clear there needs to be balance, and that includes in the life of a Biblical Christian.**

Addiction is one of the toughest problems facing the Christian Church today. And that is to say nothing about how addictions are affecting the world in general. Here in the U.S. our culture has been shaped by the media and the advertising agencies that have promoted a 'feel good right now' mentality that tends to fuel the addictive process.

Ads for alcohol show only happy people drinking, never the person that is homeless or has lost their family because of an alcohol problem. Review the ads for food and see how this or that food will improve your health, tastes good, and is quick to prepare; never ads on how eating these supersized meals can make a person obese and suffer with health problems.

All the ads for casinos show happy people gambling, having fun, and making money. You too can have it all and feel good about yourself, if you will just let us take your money.

My daughter is an attorney specializing in bankruptcy and she can tell many stories of people that lost everything because they get caught up in gambling. Remember there is the other side not shown of those who have lost everything because they could not stop gambling.

A person is drawn into an addictive behavior or use of a substance because of the way it affects their emotions. Short term it feels good, or I can get something for nothing, etc.

Every person, including Christians, has a human nature which we have already determined is a sinful human nature. If a Christian lets the sinful human nature have any slack, that sin can soon become addictive.

By our very nature we tend to do that which is sin in God's eyes. Given our sinful nature it is not too difficult for a person to justify a sin because it feels good, numbs or blocks out feelings which do not make a person feel good.

And God is love, so wouldn't He want us to feel good?

So what exactly is an addiction and can a Christian, who the Bible says is a new creation in Christ Jesus, become addicted?

Sometimes the Bible refers to weakness of the flesh and that is not an addiction. If the problem is a weakness of the flesh, that will need to be dealt with differently.

Paul in Romans 13:13 & 14 puts it this way:

Let us walk properly, as in the day, not in revelry and drunkenness, not in lewdness and lust, not in strife and envy. But put on the Lord Jesus Christ, and make no provision for the flesh, to fulfill its lusts.

If the Christian lives in the flesh and runs after the desires of the flesh, then we need to deal with those issues long before they can become addictive in nature.

Paul says we are to put on the Lord Jesus Christ, or to put it another way, immerse ourselves in Jesus so deeply that there is no room to entertain thoughts and actions described by Paul in Romans 13.

What part does our sinful human nature play in the addiction of a person? Where does Satan fit into the life of an addicted person, especially if that person is a Christian? So many questions, but can we find the answers?

I will briefly address what an addiction is, but addiction is a separate study in itself so again I will not go into addictions in depth.

Our discussion will touch on addictions because every addiction sooner or later has a direct bearing on a person's health and that is what this book deals with.

Can a Christian become addicted is easily answered if you spend any amount of time in any religious fellowship or church.

The answer is an unequivocal YES!

There are many and varied types of addictions that have been identified, and then within each of these there are varying degrees or levels of addiction. This chapter will only be the tip of the iceberg so-to-speak.

My intention is for you to see what an addition is, the effect that an addiction can have on the health of a Christian, and how **Jesus Christ can help break the cycle of addiction in a person's life.**

For years when Christians talked about an addiction they have understood this to mean an uncontrollable habit of gambling, using alcohol or other types of substance abuse.

Over the past few years the church has added the sexual, especially porn to the mix as an addition that is running rampant and causing serious damage to the individual, the family, the church and the world in general. The real truth is that **anything a person does, or indulges in, or believes in that is done in excess is an addiction.**

Philip Yancey, the American Christian Author, put it this way, "what the Old Testament calls idolatry, enlightened Westerners now call addictions."

So when you are reading your Bible and come across the word idolatry consider the context, and quite often the Bible will be referring to what we now consider an addiction.

There has long been a joke within the church that the one sin that is never preached about from the pulpit is gluttony, which basically is overeating and which leads to overweight. The reason gluttony is seldom a sermon topic is that most pastors and preachers have a problem in this area of their lives.

The other reason is so many in their congregations are overweight and the pastor doesn't want to offend them. It might be better for the person sitting in the pew if they were offended to the point where they loose weight and improve their health; and maybe extend their life cycle.

For myself I will tell you that the problem is not confined to the ministry. I love to eat and while I may not be considered obese, I certainly could stand to lose some pounds.

Recently Fox News published an article entitled, "The Obesity in America's Churches" and the study's statistics suggest that the church population may indeed be in worse condition weight-wise than the general population.

A Purdue study found that of all the religious groups, the Baptists lead with a 30% obesity rate. This should not be a surprise because any religious group knows that the best way to get people to church, Bible study or religious meetings, is to offer free food.

And most often the food offered via the pot lucks or the other offerings, is good and it is filling, **but most of the time it is not healthy.**

A big thing in many churches today is to establish a restaurant or food serving area within the church.

If Christians today would take an honest look around, it would not be difficult to determine that many of the sicknesses and diseases found within the church population are due to overeating and poor diets.

Philippians 3:19 is clear that over eating is a sin which can end in our destruction. Overeating is a common sin that is separated only by degrees which can be measured in pounds.

whose end is destruction, whose god is their belly, and whose glory is in their shame - who set their mind on earthly things.

This verse is taken out of its surrounding context, but if you put these words into the overall context of the Bible, they fit. When a Christian allows the belly to become their god and allow food to rule their mind, the end could well be their destruction.

Even as night follows day, sickness and disease will follow unhealthy food and eating in excess of what the body needs.

Most of the time eating more than the body needs to sustain itself is simply a matter of the flesh. The Bible is clear on how to handle the desires of the flesh, but a person needs to take the fleshly desires under control, and here I am talking also to myself.

When fleshly desires relating to eating get out of hand, and eating becomes compulsive; the person has moved beyond fleshly desires to the point where compulsive eating becomes an addiction, and addiction is a sin.

There seem to be two symptoms that all addictions have in common. First an addictive behavior will be counter productive to the individual. Instead of helping a person adapt to a situation or overcome a problem, the addictive behavior will do just the opposite.

An example would be the person who is addicted to looking at pornographic material either in magazines or on the internet. It could have started because they were not sexually satisfied with their spouse.

It could be something that started out of curiosity and then grew from there until the individual finds that he or she cannot stop watching, thinking, or lusting about sexual exploitations.

For me it began in my preteens as an innocent action. I grew up on a truck farm and irrigation was a requirement. Our farm needed a new irrigation well. The family hired a man to come to the farm and by using a forked stick he would locate the best place to drill a well for the water we needed.

He walked around holding the forked ends of the stick and when the other end of the stick bent toward the ground, water was available at that spot.

A well was drilled into the ground at that point, and sure enough a good water producing pocket was found.

As a young preteen, this water dousing really fascinated me and I got my own forked stick. I ran all around trying the make the stick quiver downward. At the time I really thought this was fun but I never knew the consequences that were to follow.

As I grew older I developed a fascination with improper magazines showing the female anatomy in various degrees of undress. I could not walk in front of the magazine rack without having to look at these magazines. I could not stop this activity although I tried, I prayed about it, but to no avail. Then one day I was reading a small book written by Hobart Freeman entitled Angels of Light. Buried in a short paragraph I read where water-witching could open up a person's life to this sexual addiction.

I found a group that believed in what is called casting out of demons. They prayed for me and the power of that addiction was broken.

After that when the problem would surface I knew it was my sinful human nature and not a problem in the demonic world.

Oftentimes sexual pornographic or mental fascination with pornography can and often will lead to more serious behavior

Or a person might wish for more money, or easy money, and start gambling. Often this obsession for wanting more will lead instead to a drain on his or her financial resources.

Many times gambling will lead to destruction for themselves and those around them, especially family members. At some point in time a person who started gambling for fun can cross the line and not be able to stop gambling.

Gambling according to the Bible is sin, but even if you do not think gambling is a Biblical sin, when gambling becomes an addiction it is definitely a sin.

A person may start out having an occasional drink when they are feeling blue. Or they find themselves in a situation where drinking is part of the environment. Then they find more situations where a drink makes them feel good.

Eventually alcoholic drinking gets out of hand and what started out in a small way leads to excessive drinking because a person has to have it to survive.

And in many instances, this alcohol addiction can also lead to depression.

Or consider a person that has developed into a sex addict who only started out craving intimacy. But the sexual acts became the focus and eliminated any real closeness from ever developing.

A person becomes an addict when their behavior becomes persistent, in spite of it causing them trouble.

Just as overeating can become addictive, an obsession to being skinny can also become addictive. Both can cause harm to the body and lead to health problems.

Addiction such as drugs (both legal and illegal) is the continued use of mind or mood altering substances that cause adverse consequences, or a neurological impairment. A person can become addicted when the body needs more and more of whatever in order to function.

A gambler keeps thinking that the next time will be the big payoff. The sex addict thinks the next sex act will provide the intimacy they crave. The drug addict thinks the next use will provide the permanent fix.

Just one more and I will be feeling really good and I can handle the problem.

And in order to feel good for the immediate future a person ends up sacrificing the future.

Often we are told that genetics are responsible for a person's addiction. Genetics can often cause a person to lean in a certain direction, but what does the Bible have to say about genetics leading to an addiction?

Way back at the beginning of creation God created man good and without sin. Sin entered into the equation in the Garden of Eden and the nature of mankind became sinful.

Our sin nature is such that we often seem hell-bent on running towards sin. Sometimes as Christians even when we do not want to sin, something seems to be dragging us in that direction.

Paul says it this way in Romans 7:19:

For the good that I will to do, I do not do; but the evil I will not to do, that I practice.

Getting back to genetics; we start out life with a nature that is genetically sinful and then our family history can often influence the nature of an addiction.

In the Old Testament at the time God gave the Ten Commandments to Moses, God made it very clear that He would forgive sin. But if the sin was not repented of then He would pass on the sins of the fathers.

You can read Exodus 34: 6,7, Exodus 20:5 and Numbers 14:8 but they all say basically the same thing:

The Lord God is merciful and gracious, long suffering, and abounding in goodness and truth, keeping mercy for thousands, forgiving iniquity and transgression and sin, by no means clearing the guilty, visiting the iniquity of the fathers upon the children and the children's children to the third and fourth generation.

These words were given directly to Moses by God Himself for His special chosen ones. God starts out by reaffirming the kind of God He is to His kids.

God considers Himself to be merciful, gracious, long-suffering, with an abundance of goodness and truth. He has mercy for thousands, forgives iniquity, transgressions and sin, **but even though the Israelites are His children, He would not automatically clear them of sin.**

God said to Moses that the sins the fathers commit will carry down unto the third and fourth generation. The Christian is a child of God but the same principal holds true.

God will forgive you when you sin, but He will not do so automatically. If you do not repent and ask forgiveness of a specific sin, that sin will be passed on to the next generations.

A word study of iniquity and transgression indicates these are specific sins. From my personal experience these specific sins will be passed on to subsequent generations.

Sins like divorce, alcohol, drugs, anger, temper, sexual sins, and so forth are passed down from generation to generation.

I am going to add depression to the list of what is passed down from generation to generation, but I will hasten to add that I do not think depression 'per se' is a sin.

Staying in depression for the Christian can become a sin because God has made a way out. If we do not have enough trust in God to fight our way out of depression, then I think it becomes a sin.

However, looking at depression in my family lineage made it very clear that depression has been passed on to a number of my family members.This generational thing called depression needs to be broken or it will continue to be passed on.

Always remember that while all of these sins listed are, or may become, addictive in a person's life, God has said that He is merciful and He will forgive will you; **but you must repent, confess, and turn from the sin.**

As I reviewed my life looking back to my parents and grandparents, I realized how true these scriptures are. Anger and temper were passed on to me, and when I looked at my children I realized that these sins were continuing.

I am so thankful that some years ago I was made aware of the teachings of Neil Anderson and his books on spiritual warfare. I learned that these generational sins can be broken, both in my life and in the lives of my descendants.

As I looked around at others in my circle of family, friends and acquaintances, I noticed a pattern. Divorce seemed to follow from one generation to the next. Depression seemed to flow from one generation to the next. In my case, anger and temper flowed to me and then to my children.

Prove this to your self by looking backward and then forward and see if you notice a similarity in your family. Fortunately these generational sins can be broken and I invite you to read the books by Neil Anderson and find out how you too can break the chains, personally and generationally.

Neil Anderson in his book Victory over the Darkness states there is one common denominator for all struggling Christians, It is that they do not know who they are in Christ; nor do they really understand what it means to be a child of God.

In an early chapter we took a look at Scriptures and learned that in God's eyes we are saints. It doesn't matter how the world sees us. What is important is how Father God sees us, and we need to start living our lives consistent with the way in which Father God sees us.

Our study has taken a look at Biblical promises where Jesus Christ suffered at the cross so that His adopted brothers and sisters could be set free from sickness and disease.

This section is dealing with addictions, and when you examine any addiction, whether it is gluttony which is overeating, alcoholism which is the same as drunkenness in the Bible, drug addiction, sexual addictions, addiction to exercise, hooked on gambling, or compulsive spending, it becomes clear that any indulgence taken to excess, is an addiction. **Anything taken to excess can quickly become an addiction, and addiction is a sin.** The body has to have food, so we eat. Eating is not a sin. The Bible does not say it is wrong to have an alcoholic drink, but drunkenness is considered a sin.

The Bible has much to say about sex, but within the proper context of husband and wife relationships, sex is not a sin.

Buying and selling are not wrong in themselves, but compulsive spending violates the Biblical mandate of stewardship of that which God has entrusted to you.

Lying or cheating when you sell something is a sin. Habitual lying can invite a lying spirit into your being, and it then becomes next to impossible for the person to tell the truth.

When any of life's activities become counter productive and you cannot function without depending on them, or you find yourself in the position of not being able to stop, then you are addicted. No one starts out with the intention of becoming addicted to anything. So what happens and how does a person end up addicted to something? People often begin an addition by getting pleasure from something that develops into a habit. It has been estimated that if a person does something for thirty days it will become a habit, either a good habit or a bad habit. Once a bad thing becomes a habit, it is easy to increase the habit until the habit becomes an addiction.

For example, a person decides to have an alcoholic beverage with a meal on special occasions. The special occasions become a drink with every evening meal. In thirty days, this becomes a habit.

The same thing is true with eating. Eating more than the body needs to sustain itself can become a habit.

Neither eating nor drinking in moderation would be considered a sin, But the Bible addresses both of these issues when taken to excess, and excess taken to the next level becomes an addition.

Improper sexual activities in any shape or form are sin from the beginning and God has plenty to say about a person sinning sexually. When the activity is sin from the start, Satan will be right there to encourage that person. **Especially if you are a Christian he will argue that the sin is not so bad, and after all you deserve it.**

The devil will be only to happy to tell you that pornography or an extra-marital affair is okay, and God will forgive you because you are being short-changed in that department.

Once the devil gets a person to cross the line and justify the sin, he then works to get his claws deeper and deeper into a person, until the excess becomes an addition.

This book is about divine healing and I have spent some time describing addictions only because addictions of any kind most often have a negative influence on the health and well being of a person, including Christians.

Reading about addicts and addictions, talking with addicts, and observing addicts, it is obvious the devil or demonic oppression always seem to be involved.

The beginning of the path that leads to an addiction **always** begins in the mind. Sometimes it is our human nature that plants the seed in our mind and sometimes the seed is planted by the enemy.

If the mind of the Christian is 'stayed on the Lord' that thought will not remain, nor will the Christian spend any time on the thought.

Paul in Second Corinthians tells the Christian to bring every thought into captivity.

For the weapons of our warfare are not carnal but mighty in God for pulling down strongholds, casting down arguments and every high thing that exalts itself against the knowledge of God, bringing every thought into captivity to the obedience of Christ.

There is no question Biblically that Christians will find themselves in a fight with the enemy of God; which we have identified as Satan and his demonic realm.

Paul says the Christian cannot fight this enemy except in the spiritual realm. Paul goes on to tell us where this battle is to be fought when he tells the Christian to bring every thought into captivity.

The word 'thought' identifies the area of that battleground is the mind.

There are numerous scripture verses where we read that Jesus Christ has defeated the devil with His death on the cross. After Jesus had defeated the devil He turned this authority and power over to the Christians.

There has been, and continues to be numerous times when I have to take authority over my thoughts that the devil would like to have me dwell on.

Over the years there have been far too many instances where to my shame, I should have confronted the devil as he played in my mind. I allowed the enemy to move into a room in my Father's house, and when I was finally willing to confront my sin he then had to be ordered out. And that was much more difficult and time consuming than if I had dealt with the thought originally.

I have learned that I can use the Name of Jesus and command the enemy to get out of my mind. Or if I did not catch him soon enough, then in the Name of Jesus I can order him out of my body.

If I know the name, or the nature of the demonic spirit I am confronting, I call it out by name when I command it in Jesus' Name to take a hike.

It may sometimes take more than once before he knows that I really mean it; but in every case the power Jesus has conferred on me to use His name is sufficient.

In my experiences of dealing with the devil I can tell when the demon leaves, as it leaves in the midst of a gut-wrenching yawn. For others the experience of the demon leaving may well be different, **but when the devil is confronted with the Name of Jesus, he has to leave.**

However, with a sin that has become an addiction or depression, it is too late to bring the thought or thoughts into captivity. This spiritual warfare will most often require a different approach.

Once the devil has moved in to these addiction extremes, getting him out will often require the help of believing Christians.

The power of the Name of Jesus is more than enough to free the person from the clutches of the enemy. However it may require time and interference by those involved in the deliverance ministry.

There are times when getting free from demonic oppression will be like peeling an onion, one layer at a time until finally getting to the bottom of what caused the problem.

Okay what about medicine, counseling, AAA, and all the other help that is available to a person who is addicted or suffering from depression? In my opinion these are just band aids and while they may help or provide some relief, these do not solve the basic problem.

I heartily endorse the use of medicines, counseling, or group therapy, as these aids can provide time for the depressed or addicted person to deal with the root problem that is spiritual in nature.

But you will not be fully free of the problem until you resolve the spiritual issue that got you there in the first place.

Every single writer in the New Testament makes mention of the demonic, but in every case the believer is told to do something about the devil.

The Bible is very clear that it is the will of God to heal the sick person, and as Christians we **are** **not** to pray, "If it be your will, please heal me, or heal so-and-so."

And when the problem is demonic in nature, we are not to pray and ask God to get rid of the devil that is causing a problem.

Oh you say, that cannot be right; of course God will remove the devil. Really, let's take a look at what God's Word tells us regarding how we need to interact with the demonic forces.

Some years ago Kenneth Hagin wrote a short book entitled Demons and how to Deal with Them. He tells of a time he was praying and communicating with Jesus, when this little spirit ran between him and Jesus. This little spirit pulled out and began waving something like a black cloth, kicked his legs, waved his arms, and hollered. This distraction kept Hagin from hearing what Jesus was trying to say to him.

Hagin kept waiting for Jesus to do something about this spirit but nothing happened. Finally Hagin got mad and pointed to the spirit commanded him in the Name of Jesus to shut up.

The spirit stopped his antics, the cloth disappeared and the spirit fell to the floor shaking and whimpering. The spirit said he did not want to go, but if Hagin told him to, then he would have to leave. Hagin told that spirit in the Name of the Lord Jesus Christ to get out of there and he did so.

Kenneth Hagin then resumed his conversation with Jesus and he asked Jesus why He did not tell that spirit to stop. Hagin said that Jesus told him that if he, Hagin had not done something about the situation, He, Jesus could not have.

Notice **Jesus did not say He would not have**, but the words Jesus used were He **could not have done anything about the evil spirit**.

Jesus went on to tell Hagin that there was not one single place in the New Testament where a believer is told to pray against the devil.

Jesus also said that there was not one single place or time in the New Testament where it is stated that if a believer prays to God the Father, or to Jesus Christ, that They will do anything about the devil.

Jesus added that to pray against the devil is a waste of time for the Christian. Jesus also said that every single writer of the New Testament mentions the subject of the devil, or the demonic, but every writer tells the believers they are to take the action against the devil themselves.

In Matthew 28:18-20 we read that all power and authority was given to Jesus.

And Jesus came and spoke to them saying, "All authority has been given to Me in heaven and on earth. Go you therefore and make disciples of all the nations, baptizing them in the name of the Father and of the Son and of the Holy Spirit, teaching them to observe all the things that I have commanded you; --

Mark picks up on this commandment that Jesus gave in the 16th chapter were we read:

Go you into all the world and preach the gospel to every creature and these signs shall follow; In My name <u>they will cast out demons;</u>-- they will lay hands on the sick, and they will recover'.

God will use some people to a greater degree in special ministries. But from these two passages it seems to be quite clear that to use the Name of Jesus for throwing out demons or in healing the sick; **that power and authority belongs to each and every Christian**.

Jesus' power and authority can be used by the Christian for personal needs and the Christian is also instructed to use the power and authority inherent in the Name of Jesus Christ to help others.

Scripture makes it clear that when it comes to overcoming Satan it is the Christian who must do the actual work? In Mark we have already quoted the scripture were Jesus said specifically that His disciples were to use His name to cast out demons.

In James 4:7 we read that action against the devil is also the responsibility of the Christians:

Therefore submit to God. Resist the devil and he will flee from you.

It is you who is to do the resisting? Peter in I Peter 5:8 adds to what James said with the words:

Be sober, be vigilant; because your adversary the devil walks about like a roaring lion, seeking whom he may devour.

Again it is you who needs to be sober and watchful? There are a number of things to learn from these two passages.

First how could we as Christians resist the devil if we did not have authority over him?

The word James used was to flee. Webster's explains the word 'flee' is to '**run from as in terror**'. Far too often it is the Christian that flees the devil in terror.

The passage in first Peter makes it clear the devil is like a lion walking about with no teeth, no claws, with only a big mouth.

You want the devil to shut up and leave you alone; try using the authority and power you have when you use the Name of Jesus.

I would like to say, 'try it and you will like it', but that sounds a bit flippant, and where the Word is concerned the Christian should not be flippant.

Instead I will suggest that the next time Satan tries to make a suggestion or tempts you in any other way, try using the Name of Jesus and tell
him to get out of your mind and out of your life.

He will leave, but be watchful as he always tries to get back in.

In Colossians 1:13 and 2:15 we read that when Jesus Christ died on
the cross His death delivered us from the power of darkness. But Jesus
was not satisfied with just delivering us from Satan's power.

He spoiled Satan not only by taking his power, Jesus took everything else from Satan as well, and Jesus did this openly and publically so
everyone could see what He had done.

*He, Jesus has delivered us from the power of darkness and con-
veyed us into the kingdom of the Son of His love. – Having disarmed
principalities and powers, He made a public spectacle of them tri-
umphing over them in it.*

Finally in Ephesians 4:27 we read that the Christian is to give no
place to the devil. When the devil does what he does best and tries to
make you do something you know is wrong, command him to leave in
Jesus Name.

<u>Don't even take time to think about it, you just do it.</u>

Jesus did what needed to be done to defeat the devil. Then shortly
after completing His work, Jesus turned all of the power and authority
He had in this area over to those disciples who would follow Him.

In the legal profession this is known as giving us His 'Power-of-Attorney'.

**Until that power-of-attorney is taken back by Jesus, it is our
<u>responsibility</u> to use it.**

As far as I can tell Jesus has never taken His power-of-attorney back,
and when Jesus returns we probably won't need it any more.

As a Christian disciple of Jesus you may not be called or gifted with
the full time ministry of deliverance. But Jesus and the Word make it
very clear that as a disciple you are expected use His Name personally
and in ministering to others.

Philippians 2:12 makes it very understandable that the Christian is
to work out his or her salvation while they are here on this earth. That
work involves both the daily battle against the devil, and in building up
our faith for healing.

Neither is an automatic done deal. Jesus has done everything to make the Christian a winner, but **how you or I use what He has made available to each of us, is up to each of us.**

Addiction is a sin that will affect the health of a person in a number of different ways depending on the addiction. And I have not found any addiction that does not affect the health of a person, physically or mentally.

God is a God of forgiveness and He will forgive the sin. God is also the God of healing and He will heal you if you ask.

James tells the sinner to confess their sins one to another and in the case of an addict, the help of Christians to break the cycle of addiction will often be needed.

If an addict, or the depressed person, is not willing to be cured and healed physically and spiritually, it will be almost impossible for God to move, forgive and heal.

If you are a Christian involved in the life of an addict, what you can do is take authority over the evil spirit, or spirits, within the addict and bind them. Then ask the Holy Spirit to open the heart and mind of the addict to recognize the problem and seek help.

Father God is able to help. Father God wants to help. And Father God will provide the help if you will ask.

Christian or non-Christian, God wants to help you overcome your addiction or depression; but only if you want to get rid of it and only if you will allow Him to do so.

Once again it is your choice.

THIRTEEN

The hardest question many sincere Christians ask is the question of what is God's will for me in a given situation.

This book is based upon the concept of finding a Biblical balance as it relates to God's plan for our health and our healing, and I will address this "God's Will" issue from this direction.

Throughout this book you have read of incidents where God has healed me, or has used me in the healing of others. Once I knew what the Bible had to say on the issue of health and healing, it was no longer an issue of what was God's will for my life as it related to healing.

It then became 'how-and-when' He wanted to move in the health situations both personally and in the lives of others.

As I began to know God's Word better as it related to healing, it became clear that God's will is to heal, not only in the life of the Christian, but for all mankind.

The best way for a Christian to know God's will in any area is to become familiar with the Bible. If you get to know God's word and understand God's word, then you will know the will of God for your life.

God's will for your life will be different than God's will for my life. However in either case, **God's will for anyone will always line up with God's word.**

It is not what you think you know that counts. You cannot pray what you think, or what you want, and expect that to line up with what God wants.

If what you want lines up with what God wants, then you will not only be in the will of God, but you will also be at peace with it.

Colossians 3:15a,16a puts it this way:

And let the peace of God rule in your hearts, -- Let the word of Christ dwell in you richly in all wisdom --

Another way you can discern the will of God for you is through prayer. When you sincerely pray and read His word you will learn what pleases Him.

When you are in the center of the will of God you will have the peace of God in your heart.

The peace of God is like a regulator and when you violate His will, the peace will leave you and you will find yourself having inner turmoil.

God will never puts His child under pressure to do something for Him. At times you may feel urgency, but if God is in it, the Christian will not live with a 'pressure-cooker' feeling.

God will also reveal His will to you through other means as well. Proverbs 19:20 informs us that God will work through godly counselors:

Listen to counsel and receive instructions, that you may be wise –

God will also reveal His will directly from His Spirit into the spirit of His kids. Isaiah 1:1, Joel 2:28 and Acts 2:17 are three Biblical verses that support this:

The vision of Isaiah the son of Amoz, which he saw concerning Judah and Jerusalem. -- And it shall come to pass in the last days, says God, that I will pour out of My Spirit on all flesh: your sons and daughters shall prophesy, your young men shall see visions, your old men shall dream dreams.

The Christian needs to be careful in the understanding of these passages. The children of Israel had drifted far from the God that loved them and He sent Isaiah a vision of the judgment from God that was coming.

Peter quoted the words found in Joel to explain the purpose of this outpouring of the Holy Spirit in explaining the events that surrounded the ministry and crucifixion of Jesus.

The purpose of these events was to announce the arrival of the Holy Spirit for all flesh. Peter goes on the say that God will send dreams and visions to His own kids to help prophesy or preach the Kingdom.

Dreams and visions can also come into your spirit from the Holy Spirit so that you may know God's will or direction in a given situation.

But the dream or vision must line up with God's written word found in the Bible.

If your dream or vision does not line up with what you read in the Word of God, you can rest assured it did not come from God.

Some years ago I was scheduled to go on a church sponsored mission trip to LaCeiba, Honduras. At the time I had been told I had a heart problem and should not go on this trip.

I do not recall asking God what I should do because I responded to the doctor's admonition very quickly that I was going.

The disciples of Jesus are told to go into all-the-world and preach the good news. The good news included teaching, preaching, healing and casting out the demonic.

What I wanted to do lined up with God's instructions and I had absolute peace in my inner man with my decision.

If the circumstances of the situation line up with the Word of God, then you may rest assured that you are in God's will in your decision.

I went on this mission trip and during this trip I experienced two distinct visions from the Holy Spirit. In the first vision I saw myself being prayed for by the same Honduran church people that I would be teaching regarding Father God's healing scriptures.

I saw myself kneeling before the pulpit area and these Honduran saints were praying for the healing of my heart. This vision came to pass, but as I did not understand the language I have no idea what words were prayed.

The next day as I was praying and thanking God for what I felt had to be a physical healing, the Holy Spirit provided the second related vision. I literally saw myself being wheeled into surgery on a gurney where the doctors would provide open heart, or heart-by-pass surgery.

Would it have been wrong if I had canceled the mission trip in order to have by-pass surgery?

No I don't think so, but it wasn't until I was in Honduras that God revealed His purpose for the direction He wanted me to take.

If I had not gone on the mission trip, I would have missed the blessing when those saints in LaCeiba, Honduras prayed for me. I would not have had the opportunity to preach the healing Word to them and to pray with them.

In short, I would have missed the best that God had in mind for me. God's subsequent direction was to have the surgery, but having the God-given vision of the surgery was a spiritual experience I would have missed.

There have been numerous times in my life where I will awaken and immediately recall the dream in which God provided an answer to a question that had been running through my mind.

Peter quoted Joel when he said the purpose of God pouring out His Spirit to His menservants and His maidservants was to provide what would be required for them to teach and preach.

How did God expect His menservants and maidservants to preach? How did Jesus teach and preach when He was here?

The Great Commission found in Mark 16 sums up how Christians should teach and preach.

Go into all the world and preach the gospel to every creature. - And these signs will follow those who believe; in My name they will cast out demons; - they will lay hands on the sick, and they will recover. And they went out and preached everywhere, the Lord working with them and confirming the word through the accompanying signs.

If you are a child of God, this condensed passage should make it clear what is the over-all will of God. We are to preach, and if you remember my Honduran experience, I was in God's will to preach, and even though medically maybe I should not have gone at this time, I had peace with my decision.

The way in which Jesus taught was the same way a kindergarten teacher teaches; **show and tell.** Jesus' show part of teaching included healing the sick and by casting out the demonic he freed the captive.

Then Jesus would teach with words. Sometimes Jesus would reverse the order, but I can recall very few times where Jesus taught or preached without using this method.

Sometimes the word-teaching came a bit later when He was alone with His disciples, but He always explained His 'show' parts of His teachings. The 'show' part of Jesus' teaching always turned the attention to His Father.

Do you think if the disciples of Jesus today were to teach in the same manner in which Jesus preached and taught the church would be more or less effective?

Dreams and visions from God will oftentimes direct us in the way in which God wishes to move in our lives. This is true for both our personal needs and the direction God wants His disciples to move or intercede in the lives of others.

I will say it again; if a dream or vision is from God, it will never be contrary to what is written in God's Holy Word, the Bible.

George Mueller who lived over one-hundred years ago and founded orphanages by faith put it this way, "I seek the will of God through and in connection with God's Word. The direction of the Holy Spirit and God's Word as found in the Bible must be in agreement.

If the Holy Spirit is guiding me, He will do it according to the Scriptures, never contrary to them."

Mueller went on to say, "Next, I take into account the circumstances I find myself in. Often the circumstances will plainly indicate the will of God and the direction of the Holy Spirit; both of which will be in agreement with God's word.

Paul in the first two verses of Romans 12 puts it this way:

I beseech you therefore brethren, by the mercies of God that you present your bodies a living sacrifice, holy, acceptable to God, which is your reasonable service. And do not be conformed to this world, but be transformed by the renewing of your mind, that you may prove what is that good and acceptable and 'perfect' will of God.

Notice that Paul is writing to fellow Christians when he tells us it is a reasonable service to God for us to present our bodies to Him.

Paul goes on to say that the Christian should not be like those found in the rest of the world; the Christian is to be different by the renewing of the mind.

What does Paul intend when he says, 'renew our mind'? To renew something is to restore the object to what it once was. Our mind at the time of creation was pure in nature, and Paul is telling the Christians that we need to work to clean up our minds.

The Christian is a new creature in Christ Jesus, but the truth is our fleshly body is still being controlled by our mind. Our body does what our mind tells it to do. To renew the mind, a Christian through Jesus Christ works to change the mindset.

Sin always begins in the mind with thoughts, images, and other things that are not from God.

If you are willing to change how you think, and are willing to work at getting rid of wrong thoughts when they occur; then Jesus Christ and the Holy Spirit will be only too willing to work with you.

We said in the last couple of chapters that the devil can only get to us and control us through our mind. Because of this Paul is writing to the Christian begging them to allow Jesus through the Holy Spirit to renew his or her mind.

These two verses in Romans 12 tell us three things regarding how we may know God's will in our lives.

1. **Body:** God has shown His mercy to us through the sacrifice of Jesus Christ. In return we are to present our body a living sacrifice in response to His great mercy.

2. **Mind:** The Christian must renew his or her mind and in so doing we will find ourselves different from those who have not accepted God's great mercy.

3. **God's Perfect Will:** If the Christian does these things; **then by what we do, we will be walking out God's good and perfect will in our lives.**

Paul writing in Philippians the second chapter puts it this way:

Work out your own salvation with fear and trembling; for it is God who works in you both to will and to do for His good pleasure.

From the time you invite Jesus Christ into your life and have accepted the salvation offered by God, the Christian begins to work and to live out what that salvation means in their life.

Each Christian will need to work out their individual personal relationship, but it is God who will do the work in you. And the work He does in you will be for His own pleasure, or delight and joy.

In walking out God's perfect will in our lives there are two decisions that God never wants us to make.

God never wants the Christian to make a decision to sin, or to resist His will.

God wants you and I to make choices that agree with His will. If we know His word as found in His Holy Book, and if we are walking closely with Him, God will place His desires in our heart.

One key to knowing God's will for your life is to want God's will and not your own.

Psalm 37:4,5 puts it this way:

Delight yourself also in the Lord, and He shall give you the desires of your heart. Commit your way to the Lord, trust also in Him, and He shall bring it to pass.

If as a child of God you want to do His will and find your greatest pleasure, it will be when you are doing what is right according to the direction you find in His Holy Word.

Then God will give you the desires of your heart. **One word of caution;** the desires of your heart must line up with Father God's.

Desires of the heart should not include worldly things, through God may choose to give those to you as well. When the desire of your heart is for healing, or the healing of another, this always lines up with God's will.

Healing is a desire of the heart that always lines up perfectly with God's will.

If the Bible does not speak specifically against something and that something will benefit you spiritually, then it is Biblical to make decisions and to follow your heart.

I will repeat myself. '**Never seek the leading of the Lord concerning an act that is specifically forbidden in God's Word**'.

If you will line up your asking with the written Word of God, you will not have to ask God's permission on anything where He has already provided a positive 'YES' in His Word.

The opposite is also true; do not ask for a leading when God in His Word has made it clear the direction you are inquiring about is a NO.

This could get me in trouble, but as we search to know God's will for our lives, **we often forget that in the majority of decisions touching our lives, God doesn't really care which choice we make.**

Some Christians worry about which profession they should enter, what car they should drive, what school they should attend, where they should live, and other such matters. God doesn't really care which color shirt you wear or what color car you prefer.

God does care if you select a car or home without considering His guidelines regarding stewardship or pride. God has already given direction to the Christian in both of these areas.

God has also given guidelines in His Book on the requirements for the selection of a mate.

I am going to get a bit personal here. I was not a Christian when I started courting my wife. If it would not have been for lust which I thought was love, I do not think we would have gotten married.

But Father God loved me even then, and He knew that Linda was exactly the kind of wife and partner that I was going to need throughout my life.

Linda and I have been married for over fifty-five years and the times were not always smooth. Sometimes the waters became boisterous, but often I have looked back and thanked God for putting us together.

God loved me so much that even before I knew Him personally, He knew what I would need in a life partner.

God also allows great latitude in career or job selections.

I remember our middle son came to me one day and said that he wanted to do something, career wise, but he didn't think I would like his choice.

At the time he had just gotten out of the Army and what he wanted to do was to become a Paramedic. My response was not what he expected from me. I told my son that if he wanted to be a Paramedic then just go and be the best Paramedic he could be.

I am going to brag a bit here when I tell you that this young man had come to my wife and me in his last year of high school. He told us he wanted to quit school and join the military.

We finally agreed and he left school, but while in service he earned a GED diploma. After serving for several years in military service he left and became a Paramedic for a time.

Then the day came when he came to me and told me he wanted to go to school and become a male nurse. My response was the same as when he wanted to become a Paramedic.

Since the day when he wanted my input on becoming a Paramedic, he has never stopped studying and today he is a Physicians' Assistant, a Nurse Practitioner with a goal of earning a PhD.

How does this personal story fit into knowing God's will for your life? Simple, our son knew the Lord and the desire of his heart was to help other people. This was in line with the words and direction found in the Bible.

God honored the desire of his heart and God also allowed him to choose his own direction.

Please do not misunderstand, the road was not always easy or straight, but he has persevered.

Just because you know the direction of the Lord's leading does not mean it will be straight, well paved, and with no potholes. More often than not you will find the opposite to be true.

The same guiding principal has been evident in the lives of our other children as they made career decisions. As long their choice was not in opposition to what is found in God's Word; and it was something they felt comfortable with, God did not have a problem with it.

However, when the direction was in opposition to what God requires of His kids, the outcome was not the same.

The Bible is very clear we are not to do those things that have been specifically commanded or forbidden to us.

God has also made it very clear that mankind has a free will. And it follows given the fact that we have a free will, we are also free to choose.

There are many stories in the Bible that include the shepherd, or shepherds. Jesus several times referred to Himself as the great Shepherd.

Most of us have never had the occupation of shepherd in our resume, but it is my understanding the shepherd leads the sheep to grass, but the sheep decides which tuft of grass he chooses to eat.

Just like those sheep, we make those decisions as to what grass to eat, not the Lord. However it was the shepherd who led the sheep to the grass.

In the tenth chapter of John, Jesus says that He is the good shepherd and His sheep will hear His voice, and His sheep would hear Him and they would follow Him.

Isn't that really the role and function of a shepherd?

In addition to the No's and Yes's, there are the areas where if you know His word and hear His voice, the choices you make will please Him. **And God is pleased when we make those choices.**

But what about those times when there is a significant choice to make and you cannot find a clear spiritual instruction or direction. You are now forced to choose between two or more possible directions.

In those cases we have God's promise to guide us correctly. Ask Him, seek His answer, and then listen for His direction.

This book is about God and our health, so let's take a look at it from that perspective.

A number of years ago cancer was discovered in my body and I was confronted with having to make decisions that effectively were life and death; **my life and my death.**

What was the Will of God in this situation for me? I knew His Will for His kids was health and life, but how was that to be worked out.

Philippians 2:12b and 13 became very real at that point in my life. Paul said it this way:

Work out your own salvation with fear and trembling: for it is God who works in you both to will and to do for His good pleasure.

I am sure there are other applications for these verses, but for me at that time, and facing difficult decisions, I wanted to be found in God's perfect will.

When you as a child of God find yourself in a difficult health situation, whether it is physical or mental in nature, finding God's will at that point of your life becomes quite urgent.

Once I came to grips with the diagnosis, I started to pray and ask Father God for direction. He reminded me of the scripture verses found in the book of James:

If any of you lack wisdom, let him ask of God, who gives to all men liberally, and upbraideth not; and it shall be to him. But let him ask in faith, nothing wavering.

There were other verses that the Holy Spirit brought to mind, but these two passages became the rock upon which I based my subsequent decisions.

Would it have been wrong for me to follow the doctors' advice and have had the surgery and radiation treatments that were recommended? **No it would not have been wrong, but remember I had gone to God and asked Him for His wisdom and leading in this situation.**

Father God had made it clear to me that I was not to have surgery, and subsequently God closed a number of doors as I worked out His perfect will for me.

Because of the medical prognosis I felt I needed to be in Father God's perfect will regardless of the pressure put on by the medical profession, family, friends and even spiritual leaders.

God's path was not straight and it was not always clear what the next step was to be. And given the context of the time frame for the disease, for me God's path was not short nor was it quick.

The Holy Spirit always provided an answer that was confirmed by God's Word. I give thanks to the Holy Spirit for the faith He provided which carried me through those three years of twisting and turning.

Every time I had a doubt or I started to waver, the Holy Spirit brought a verse to my mind or a spiritual word from someone that kept me on the path.

In my case the God provided healing for the prostate cancer was not a one-time deal. The cancerous tumor has persistently returned to life. The first three times God took care of the problem using the same manner each time.

The fourth time the cancer returned and God's direction was the same, but He confirmed the direction only after a time of prayer and seeking. This fifth time God's perfect will for me has taken a different direction and I will just have to follow where He leads.

But this I know; my desire is to be in His perfect will and if His perfect will for my life is for me to come home, then that is where I will end up, sooner rather than later.

I believe He will once again heal me, and while this may sound a bit strange, I believe that God has told me I will not be coming home with sickness in my body.

In hindsight I can only say that I am glad that I have sought, and by faith, followed His perfect path. With both the cancer and the heart problem I am glad that He allowed me the choice of which path to take.

With the heart problem the path taken was the one that allowed me my hearts desire, whereas with the cancer the path taken has sorely tested my faith. But as I look back I would not have wanted it any other way.

Because I am human and as such I have a sinful nature, I don't always find myself wanting God's perfect will in my life. I find myself doing what I want to do, even when I know it is in direct opposition to the Biblical direction.

I would like to always be found in God's perfect will for me, but I miss it more often than I find myself in His perfect will. What to do?

Satan is always right there to condemn me when I miss it. And if I let him get into my thought process; he will do everything possible to convince me that I not only blew it again, but this time I really blew it.

Satan does his best each time as he tries to convince me that God will not let me back into a right relationship with Him.

The Bible says that Satan is the father of lies, meaning there is nobody that lies as often, or as good as he lies.

God on the other hand is the Father of love, grace and mercy, and He will never lie.

The choice is yours; will you choose to believe the devil and have inner turmoil, or are you going to let God forgive you when you miss it.

Are you going to get back in a right relationship with God where you once again have a Shalom peace in your heart?

In summary: As a child of God, you can know the perfect will of God for your life, and in every situation. There are many Scriptures that support this fact, and I have put some of these together in a collage:

If anyone desires to do the will of God, he will know whether it is from God or not. God's desire for you is that you might be filled with the knowledge of His will in all wisdom and spiritual understanding.

God's perfect will for you will be for you to do that which is good and pleasing in His eyes. And he who does the will of God abides forever. We are to pray without ceasing and in everything give thanks, for this is the will of God in Christ Jesus concerning you.

Take your problem to the Lord. Remind Him of these Biblical promises found in His Word. If you are dedicated to God's purpose, He will not allow you to make a mistake.

FOURTEEN

The Law of Miracles:

To determine if there is a 'Law of Miracles', we need to determine the definition of a law. To get a proper definition I turned to my Webster's dictionary and looked up the word.

The one definition that fit the context of whether there is a Law of Miracles was defined this way: 'an action recognized as binding or enforced by a controlling authority'.

Miracles are certainly a recognized action as anyone who has ever experienced a miracle in their life, or the life of loved one, would attest to. Miracles are brought to fruition or are controlled by a higher authority; and according to the Bible there is no higher authority than Father God.

In chapter seven we listed ten ways in which God heals. All of these are miracles even though some are more obvious miracles than others. The fact that God built natural healing into His human creation is a miracle law put into place at the time of creation.

God sent His son Jesus to Calvary to cover our sins, but also by bearing the stripes on His back He covered in the atonement our sicknesses and diseases.

Our health that Satan stole by virtue of fall of Adam was restored.

God did not need to set another Law in place as God's original law was for mankind to live in perfect health; body, mind and soul.

That original law of health was set aside when Adam sinned. Father God sent Jesus to Calvary to restore His original law of health for all mankind.

Sin had ruined the original natural law of health, and unless sin could be done away with, the law had to be circumvented.

God though Jesus Christ did this by instituting the Law of Miracles which restored God's original law of perfect health.

The common translation for the word miracle found in the Bible is translated as a sign. When you read many of the miracles that Jesus or His disciples preformed in the Bible, these supernatural signs were always used in one way or another to point to God.

Thus a miracle is a sign that points to God, and because the sign is an action given and supported by God's controlling power; that makes them a non-changeable law.

Jesus provided atonement for sins and atonement for sickness and health at Calvary. The restoration of that which had been stolen in the Garden has now become the Law of the Miraculous.

The Father has permanently fixed these laws and no one can move them; not man and not Satan.

The Glory of God is revealed to those who will believe in Him. Faith unlocks the door of our understanding of Scripture, and faith releases the Spirit's activity in our lives.

If you need a miracle from God, you can approach God boldly through Jesus Christ. The miracle you receive is a sign pointing you directly to Him.

The law of miracles is provided for the Christian and the non-Christian alike. Miracles are signs that point to God. For the non-Christian it is a sign that should lead the sinner to repentance. For the Christian it is a sign from God that should lead the Christian in becoming more like Christ.

In the eleventh chapter of John, Jesus had just restored Lazarus to life and He said to Martha:

Did I not say to you that if you would believe you would see the glory of God?"

In the forty-fifth verse we read that many of the Jews that saw this miracle and had seen the things that Jesus did; believed in Him.

The Law of Miracles guarantees the performance of impossible things. Miracles take place in Jesus' name with power flowing from the invisible world where God is. The power for a miracle then flows through the spirit of man where the center of our being resides.

This God-given power for a miracle-healing has to flow through the mind of man and then out to the individual in order for the miracle to take place. Whenever a miracle takes place it should bring glory to God.

So how do we pray for a miracle that includes healing for the body or mind? We have stated that miracles come from God through Jesus Christ. Every miracle is guaranteed by the authority of God Himself. So the best place to start when in need of a healing is by humbly going to God in prayer.

Your sickness or disease may have been caused by one of any number of causes, so the first thing is to determine the why or what. Once you know the why or what, then it is necessary to determine God's will in the matter.

Is your sickness just a cycle-of-life sickness? Or are you or have you done something stupid that resulted in your sickness?

Is it a sin that He wants confessed? Maybe your sickness is a test of your faith. Does God want to use this sickness as a sign for others? Or is the healing of your sickness just so that you may give Him the Glory?

Often times the Christian already knows the reason, but if not, then ask God and He will provide you with the answer or confirmation. **Sometimes the Christian may know the 'why' but prefers not to admit it, as then one has to apply the Biblical response**. Once you know God's will and direction in the situation, then base your action and prayers accordingly.

Healings are brought into existence through the power of the Holy Spirit. Praying for a healing is simply welcoming a gift of the Holy Spirit to manifest itself in your life.

When it is God's will to work a healing in your life it is the Holy Spirit who will witness this to your heart.

Then pray for the faith and the Holy Sprit's power to perform the healing God wants to bring about.

When the gifts of healing are in operation through you for others, the Holy Spirit will also witness this to your heart. You then pray for the faith and the power to perform the healing God wants to bring about through you.

Sometimes it is necessary to use the spoken word to remove demonic opposition before a healing, physical or mental, can be manifested.

In Matthew 10:1 Jesus sends His disciples out with instructions in what they are to do.

He gave them power over unclean spirits, to cast them out, and to heal all kinds of sickness and all kinds of disease.

In the last two chapters we discussed the role of the demonic in depression and addiction. In Matthew 10 His disciples were told to cast out unclean spirits. So how do you cast out a spirit?

The Bible never says we are to pray to God to get rid of the demonic. Jesus never prayed for the demons to leave, He just told them to get lost, or get out, and they did.

In Matthew ten Jesus said to cast them out. You use the Name of Jesus in conjunction with His power and spoken through your mouth.

God through Jesus Christ has given us His authority over the demonic realm. With the atonement of Jesus at Calvary, He has provided the victory over sickness, disease, mental problems as well as over storms and finances.

As disciples of Jesus we are to verbally use the power given to us in the use of His Name.

The Holy Spirit will then supply the guns and ammunition to send the enemy running. **And the enemy will not just run, but he will flee in panic.**

With the Holy Spirit supplying the anointing faith that God provides; believe with your heart, say it with your mouth, **and it will be done and you will have whatever you say.**

If the problem is demonic in origin then the only way to deal with it is **for you to speak forth the command with your mouth.**

Keep in mind that miracles and healings only come by faith in God's present power. These do not come through a ritual, or a formula of human words, or by using your will power.

God has placed the Law of Miracles in place at Calvary, and that is a done deal.

Do not put God in a box, as the miracle you hope for
may not always be the miracle you receive.

How to Hinder Your Healing:

The first way I have listed in which we can hinder our healing was not picked randomly. This hindrance is probably the one that most Bible believing Christians would prefer left alone and swept under the rug.

The hindrance that affects so many Christians in America is that of overeating, resulting in overweight and obesity. This weight problem affects much and maybe most of Christendom from the top echelons, to the back pew in the church.

In our quest for Biblical balance in the healing ministry we have determined that God can heal and God wants to heal. God sent Jesus to make atonement for our healing, and through the working of the Holy

Spirit provided all the guns and ammunition to overcome any obstacles to healing.

Having stated what God has done to fulfill His end of the healing provision, let's take a look at how you and I can hinder the work of the Holy Spirit in our healing.

From the beginning I stated this book on healing was being written primarily to believers and followers of Jesus Christ.

God's Health Care Plan is directed towards brothers and sisters in Christ Jesus, but what is written is just as applicable to everyone else.

The God of love and mercy wants to heal everyone, not just believers in Christ Jesus. However, the same things that can hinder the healing of a Christian will also hinder the healing of a non-Christian.

"Good morning, I am Pastor Doug and I am obese" were the opening words of the morning sermon. Pastor Doug Anderson of Tyler, Texas had recently been shocked by his primary care physician during his annual visit. The word 'obese' that had been attached to his name by his physician made the pastor realize it was time for a personal lifestyle makeover.

Pastor Doug's pulpit announcement was reported by Fox News in an article entitled, 'The obesity epidemic in America's churches'. The article went on to say that a crisis is looming in the pews of the churches across America.

A 2006 Purdue study found that fundamental Christians are by far the heaviest of all religious groups, and of this group the Baptists lead with a 30% obesity rate.

The article reminded me of a story where a kindergarten teacher gave her class a 'show & tell' assignment. Each student was instructed to bring an object to share with the class which represented their religion.

The first student got up in front of the class and said, "My name is Benjamin and I am Jewish and this is a Star of David."

The second student got up in front of the class and said, "My name is Mary. I am a Catholic and this is a Rosary."

The third student got up in front of the class and said, "My name is Tommy. I am a Baptist, and this is a casserole."

While this story is humorous in its content, the implication of what is important in a church setting is no longer humorous. If the church wants to have an event well attended, just include food.

The article went on to say that at the church level, pastors and clergy are burdened by the skyrocketing number of their members with chronic diseases such as cancer and heart disease.

A disproportionate amount of clergy's time is spent caring for their ill members and less time is being spent in study, discipleship, and evangelism.

The writer of the article went on to say that it is rare to hear a sermon preached on the stewardship of the physical body, and even rarer to hear a sermon preached on the sin of gluttony.

Tables at potlucks strain under the weight of casseroles, pound cakes, pizza, fried chicken and cheesecake. The scared Sunday ritual between services is donuts, bagels with cream cheese, and coffee with cream and sugar.

Restaurants are now being installed inside the walls of the church itself to appeal to its members and to entice new members.

What a way to start out the chapter on how a Christian can hinder the Holy Spirit in providing a God-given healing.

I can already hear some of you say, "How can this be? God can do anything and He has stated that He wants to heal me. Jesus Christ atoned for my sickness or disease at Calvary so that I could be healed."

And yes, you are correct in what you say.

But consider that God wants you to enjoy the top level of His ULTI-MATE health care provision. One of the ways that God heals is through what He installed in your body at the time of creation. The body is designed to heal itself, **but only if you allow it.**

You can hinder, or even stop, the body from healing itself by what and by how much you eat.

Do I think God can and will heal you if you are overweight? Yes, God can heal you because God can do anything. And to prove He meant it, He sent Jesus Christ to bear the stripes at Calvary for your sicknesses and diseases. But the question is not whether God can or wants to heal you.

There are two things the Christian needs to be aware of. **Gluttony which is overeating most often leads to obesity which is a sin.** This is a sin that can easily lead to an addiction, or compulsion to eat. Addictions are very hard to overcome for Christians and non-Christians.

As Christians we should be aware of this. When a Christian knowingly and willing is living in sin, they will find it much harder to accept the miracle gift of healing, even when it is offered.

One of the ways which God heals was built into the human body at the time of creation. The body will have a very hard time to heal itself when the body is overweight, simply because overweight blocks the natural law of healing.

When a Christian is convicted of a sin, God requires him or her to repent of the sin. God will instantly forgive and restore. This includes the sin of gluttony.

Repentance means to turn away from this sin after God has forgiven you.

The oft repeated funny saying that, 'it is easier to ask for forgiveness than it is to ask for permission' doesn't work with God. God has made it quite clear in His written word how the Christian is to view eating more food than is necessary.

This son of ours is stubborn and rebellious; he will not obey our voice; he is a glutton and a drunkard.

This verse is found in Deuteronomy 21:20 and the passage continues on to convey how serious God considered this to be, as the elders were to take this son out and stone him to death. The sin was that of stubbornness and rebellion, but this sin led to gluttony, which in God's eyes became an additional sin.

Proverbs 23:1-3 puts it another way:

consider carefully what is before you; and put a knife to your throat if you are a person given to appetite. Do not desire delicacies for they are deceptive food.

Solomon wrote the book of Proverbs and he was considered to be the wisest person that has ever lived. In this passage Solomon is suggesting that if we cannot control the appetite, we need to slice the throat.

Solomon writing under the guidance of the Holy Spirit makes it very clear how God views overeating. Solomon goes on to mention delicacies, which in today's terminology means junk food, as being a deceptive food.

Webster explains the word deceptive as having the power to mislead. **The junk food that we like and which tastes so good; may in fact be deceptive and not good for us.**

There are many Bible verses relating or equating gluttony with drunkenness, but both of these sins are sins of excess and will hinder the healing that God has for you.

Sins of excess stop the normal healing processes that God has created into the human body. Sins of excess also hinder the faith of a Christian to believe God for a miracle healing.

And these sins of excess invite sickness and disease to feel right at home in your body.

Please hear this correctly; if you have faith for God to heal you and are willing to accept a Godly miracle, God will heal you just so you may know He is able. **God is the God of grace and mercy.**

If He has provided a miracle in your life and He has gotten your attention, what will you do next? Are you willing to repent of your excessive eating or addiction and turn away, or are you going to thank God for your healing and keep on eating?

After all, God healed me this time and surely He will do so again. **Maybe, and then again, maybe He won't.**

Living in America the Christian today is being pulled in two directions. On the one hand food is available at home, in restaurants and in our churches. It is packaged to look good and includes ingredients that make it taste good.

On the other hand there are all these advertisements regarding proper eating and getting enough exercise. Focusing obsessively on exercise and being extremely thin can be taken to excess as well. Either of these taken to the extreme, is wrong.

The Bible teaches that balance is required in all things. Proper stewardship of the physical body requires both food and exercise, but with a balance.

In addition to the physical body, sometimes a Christian can be out of balance by putting too much emphasis on the physical person while neglecting the spiritual man.

The other extreme is to be so spiritually-minded that we neglect our bodies by under eating or in the lack of exercise. Philippians 4:5 states it so well:

Let your moderation be known unto all men. The Lord is at hand.

Thought for the day. '
Jesus has never been made the
"Lord of the fork."'

UNFORGIVENESS:

The Bible has much to say regarding forgiveness, the most familiar is found in the verses taken from what is known as the Lord's Prayer.

We can find clarification in Matthew 6:14,15 where Jesus deals directly with forgiveness:

"For if you forgive men their trespasses, your heavenly Father will also forgive you. But if you do not forgive men their trespasses, neither will your father forgive your trespasses."

Forgiveness and Unforgiveness is a study all by itself. For our purposes we will only look at how the lack of forgiveness can hinder a Christian's healing.

If a Christian fails to forgive, he or she will block the flow of God's power to heal. Unforgiveness in the life of the Christian will hinder and block the faith and trust needed to receive what God wants to provide.

Forgiveness is a commandment directly from a loving God who loves us so much that in spite of the sins you and I commit, God is willing to forgive us.

He expects no less of us; He is willing to forgive and in return He expects us to be willing to forgive.

Bitterness, wrath, desire for revenge are all forms of unforgiveness involving others, and those feelings must go. If a Christian is not willing to forgive others for what they have done, it is like a steel door has been pulled down between the Christian and the gift of healing.

Sometimes God will heal in spite of the sin of unforgiveness just to get the attention of the Christian. But if the Christian continues in the sin of unforgiveness, it will only be a matter of time before the enemy once again steals your healing.

Forgive and forget is how the old saying goes. But it is not that easy nor is it that simple? Nor does God say the Christian has to forget, only to forgive.

My years of personal experiences have taught me that it is easier to ask for forgiveness, or to forgive, than it is to forget.

You do not have to forget, but if you let the bitterness or the lack of forgiveness back in, you will have to forgive all over again.

Please do not misunderstand what I am saying. Forgiving is not easy in any situation, and some situations where I needed to forgive were extremely difficult because I really felt that I was in the right.

Even after God would get my attention and I would forgive the person or persons, the devil would catch me in a weak moment and try to sneak the bitterness of the thing back in.

The thought would just slide into my mind as to how I had been unjustly treated or sinned against.

If I do not catch this thought, or thoughts, immediately I quickly found myself back into the area of unforgiveness.

There have been far too many situations where I have had to ask God to forgive the same thing way too many times. The only bright spot in all of this is that it gets easier each time to catch the problem trying to sneak back in and to get rid of it quickly.

I have also learned that if I am faithful in dealing with the bitterness creeping back in, eventually the period of time between the returning thought is longer.

But the enemy never stops trying, and I have learned how to put the armor on quicker. I have also learned to keep the armor close at hand at all times. And finally I am learning how to bring every thought into captivity.

I will state this as clearly as I know how. **Lack of forgiveness, regardless of the offense is a sin.** Sin that is not confessed comes between us and God. Sin that is not repented of damages your relationship with the Lord who wants to heal you.

Do not let the sin of unforgiveness keep you from your healing. And if God heals you in spite of your sin, do not allow the lack of forgiveness on your part to permit Satan to steal back what God has freely given.

Doubt and Unbelief:
Doubt or unbelief according to Mark 6:5,6 can limit the work of God. *Now Jesus could do no mighty work there, except that He laid hands on a few sick people and healed them. And He marveled because of their unbelief.*

Sometimes God will move to heal someone who has a very low level of faith in Him, but there will be other times that God will delay His healing miracle so that you may have your faith level increased.

The Scriptures are full of passages dealing with doubt and unbelief and in every case these are a hindrance. Deal with them as the scriptures and the Holy Spirit indicate.

Pride:

The Catholic Church lists seven sins they see as the origin of the other sins. The seven sins are identified as wrath, greed, sloth, pride, lust, envy, and gluttony.

The first hindrance to healing addressed was listed as gluttony and applies more to the developed Western countries because food is so readily available. There are many countries in the world where gluttony would not be considered first.

Lack of forgiveness was considered next, and five of the Catholic 'caput' seven sins often are caused due to lack of forgiveness by the Christian.

Pride is the most deadly of sins, and is the sin that began even before the creation of the human race. The Bible informs the reader that pride originally reared its ugly head with Satan, and it was pride that brought him down.

Pride is emotion that is inwardly directed, and pride carries two common meanings. We will only deal with the negative connotation and in this aspect pride relates to an inflated sense of one's personal status or accomplishments.

Return to an earlier chapter in this book where Naaman's healing was discussed. Naaman was upset with the way in which God wanted to heal him. Naaman was an important person in his own eyes and even in the eyes of King of Syria.

Naaman's pride almost cost him his healing.

Pride can keep a Christian from coming to God for healing. Thinking or believing, that because of what you have done for God, or your position in the religious order, this should automatically require God to heal you is pride, and will surely hinder your miracle.

Stated in another way, pride is the excessive belief in one's own abilities.

Pride will interfere with your recognition of the grace of God, which in turn will slow or block your healing. And oh-by-the-way, through you own doings, you are nothing and you can accomplish nothing.

Everything you are, everything you have, everything you have accomplished, everything flows from God. He can strip you of any, or all, of who you think you are, or what you think you have.

Pride can also block the Gifts of Healing from flowing through you. Often religious leaders, pastors and teachers, because of their 'exalted' earthly status, believe if God is going to do anything it would have to flow through them.

This is pride at its ugliest and God will have no part of it.

With this type of thinking religious leaders can block the healing God has for you. God will choose to use the hands, the feet, and the mouths of any disciples that are willing to be used.

It is God who honors His word, both in salvation and in healing. It is God who saves, and it is God who heals.

You and I have nothing to do with either; **except as pass-through-vehicles of God in expanding His kingdom through words and works.**

Father God is willing to heal. Father God wants to heal. Father God commanded His kids to heal and set free those in bondage or sickness.

God sent Jesus to restore the health which Satan stole from mankind in the Garden of Eden.

Father God has even made a promise to keep His kids healthy so they do not need healing; **but only if they will only obey Him.**

Pride will cancel out and hinder all Father God
has created, promised, provided, and restored.

Do not let your pride be your hindrance to what
God is willing to give to you.

FIFTEEN

And Jesus said to them, "Go into all the world and preach the gospel to every creature. He who believes and is baptized will be saved; but he who does not believe will be condemned. <u>And these signs shall follow those who believe</u>; In My name <u>they will cast out demons</u>; they will speak with new tongues; they will take up serpents; and if they drink anything deadly, it will by no means hurt them; <u>they will lay hands on the sick, and they will recover</u>.
Mark 16:15-18

Jesus was speaking to those whom He had called and trained in proclaiming the Good News of the Kingdom of God. Those early apostles and disciples did indeed go out into all the world and huge numbers were saved, healed, and baptized.

Throughout the New Testament period following the ascension of Jesus into heaven, signs and wonders were a normal part of those believers in Christ.

The Holy Spirit provided these early Christians with the anointing to preach with boldness, cast out demons and to lay hands on the sick, and to glorify God when people were saved, delivered, and restored.

I have read the New Testament from cover to cover looking for a time when the Great Commission was changed, but I have never read where Jesus said His disciples could back off, or that He would take over.

There are numerous verses and passages where the disciple is told to move out and God would move with him. **BUT, never did I read where God would walk the walk, nor do the work for us.**

The life of a Christian disciple is to bring glory and honor to God. There is only one way to do this that I have found in Scripture, and that is to become more like Christ.

Pastor and teacher, Ray Vander Laan of 'That the World May Know Ministries' has said that a disciple is one that teaches what the Rabbi taught, and mimics what the Rabbi did.

As disciples of Jesus Christ, we are to teach what He taught, and we are to do what He did. And isn't this the Great Commission in a nut shell?

I refer to again to Billy Graham in his book, "The Journey" where he said, "Whenever Christians have lost sight of the 'teachings' of Jesus, they have betrayed their Lord and brought dishonor to His Name.

The Christian Church by-and-large has condensed the Great Commission down to the first two sentences. The Church and the disciples within the church have for the most part been willing to go out and to preach with words.

But it is the how and what that Jesus did when teaching and preaching the Good News of the Kingdom that Christendom has lost sight of.

The Christian church is willing to send out workers to build, repair and paint. And please do not misunderstand me; these are good things to do. But building and painting were not something that Jesus or His disciples did. Neither were these listed in the Great Commission.Somehow two-thousand years later, something is missing or has been thrown out. Assuming Mr. Graham's statement is true; the Christian disciples are betraying the teachings of Jesus and as such are bringing dishonor to His Name.

Christian disciples willing to do God's work do not seem to be comfortable with doing the good works found in Mark the sixteen chapter. Maybe it is because they have not been trained in the Word or taught to trust God for the results. It could also be possible that the Christian, leader or layman, is afraid of looking like a fool in the eyes of man.

For whatever the reason, preaching the Kingdom of God as Jesus did by using works as well as words has been shelved.

The challenge to the churches today is to provide the atmosphere and training for a healing ministry that includes deliverance of the captives.

Churches in America need to rise up and take the lead in providing God's Health Care Plan as given to us through Jesus Christ.

Many local churches are providing food and clothing through their outreach programs, and this is good.

But how many are offering a free health care benefit program to their parishioners and expanded through their local and foreign mission programs.

In Proverbs God said that He has called His disciples to go and to do, but we have refused. He has offered to heal with His outstretched hand in partnership with Him and we would not grasp it.

Isn't it time as Christians we step up to the plate and take His outstretched hand?

I have called and you refused, I have stretched out my hand and you did not regard.

Proverbs 2:24

No one that has ever come to the Father for healing has been denied. God may have delayed your healing in order to give you time to hear what He has to say to you.

But if you ask in faith, and listen for what God has to say to you when you ask, **you will not be denied**. God has said His Word would not return unto Him empty, but fulfilled.

God at the time of creation created man and woman in perfect health. There was no sickness or disease until Satan entered the picture and stole that perfect health.

But God had a plan B, and His plan B provided a way of restoration. God put Plan B into effect when He sent His son Jesus to die for our sins and restore eternal life.

Plan B also included the crown of thorns on His head and the stripes Jesus bore on His back which He suffered for our sicknesses and diseases. In so doing Jesus restored God's health for our physical bodies.

The sufferings of Jesus were enough to atone for mankind's sicknesses and diseases, but God didn't stop there. In the process of the Cross at Calvary, Jesus took on Satan and defeated him.

And even then God did not stop there. Jesus then took all of the power and authority He had displayed at Calvary and transferred all of this to His disciples.

But did Jesus stop there? <u>No He did not</u>; in addition to giving His disciples the power and authority, He sent the Holy Spirit loaded for war, to work and fight with His disciples.

God had done His part once Jesus had completed Plan B. Jesus then turned it over to His saints to carry on. The Holy Spirit in carrying out His Plan B work assignment did not bypass humans; instead He was instructed to do the work through them.

The problem that has arisen over the years is that the Christian clergy has closed the door to the miracle operations of the Holy Spirit. My wife has a favorite saying that the fish rots from the head down. If those in religious or spiritual authority choose to close and lock the door, it is almost impossible to open it without access to the key.

It is time for the clergy to open the door and allow the Holy Spirit free access. Granted the doors can open in individual hearts and the Holy Spirit will work through those open hearts, but God has said that to those to whom much has been given, much is also required.

If you are in Spiritual leadership then providing leadership in fulfilling ALL of the Great Commission is required of you.

During my reading I came across a verse in Psalm 35:27 that was written before believing in Jesus Christ made it possible for man to become sons of God through adoption. The verse reads:

Let the Lord be magnified, who has pleasure in the prosperity of His servant.

The original word translated prosperity meant: Happy, Holy, Healthy, and in Peace. It also means safety, wellness, happiness, healthiness and peacefulness.

God's desire for the Christian is to be happy, holy, healthy, and to live in peace; but how is that to come about?

This book is about a balanced Biblical approach to healing, and is written primarily to Christian brothers and sisters.

When a child of God is healthy in mind, body, and soul, it will be a lot easier to be happy, to live holy, and to have peace within.

The Bible is quite clear that the Body-of-Christ is comprised of many members and each member supplies a different function. However, if a little finger were to be cut off, something would be missing and the body could not function as God created it.

That is what has happened in most Christian denominations and fellowships. The entirety of the Great Commission which was to spread the good news of the Kingdom of God by healing the sick and setting captives free has been shoved behind the door.

Sure from time to time the Biblical words are read, but as Christians by-and-large we have denied the power thereof. **A part of the body has been allowed to die from lack of use.**

The apostle Paul was aware that this was going to happen and he wrote to Timothy about it. You can find those words in Second Timothy the third chapter verses 1 and 3:

Know this, that men will become lovers of themselves, lovers of money, -- unloving, unforgiving – lovers of pleasure rather than lovers of God, having a form of godliness, but denying its power.

Our churches, parishes, and fellowships, are full of people that say they love God, but when God looks at their everyday lives what does He see?

Far too often God sees Christians who are too busy pursuing their own agendas to be bothered with God's agenda. Clergy members who are too busy building the size of the church membership, building bigger buildings, and inflating their own egos to be slowed down with what God desires.

Much of Christendom has fallen into Satan's trap. Paul in II Corinthians 11:13-15 described it this way:

For such are false apostles, deceitful workers, transforming themselves into apostles of Christ. And no wonder! For Satan himself transforms himself into an angel of light. Therefore it is no great thing if his ministers also transform themselves into ministers of righteousness, whose end will be according to their works.

Christians, both clergy and lay people, read these words written by the apostle Paul and let the Holy Spirit apply these words to your spirit.

Have you been deceived by the angel-of-light who only brings darkness and misery? Has this angel-of-light stolen the power of God from your life or ministry?

Evangelist Herb Stewart in his book the Mighty Hand of God said that a God-ordained teacher does not rely on self-satisfying displays of theological jargon or endless definitions of Greek and Hebrew root meanings.

The God called priest, pastor, or teacher differs from the merely educated teacher because of the anointing of the Spirit of God.

The preacher and teacher's calling and ministry is to show people the benefit of living out God's word and not to promote himself or his ministry.

Pastor Stewart went on to say that the teacher needs to communicate to the students that they are expected to take their newly acquired knowledge and know-how and apply it fruitfully in their own lives, their family, and move outward from there.

For forty years Israel had failed the first test of their faith. they had let their faith fail them because their trust in God was allowed to die and shrivel up. An entire generation missed the opportunity to enjoy and experience what God had prepared for them.

How many generations of Christians have missed out on the healings that God has had for them to enjoy and experience? How many Christians have suffered and died prematurely?

Which then brings up the Biblical question of what are the churches and fellowships who are called to be Rabbi Jesus' Talmidim or disciples going to do to bring the dead body part back to life?

If you are called by His Name, shouldn't you be doing what He said to do?

Jesus Christ made healing of the body, mind and soul, the foundation for the Kingdom of God He brought to earth. Jesus Christ did His part in the atonement for our sins with His death at Calvary. He also did His part in the atonement for sicknesses, and diseases when He bore the stripes on His body for our healing.

But Jesus Christ did not stop there. He also defeated the devil and made it possible for the captives to be released.

Jesus then went to heaven to sit at the right hand of Father God. But before He did that He reminded His disciples of what He had been doing and told them to; Go and Do Likewise.

Jesus said that He would send the Holy Spirit to provide all the necessary tools to accomplish what He had started in the three years of His ministry.

He instructed His disciples at the time to go and make lots more disciples.

Teach them to use the power and availability of the Holy Spirit to do what He had been doing.

How can you be a part of the Mighty Hand of God when it comes to healing? Start with yourself. Read what God has to say in His word the Bible as it relates to healing.

Believe what you read and ask the Holy Spirit to provide you with the faith to trust God for your healing. Then move out from self to your family, to your church, and finally, move out beyond as near or as far as God directs you.

Jesus never said that He would do it Himself, but that He wanted His disciples to preach the good news as He had preached the good news. That good news included the instruction to heal the sick, cast out demons, and to free the captives.

The Holy Spirit has more guns and ammunition than the Christians could ever use. The Holy Spirit is also the provider and giver of the boldness to use the guns and ammunition.

Paul in the twelfth chapter of I Corinthians lists nine (9) Spiritual Gifts, and in Romans twelve Paul lists seven (7) more special gifts of the Spirit. **These special Holy Spirit empowered gifts are available to the entire church through the individual church members.**

Many of these gifts are designed to work in conjunction with other gifts. Some of the gifts are also given as a full time gift for church leaders, such as prophets, pastors, teachers, and evangelists. But most of the gifts are given to ordinary Christians for the benefit of everyone.

All of the Gifts of the Spirit are given to anyone who is willing to be available for God to work through.

The Holy Spirit will anoint a child of God to function in any of the gifts and with a special dispensation of His Holy Spirit's power for a given need at any time.

It is well and good if a pastor has the gifts of healing in operation within his calling, but it will benefit his church followers just as well and possibly even more so, if the gifts of healing are flowing through several of his church members.

To the clergy God would say, establish, encourage, and support, a nucleolus of your members to make the healing ministry available for and through your members.

Then make the healing ministry available to the community at large. Train your mission out-reach workers so they feel comfortable in laying hands on the sick and to trust that Jesus will heal the sick.

Send these workers out on the mission field along with the physical workers who will build and paint. Make the mission blessing two or three fold, by preaching, healing, and building.

If the clergy member is not comfortable in training and teaching this part of the ministry of Good News, bring in a Spirit anointed trainer and then move out of the way bodily, while supporting the healing ministry.

Encourage those involved in the healing and deliverance ministry to reproduce themselves and enlarge the ministry as the need is very great. The Holy Spirit will take it from there and move into the lives of Christians imparting the Gifts of the Spirit as found in Corinthians.

- The Holy Spirit often provides a special anointing to meet a need and when that need is met, the Holy Spirit anointing may be lifted.
- The gifts of healing are available to flow through any disciple of Christ.
- Disciples must recognize the teaching contained within the Bible, and be instructed on how to invite the Holy Spirit in when he knocks.
- The clergy are the spiritual leaders of the Church, and as such it is their God given responsibility to expose and train disciples to understand the Bible related teachings regarding God's Health Care Plan.

The question each individual Christian must answer is this: **Am I willing to be used in the gifts of healing?**

The question each church or fellowship leader must ask is this: Am I willing to allow the Holy Spirit the freedom to provide the gifts of healing to work in and through Christian disciples within my church, or will that make me insecure in my leadership position?

The Church from the top down is failing to bring honor to God by not providing ALL of what He has provided through the death and suffering of His Son, Jesus Christ.

The power of the Holy Spirit during the earthly ministry of Jesus provided boldness to preach and power to teach the Kingdom of God by healing the sick, by casting out the demonic, and in setting captives free.

That same Holy Spirit power and authority recorded in Acts 2 was transferred or passed on to all disciples to use until Jesus returns; when it will no longer be needed.

Priests, pastors, bishops and teachers, are you willing to open the door and then to get out of the way? Are you willing to support and

encourage the Holy Spirit to bring the dead body part back to life in your church, parish, or fellowship?

If you are willing to bring honor back to God with the gifts of healing and all that entails; then ask the Holy Spirit to raise up anointed individuals under you, encouraged by you, and if necessary taught by you.

Read Acts 4:29-31 because that is how Christian disciples are supposed to react to the teaching and preaching of the Word; and when they react scripturally, **God will heal and set free.**

Now, Lord, grant to Your servants that with all boldness they may speak Your word, by stretching out Your hand to heal, and that signs and wonders may be done through the name of Your holy Servant Jesus. And when they had prayed, the place where they were assembled together was shaken; and they were all filled with the Holy Spirit, and they spoke the word of God with boldness.

A quick reading of this scripture passage would indicate that everyone asked for boldness to speak the Word and for God to stretch out His hand through them to heal.

And through the Name of Jesus, signs and wonders which included healing, casting out the demonic and freeing the captives would follow. The passage states that they were all filled with the Holy Spirit and moved out with boldness.

Not just the leaders, but all who were there received a new and fresh anointing of the Holy Spirit to fulfill Mark sixteen in its entirety.

I say again that priests, pastors, teachers and spiritual leaders in positions of responsibility should prayerfully consider adding, encouraging, and supporting a healing ministry within the walls of your area of spiritual purview.

Ask the Holy Spirit to anoint individuals within your fellowship to become involved in this healing ministry. Remember Steven was first given responsibility to wait-on-tables before God moved him out from there and the gifts of healing became a part of his ministry.

The same will happen in your church, parish or fellowship if you will pray for the Holy Spirit's moving.

God wants balance within the church body and the healing ministry should be only one part of your ministry. Do not neglect the ministries that God has called you to be involved in.

But neither should you neglect the healing ministry that Jesus ordained and embraced from the beginning of His ministry.

Jesus showed His disciples how to preach the Kingdom with power; He defeated the devil, and then provided the Holy Spirit to make the healing ministry effective.

Most church groups have a local mission outreach as well as a global mission out reach. The healing ministry and the gifts of healing are needed in both outreaches.

Under the healing ministry umbrella the pastor might consider having two groups involved with specific targets and training for each, one for the church body and local outreach, and the other for the foreign outreach mission program.

Jesus Himself in the first chapter of Acts told all those who were gathered together what was to come, and what they were to do with it.

You shall receive power when the Holy Spirit has come upon you; and you shall be witness to Me in Jerusalem, and in all Judea and Samaria, and to the end of the earth.

The power of the Holy Spirit provided the wherewithal to bring the witness of Jesus, and that included the power to do all which Jesus had been doing.

Jesus said that by so doing we will be doing it to Him, or if you prefer, for Him. In other scriptures we are to start in our own homes and with our own families.

If God can find us faithful there, then the Christian is instructed to move out locally, nationally, cross-culturally, and finally internationally. The healing and freedom ministry is to move in exactly the same manner.

Christian brothers and sisters, Proverbs 2:24 says that God has called, but you have refused. Do not refuse to be used by God in the healing of your immediate family, your brothers and sisters in Christ, and in the witness of Jesus to others.

Jesus said that He transferred His power and authority to each one of us to be used in the body of Christ and to expand His Kingdom here on earth.

Christians are hurting physically, mentally and spiritually, and if you claim to be a disciple of Jesus Christ, then you have no option but to do as He did. Step out in faith and boldness and the Word will not return unto God without a handful of fruit.

Absolutely, sinners receiving Jesus are the most important of the produced fruit. But God has provided for more than just one kind of fruit.

Sinners and saints being healed as well as saints and sinners held in captivity being set free, are another kind of fruit that God wants from his kids.

Having spent several years in the fruit and vegetable business I can assure you that picking, packing and selling only one kind of fruit gets a little stale.

When I go to the store and find myself in the fresh fruit and vegetable section, I would not be too excited if the only fruit available was apples. I like apples, but I also like oranges, bananas and a whole lot more.

God has instructed His kids to produce spiritual fruit, not to become religious nuts. Keep everything in balance and do not become a religious nut when it comes to healing.

Remember the gifts-of-healing is only one of the nine gifts that Paul lists.

If you feel the nudging or calling of God to move out in the area of healing, learn through the Word what is God's will and what are His promises regarding healing. Then put His word to the test.

Invite the Holy Spirit to use you in the manifestation of the gifts of healing, in your family, in your church, in your fellowship, and in your "all-the-world" mission outreach.

As this chapter titled "Are You Willing" comes to a close I am reminded of a few songs that are sung by those who refer to themselves as Christians:

Oh Lord my God, How Great Thou Art.
And when I think that God, His Son not sparing,
Sent Him to die, I scarce can take it in;
That on the Cross, my burden gladly bearing,
He bled and died to take away my sin;

The Christian can add that, '**For my sicknesses He was whipped**'!

Then sings my soul, my Savior God, to Thee:
How great Thou art, How great Thou Art.

The Swedish writer of this great song could also have added a verse that for my sicknesses and diseases Jesus was whipped and beaten. When you are suffering in sickness or depression, always remember just How Great He Is!

What a friend we have in Jesus, all our sins and griefs to bear.
What a privilege to carry everything to God in prayer.
O what peace we often forfeit, O what needless pain we bear,
All because we do not carry everything to God in prayer.

Griefs can be understood as sicknesses and diseases, and yes, Jesus bore those at the Cross as well as my sins. The writer of the song goes on to chastise the Christians because we do not avail ourselves of the privilege we have to give EVERYTHING to God in prayer.

The peace of God is offered, but we do not have this Shalom, and the pain of sickness and diseases we have to bear because we are too stubborn to give them to God.

This small verse says it all:

Blessed Savior, Thou hast promised Thou will all our burdens bear
May we ever, Lord, be bringing all to Thee in earnest prayer.
Soon in glory bright unclouded there will be no need for prayer,
Rapture, praise and endless worship will be our portion there.

The chorus of the song, 'It Is No Secret' goes like this:

It is no secret what God can do.
What He's done for others,
He'll do for you.
With arms wide open
He'll pardon you.
It is no secret what God can do.

What God has done in the realm of healing, He has not hid under a bushel. No, He has proclaimed it from the highest mountain tops so all could see, and all could hear.

God has no favorites, He loves us all and what He has done for others He will also do for you.

I am not given to the prophecy of things to come, but there are signs that the health care needs here in the United States of America are changing. Already many within the church bodies do not have health care and can not afford to go to a doctor or a hospital.

The need for the healing ministry was great in the early Christian church when Jesus ushered in the Kingdom of God which included both healing and setting the captives free.

Let's not wait to resurrect the healing ministry as our brothers and sisters have these same needs now. It is imperative that as disciples of Jesus we once again do it God's way.

And the best news is that God's Health Care Plan is free in terms of money, and His healing is given in love instead of given for money.

The other difference is that doctors are practicing medicine and Father God does not need to practice.

If the people of God, who are called by His name, will resurrect the God given healing ministry, both within the body outreach locally and in their global mission outreach, only then will Christians again be providing for needs within the Kingdom of God on this earth.

Are We Willing?

The second Secretary General of the United Nations
Dag Hammarskjord once wrote:
"He who has nothing - Can give nothing,"

Jesus has everything and has offered to give His disciples much
so that they may give much

SIXTEEN

The ULTIMATE Healing Experience

This book titled, 'God's Health Care Plan' is coming to its end. **There is so much more that could (and probably should) be said; so let this book be only the beginning for you.**

Every child of God that is in need of a healing and asks of the Father will never be denied; as that is Father God's will for His kids. Perfect health for His created beings was the plan from the beginning of creation.

When God's original plan was thwarted by Satan, God had plan B waiting in the wings. Father God loved us so much that He sent His son to implement His plan of restoration. That plan and process for the restoration of our complete health has been completed.

All the requirements have been written for all time in God's Holy Book, which we know as the Bible.

There may be a question of timing regarding the manifestation of your healing, and your healing may be delayed; but it will never be denied.

Father God loves you with a love that can never be fully explained or experienced by His sons and daughters while here on this planet.

Father God wants you to experience His absolute best for you, starting from the day you trusted Him for eternal life through His son Jesus.

Your manifested healing may be delayed for a time while God works through the Holy Spirit to make you more like Christ, or God may use this time to use the witness of your faith and trust in Him to others.

Even as I write this last sentence, I felt my spirit flinch. While God may delay your healing for this reason, do not use that for a 'cop-out' for why you have not received the healing you asked God for.

I have touched on numerous reasons why God may delay your healing, and that it is Biblical to ask God why. God will make the 'why' known to you.

What you choose to do with the 'why' will determine the time frame of your healing. **If you choose to ignore what God tells you, or if you rebel against what God has shown you, there will be a delay in receiving what God wants to give you, <u>and it may be long</u>.**

If a child of God procrastinates in following God's instructions long enough, he or she may never experience the healing that they asked God for

Does that mean that God will not keep His promise to heal everyone that asks in faith and trusts in His promises?

No, God will keep His promise, but the Christian may not collect on the promise until the time of transition from this earthly world to a place known as heaven. In heaven there will be no sickness, no diseases, no sadness and no sorrow.

Father God loves each of us so very much that He has given directions on how to get to heaven. Then He has provided both the road and the road map to get there.

While traveling this road there will be a number of paths that branch off. The choice to veer off onto a path that looks appealing is a choice that the Father allows each of his children to make.

Once a child of God chooses to leave the road for a path, many times the path will take the Christian into a maze. It is the Christian's choice as to how long they wish to remain in the maze. The Father wants to show you the way out, but the enemy would like to keep you in the maze as long as he can.

Along the edges of the straight road to heaven, God has placed a number of gifts and presents, the gifts of healing being just one. Staying on the road is the quickest way to get where the gifts and presents are. Picking a side path of sin or rebellion leads into the maze where there are no God-given gifts or presents.

Time spent in the maze that leads nowhere, depends on how long the Christian fights against doing it God's way.

There is a restaurant chain that advertised you could, "Have it Your Way." Yes you may choose to have it your way, but in the long run it will be considerably easier on you if you would choose to, **"Have it His way".**

Throughout the course of this book I have shared a large number of Scripture verses and Scripture passages pertaining to healing. Some of the Scriptures were mind-boggling in what they said, or how they should be understood.

Paul during his years of ministry was writing to early Christians who often suffered greatly, even though they had all the authority of Jesus, and all the power that accompanied the use of that Name.

These early Christians having all the same power and authority that is available to disciples of Jesus Christ today, still suffered and often their lives ended up in an unpleasant death.

Should we as Johnny-come-lately-Christians expect anything different? The apostle wrote to these persecuted Christians in Romans 8:28, words that are very applicable to Christians when they are struggling with health issues.

And we know that all things work together for good to those who love God, and to those who are called according to His purpose.

Christians have often used this verse in Romans to justify the situation they find themselves in? Don't worry about it; just suffer along as God is going to use this for good.

There is truth in this and God (if we let Him) will take bad things and make them work for good, **but it will be for His good.**

If a Christian is sick in body, mind, or soul because of sin or rebellion and will not repent, then God may elect to provide the ultimate healing by taking this person home. God may choose to use your sickness to take you home, before something worse could take place.

Dr. Ed Dobson once said that, **"Sickness, disease, or time, may be the reason, but death is going to get us all."** There is a time to be born and there is a time to die, and as Dr. Dobson said we do not control either.

As far as time-of-death is concerned the Christian does have a certain amount of control over the time of death.

God has provided Section I. in His Health Care Plan whereby we may live in health. God has provided Section II in His Health Care Plan whereby He will heal us, but we may have to take His medicine.

If we strive to live under Section I of GHCP (God's Health Care Plan) our time-of-death will be according to God's time table. And as we saw with Hezekiah, God has been known to change the original T-O-D when asked.

Living within the guidelines of Section I of GHCP is not easy and Christians often find this too difficult, given the seductive ways of the world and the helpful temptations provided by the enemy.

When you find yourself fighting sickness, disease, or mental health type problems, then you need to turn the page to Section II of GHCP and follow the directions for getting better.

There is a Section III in God's Health Care Plan. God's I, II and III sections of His health care plan cover all the bases for a Christian. Kind of like the good, better, and best scenario in reverse.

The best coverage can be found in Section I, but if rebellion, sin or circumstances preclude the best, God has provided the second best which isn't all that bad, and Section II coverage can at any time be upgraded to Section I.

For one of any number of reasons the Christian is unable or unwilling to meet the requirements of Section I or II, Father God has provided a final section that is good, but not as good.

Just a note of caution; unfortunately sections I and III are only for the Christian. If you are outside of the Kingdom of God you will never be able to live according to the requirements of Section I of God's Health Care Plan.

And if you have not invited Jesus Christ into your life, God will not take you into His home anyway.

God's purpose is for mankind to bring Him glory and to give Him glory. The greatest glory a person can give to God is to accept Jesus Christ as their Lord and Savior and become one of His kids.

As a child of God we can bring glory to God in thoughts, words, and deeds. For a Christian striving to become more like Christ this is a life-long journey which is intended to also bring glory to God.

Section III of God's Health Care Plan is often the least desirable but may be the only option left to God. God's desire is to provide a healthy life style for His kids during their stay on this earth. **However, God is most interested in His kids making it to heaven for an eternity with Him.**

There will be no sickness, disease, sorrow, or tears in heaven, so once we get there all these earthly struggles will be over.

If a Christian chooses to continue in sin or rebellion, that sin or rebellion will lead to sickness or disease,

God may send sickness and disease to the back-sliding Christian in His desire for His child to get back on track. Get your life right with God and go for His healing offered in Section II of His health care plan.

When sickness or disease overtakes you, it might be God's way of getting your attention. If sin is the cause for your illness, confess it, repent of it, and accept God's forgiveness so that He can also supply your healing.

Should the Christian fail to yield to God's nudging in His desired response, God may have no choice but to implement Section III of His plan; which is to take His child home before things get worse.

My understanding of Eternal Security goes something like this. As long as we are willing to hold on to God, He will never let his child go. **But if His child no longer wants to be held, God will let go.**

Before His child can get to that point of letting go, God would prefer to provide healing under Section III and take His child home.

God knows the future and God may decide that it is better to implement Section III for the protection of His child.

Some years ago I worked for a successful businessman that in my opinion knew the Lord personally. For many years my boss had a problem with alcohol; frankly he was an alcohol addict.

There were periods he would disappear for two or three weeks at a time. His wife was a very 'devout' Christian lady that put up with him and prayed for him daily.

There came a time when Jesus Christ answered his wife's prayers and my boss turned his life around. But he only lived for a couple of years in this sober state. Alcohol had destroyed his liver, and probably caused some other health issues.

God could have healed his ravaged body, but it is also possible God knew the possibility of my boss returning to his old ways, and allowed the disease to shorten God's original 'time-of-life for him.

Just as God's 'time-of-life' can be extended, our life style can also shorten our life span. Yes, God is love, but God also allows mankind to choose between having it our way, or doing it His way.

When a person lives the life of sin and excess, then the body will suffer. Repentance will bring God's forgiveness and acceptance. But the damage done to the body will not automatically be corrected.

The sinner may enter the kingdom and the saint may be restored, but that does not necessarily result in the body being cured.

James said that we have not because we have asked not. Don't stop with being forgiven or restored; ask God to cure your body as well.

I will leave you with this Biblical passage found in Hebrews10:36-39.

Do not cast away your confidence, which has great reward. For you have need of endurance so that after you have done the will of God, you may receive the promise. And He who is coming will come and will not tarry. Now (Until then) the just shall live by faith. But if anyone draws back, My soul has no pleasure in him.

The Father's Health Care Plan

- God wants you healthy, body, soul, and mind.
- God can keep you healthy, body, soul, and mind.
- God wants to heal you when you need it, body, soul, and mind.
- God wants your restoration to be complete, body and spirit.

God's Health Care Plan is:

Biblically Balanced and Absolutely Affordable

The ULTIMATE healing for the Christian will be realized when we go to heaven to spend eternity with the Father, Son and Holy Spirit. God's eternity is complete and lasts forever; and with no sickness or sorrow.

Before I leave the pages of this book I would like to leave you with an excerpt of a sermon preached in Detroit by the late Dr. S.M. Lockeridge about my King, and if you know Jesus, your King as well.

My King was born a King. The Bible says He is a Seven Way King. He is the King of the Jews – that's an ethnic King. He is the King of Israel – that's a national King. He is the King of righteousness. He is the King of the ages. He is the King of Heaven. He is the King of glory. He is the King of kings and He is Lord of lords.
Now that's my King!

He is enduringly strong. He is entirely sincere. He is eternally steadfast. He is immortally graceful. He is imperially powerful. He is impartially merciful. He is God's Son. He is the sinner's saviour. He is honest. He is unique. He is unparalleled. He is supreme. He is the grandest idea in literature. He is the highest personality in philosophy. He is the supreme problem in higher criticism.
Now that's my King!

He is the miracle of the age. He is the only one able to supply all our needs simultaneously. He supplies strength for the weak. He sympathizes and He saves. He is the Almighty God who guides and helps all his people. He heals the sick. He frees the captives. He

forgives sinners. He defends the feeble. He blesses the young. He saves the unfortunate. He regards the aged.
Now that's my King!

His promise is sure. His light is matchless. His goodness is limitless. His mercy is everlasting. His love never changes. His Word is enough. His grace is sufficient. His reign is righteous. His yoke is easy. His burden is light. He is incomprehensible. He is invincible. He is irresistible. I wish I could describe Him to you, but He is indescribable.
That's my King!

The Pharisees couldn't stand Him, but found they could not stop Him. Pilate couldn't find any fault in Him. Herod couldn't kill Him. Death couldn't handle Him, and the grave couldn't hold Him.
That's my King!

And He is so much more. The heavens of heavens can't contain Him and no man can explain Him. You can't get Him out of your mind and you can't get Him off your hands. You can't outlive Him and you can't live without Him. He is the Prince of princes. He is the King of kings. He is Lord of lords.
Now that's my King!

He always has been and He always will be. There is nobody before Him and there will be nobody after Him. You can't impeach Him and He's not going to resign.
That's my King!

Thine is the kingdom. Thine is the power. And Thine is the glory. The Kingdom, and the Power and the Glory forever and ever and ever and ever and when you get through with all the evers, then...

AMEN!

Appendix

All Scripture versus referenced are taken from the
New King James Bible

Healing verses with conditions:

Exodus 15:16b
Exodus 21:25,26
Deut. 7:12-15
Deut. 32:39
Psalm 91:9-11
Malachi 4:2

Healing verses:

Psalm 30:2
Psalm 34:9,10
Psalm 34:18-20
Psalm 41:3,4
Psalm 103:2-5
Psalm 107:20
Psalm 147:3
Proverbs 3:7-9
Proverbs 4:20-23
Proverbs 16:24
Proverbs 17:22
Isaiah 58:8
Isaiah 61:1
Jeremiah 17:14
Jeremiah 30:17a
Jeremiah 33:6
Hosea 6:1
Matthew 4:23,24
Matthew 7:11
Matthew 8:2,3
Matthew 8:14,15
Matthew 8:16,17
Matthew 9:20-22
Matthew 9:27-31
Matthew 9:32,33
Matthew 9:35

Matthew 10:1
Matthew 10:7,8
Matthew 11:4,5
Matthew 12:15
Matthew 12:22
Matthew 14:14
Matthew 14:35,36
Matthew 15:30
Matthew 18:19
Matthew 19:2
Matthew 20:30-34
Matthew 21:14
Mark 1:30-34
Mark 1:40-42
Mark 3:3-5
Mark 3:10,11
Mark 3:14,15
Mark 5:21-36
Mark 5:34
mark 6:7-13
Mark 6:56
Mark 7:25-29
Mark 7:33-35
Mark 8:23-25
Mark 9:23
Mark 10:51.52
Mark 11:22-26
Mark 16:15-18
Luke 4:18
Luke4:33035
Luke 4:38,39
Luke 4:40,41
Like 5:15
Luke 5:17
Luke 6:17-19
Luke 7:21
Luke 8:47.48

Luke 8:50
Luke 9:1,2
Luke 9:6
Luke 9:11
Luke 10:9
Luke 10:9
Luke 11:10
Luke 13:11-17
Luke 17:12-14
John 5:608
John 9:3-11
John 14:12-14
John 15:7
John 16:23,24
Acts 3:6-8
Acts 4:29b-30
Acts 5:16
Acts 8:6,7
Acts 9:32
Acts 9:33,34
Acts 14:8-10
Acts 19:11-12
Romans 10:17
Hebrews 10:35,36
Hebrews 11:1
Hebrews 11:6
James 1:17
James 4:7
James 5:14-16
I Peter 2:24
I John 5:14,15

Faith and Promise Verses

Psalm 92:14-16
Psalm 138:3
Matthew 14:30,31
Matthew 15:28
Matthew 17:20.21
Matthew 18:19.20
Mark 5:28-34
Mark 5:36
Mark 11:22-24
Luke 1:4
John 3:36
Acts 15:8,9
Galatians 2:20
Galatians 5:22
Ephesians 2:8.9
Ephesians 6:16
Romans 1:16,17
Romans 5:1
Romans 10:17
Romans 12:3
I Cor. 13:2
I Cor. 16:13
II Cor. 5:6,7
Hebrews 4:16
Hebrews 10:36
Hebrews 10:38
Hebrews 11;1
Hebrews 11:6
James 1:6-8
James 5:13-18